# Clic!

## Livre du Professeur

## Access 1

*Julie Green*
*Pat Dunn*
*Danièle Bourdais*
*Sue Finnie*

OXFORD
UNIVERSITY PRESS

## OXFORD
UNIVERSITY PRESS

Great Clarendon Street, Oxford OX2 6DP

Oxford University Press is a department of the University of Oxford.

It furthers the University's objective of excellence in research, scholarship, and education by publishing worldwide in
Oxford  New York  Auckland  Cape Town  Dar es Salaam  Hong Kong  Karachi
Kuala Lumpur  Madrid  Melbourne  Mexico City  Nairobi
New Delhi  Shanghai  Taipei  Toronto

With offices in
Argentina  Austria  Brazil  Chile  Czech Republic  France  Greece  Guatemala
Hungary  Italy  Japan  South Korea  Poland  Portugal  Singapore  Switzerland
Thailand  Turkey  Ukraine  Vietnam

Oxford is a registered trade mark of Oxford University Press
in the UK and in certain other countries

British Library Cataloguing in Publication Data

Data available

ISBN 978 019 912752 8

10 9 8 7 6 5 4 3 2 1

Printed in Great Britain by Bell & Bain, Glasgow

Paper used in the production of this book is a natural, recyclable product made from wood grown in sustainable forests. The manufacturing process conforms to the environmental regulations of the country of origin.

### Acknowledgements

The authors and publisher would like to thank the following people for their help and advice: Julie Green, Harriette Lanzer; Audio recordings and studio production: Nordquist Productions, Oslo; song lyrics: Sue Finnie, Danièle Bourdais; music composition: Dorothée Rascalé.

**Mixed Sources**
Product group from well-managed
forests and other controlled sources
www.fsc.org  Cert no. TT-COC-002769
© 1996 Forest Stewardship Council
FSC

# Contents

**Symbols used in this Teacher's Book:**

| | |
|---|---|
| 🎧 | listening materials |
| ▶ | video clip on the *Clic! Interactif OxBox* CD-ROM |
| 🅖 | support on the *Clic! Interactif OxBox* CD-ROM |
| C1 | consolidation and extension activities available on Copymaster |
| AT 1.1 | reference to National Curriculum attainment level |

| | Contexts | Grammar | Languages strategies and pronunciation |
|---|---|---|---|
| Unit 1 | **La France et le français**<br>• Talk about France<br>• Recognise words in French<br>• Say your name<br>• Say what nationality you are<br>• Use French in class<br>• Spell words in French | • *je suis, tu es*<br>• Masculine and feminine adjectives<br>• *tu, vous* | Listening to word endings<br>Using the alphabet<br>Pronunciation of accents<br>Not pronouncing the final *s*<br>*se* ending sounding like *z* |
| Unit 2 | **C'est la France!**<br>• Use numbers 1–10<br>• Name French things<br>• Name places in town<br>• Say what there is or isn't<br>• Name some countries where French is spoken<br>• Name the colours on flags | • *le, la, les*<br>• *c'est*<br>• *un, une, des*<br>• *il y a, il n'y a pas de*<br>• *c'est le, la, l'*<br>• *l'* before vowels | Thinking of words that help you remember<br>Asking and answering questions<br>Making your voice go up when asking a question |
| Unit 3 | **Le weekend**<br>• Talk about things you like and don't like<br>• Say what you have and don't have<br>•Say what you like and dislike doing at the weekend | • *j'aime, je n'aime pas, tu aimes …?* (verb patterns)<br>• *j'ai, je n'ai pas de*<br>• *avoir (je/tu)*<br>• *j'aime, je n'aime pas, j'adore, je déteste* + infinitive | *et, mais*<br>Checking spelling and accents<br>Accents change pronunciation of vowels |
| Unit 4 | **Bonne année!**<br>• Say numbers 1–31<br>• Name months of the year and say dates<br>• Say how old you are<br>• Talk about birthdays<br>• Say what you do on special occasions<br>• Give opinions | • *mon/ton*<br>• *j'ai* + age<br>• *c'est* + adjective<br>• Verb patterns for *-er* verbs (*je/tu*) | Asking and answering more questions<br>Question words<br>Nasal sounds in French |
| Unit 5 | **Le collège**<br>• Say what your favourite subject is<br>• Say which subjects you do and don't like<br>• Use numbers up to 60<br>• Say what time it is<br>• Name days of the week<br>• Say what day you have a subject | • Likes and dislikes<br>• *il est* + time<br>• *tu/vous*<br>• Using *on* | Working out meaning<br>Difference in pronunciation between English and French words which are the same |
| Unit 6 | **Chez moi**<br>• Say what the weather is like<br>• Describe the weather in some French regions<br>• Say where you live<br>• Give an opinion<br>• Say what there is in your bedroom<br>• Explain why you like or dislike it | • *il fait, il y a* + weather<br>• *c'est* + opinions<br>• *il y a, il n'y a pas de*<br>• *c'est* + adjectives<br>• *et, mais, parce que* | Reading strategies: look for words that are similar in English<br>Use the dictionary<br>Making longer sentences<br>Final *s*, *t* and *d* not pronounced |
| Unit 7 | **Ma famille**<br>• Introduce your family<br>• Say how many brothers and sisters you have<br>• Say what someone looks like<br>• Describe your personality<br>• Describe someone else's personality | • *j'ai, je n'ai pas de*<br>• *mon, ma, mes*<br>• *il/elle est*<br>• Adjective agreement<br>• *il/elle est* + adjectives (agreement) | Working out meaning using visual clues and logic<br>Remembering words and phrases using cards<br>Pronouncing *r* |
| Unit 8 | **On mange!**<br>• Name food items<br>• Say what you like eating<br>• Say where you go when you eat out<br>• Say what you would like to eat<br>• Name flavours and fillings<br>• Order a snack | • *j'aime/je n'aime pas le, la, les*<br>• *ça*<br>• *aller (je, tu)*<br>• *au, à la*<br>• *au, à la, aux*<br>• *je voudrais* | Words that are similar in English and French<br>Adapting sentences to say different things<br>*ou* sound |
| Unit 9 | **Bon appétit!**<br>• Say what you eat at different times of day<br>• Say what you drink<br>• Say what food there is and isn't<br>• Follow a simple recipe<br>• Talk about healthy eating<br>• Say what you are and aren't going to eat | • *du, de la, de l', des*<br>• *le matin, le midi, le soir*<br>• *il y a, il n'y a pas de*<br>• Sequencers: *d'abord, ensuite, pour finir*<br>• *je vais* + infinitive (future) | Don't panic when listening<br>Last letter of words often not pronounced |

| | CLIC! ACCESS 2 SUMMARY OF UNIT CONTENTS | | |
|---|---|---|---|
| | **Contexts** | **Grammar** | **Languages strategies and pronunciation** |
| Unit 1 | **Bienvenue à Paris!**<br>• Say your name, age and where you live<br>• Welcome a visitor<br>• Say what there is in a town<br>• Say what there isn't in a town<br>• Name different transports<br>• Say how you travel | • *il y a, il n'y a pas de*<br>• *en, a* + transport | To ask a question, make your voice go up<br>Using a dictionary for new words<br>*un, une* |
| Unit 2 | **Le weekend dernier**<br>• Say what you did earlier today<br>• Say what you did last weekend<br>• Say who you are a fan of<br>• Say what he or she has done | • Perfect tense with *avoir* + -er verbs (*je, tu*)<br>• Negative in perfect tense<br>• More perfect tense verbs: irregulars<br>• Using *il, elle* + perfect tense | Saying different things using the same verbs<br>Using connectives *et, mais, après*<br>Giving yourself time to think in speaking activities with *alors, euh*<br>Pronouncing present and past: *je trouve, j'ai trouvé* |
| Unit 3 | **Vacances et voyages**<br>• Say which country you went to<br>• Say what it was like<br>• Say where you went in Paris<br>• Talk about a past holiday | • *je suis allé(e)*<br>• *en* + countries<br>• *c'était*<br>• Other verbs which take *être*<br>• Agreement of the past participle<br>• Verbs in the past with *avoir* and *être* | Giving an opinion in the past: *c'était* + adjective<br>Asking questions: *où, quand*<br>Nasal sounds: *an* and *en* |
| Unit 4 | **Planète mode!**<br>• Name clothes and colours<br>• Say which clothes you like or dislike<br>• Say what your favourite look is<br>• Say what you normally wear<br>• Shop for clothes | • Agreement of colours with clothes, masculine/feminine<br>• Agreement of plural adjectives<br>• *je voudrais*<br>• *je peux* | English words sometimes mean different things<br>Pronouncing the ch sound |
| Unit 5 | **En forme**<br>• Say which sports you like and don't like<br>• Say which sports you play and don't play<br>• Talk about more sports you do<br>• Say how often you do sport<br>• Talk about daily routine<br>• Talk about healthy lifestyle | • Negative: *je ne joue pas*<br>• *je joue au* + sports<br>• *du, de la, de l'* + sports<br>• Reflexive verbs: *je, tu* | Frequency expressions<br>*tion* sound |
| Unit 6 | **Mon temps libre**<br>• Say what you do in your free time<br>• Say how often you do something<br>• Use numbers 70–1 000<br>• Say what you'd like to buy<br>• Say how much pocket money you get<br>• Say what you bought with your pocket money | • Frequency expressions<br>• *je voudrais*<br>• Negative: *je n'ai pas acheté de* | Using the same verbs with different endings<br>Patterns of high numbers<br>Using little words to make longer sentences: *et, mais, alors*<br>Nasal sound *in* |
| Unit 7 | **Premiers contacts**<br>• Find out about someone you have just met<br>• Tell someone a bit about yourself<br>• Ask someone out<br>• Accept or refuse an invitation<br>• Say how you will keep in touch with friends | • Useful question words<br>• *tu veux …?*<br>• Say what you are going to do in the future<br>• Using *on* | *qu = k* |
| Unit 8 | **Les médias**<br>• Name types of TV programmes<br>• Say which programmes you like and don't like<br>• Name different types of film<br>• Give your opinion of films<br>• Say what you can and can't do | • Revision of some perfect tense<br>• *c'était* + adjective<br>• *je peux, je ne peux pas* | Remember new words by making connections<br>*j* sound |
| Unit 9 | **L'avenir**<br>• Say what subjects you do at school<br>• Say what subjects you will do next year, and why<br>• Say what part-time job you are going to do<br>• Give opinions of jobs<br>• Say which job you would like to do<br>• Say why you would or wouldn't like a job | • *je vais* + infinitive (immediate future)<br>• Masculine and feminine adjectives (revised)<br>• *je vais, je ne vais pas* + infinitive (immediate future)<br>• Masculine and feminine forms of job titles | Giving reasons<br>Finding new words in a dictionary<br>*c, ç* and vowels |

| Year 7–8 Long Term Plan Access 1 | | | | | | | | | |
|---|---|---|---|---|---|---|---|---|---|
| Framework objective | Unit 1 | Unit 2 | Unit 3 | Unit 4 | Unit 5 | Unit 6 | Unit 7 | Unit 8 | Unit 9 |
| **Listening and speaking** | | | | | | | | | |
| 1.1 Understanding and responding to the spoken word | • | | | • | • | | | | • |
| 1.2 Developing capability and confidence in listening | | • | • | • | • | • | • | | • |
| 1.3 Being sensitive to the spoken word | | • | | • | • | • | • | | • |
| 1.4 Talking together | • | | | • | • | • | • | • | |
| 1.5 Presenting and narrating | | | | • | • | • | • | | • |
| **Reading and writing** | | | | | | | | | |
| 2.1 Understanding and responding to the written word | • | • | • | • | • | • | | | • |
| 2.2 Developing capability and confidence in reading | | • | • | | • | • | • | • | |
| 2.3 Being sensitive to the written word | • | | | • | • | | • | • | |
| 2.4 Adapting and building text | • | • | | • | | • | | • | |
| 2.5 Writing to create meaning | | | | • | • | | • | | • |
| **Intercultural understanding** | | | | | | | | | |
| 3.1 Appreciating cultural diversity | • | • | | • | • | • | | • | |
| 3.2 Recognising different ways of seeing the world | | • | | | | | | • | |
| **Knowledge about language** | | | | | | | | | |
| 4.1 Letters and sounds | • | | • | • | • | • | • | • | • |
| 4.2 Words | | • | | • | • | | • | | • |
| 4.3 Gender, number and other inflections | | • | | • | | | • | • | |
| 4.4 Sentence structure | | | • | • | • | • | | • | |
| 4.5 Verbs and tenses | | | • | • | | | • | • | • |
| 4.6 Questions and negatives | | • | • | • | | | • | | • |
| **Language learning strategies** | | | | | | | | | |
| 5.1 Identifying patterns in the target language | • | | • | | | • | | | |
| 5.2 Memorising | | • | | | | • | • | • | |
| 5.3 Using knowledge of English or another language | • | | • | | | • | • | • | |
| 5.4 Working out meaning | • | | • | | • | | • | | • |
| 5.5 Using reference materials | • | • | • | | | • | • | • | • |
| 5.6 Reading aloud | | | • | | | | • | | |
| 5.7 Planning and preparing | • | • | | • | • | | • | • | |
| 5.8 Evaluating and improving | | • | • | • | • | • | • | • | • |

| Framework objective | Unit 1 | Unit 2 | Unit 3 | Unit 4 | Unit 5 | Unit 6 | Unit 7 | Unit 8 | Unit 9 |
|---|---|---|---|---|---|---|---|---|---|
| **Year 8–9 Long Term Plan Access 2** | | | | | | | | | |
| **Listening and speaking** | | | | | | | | | |
| 1.1 Understanding and responding to the spoken word | | | • | • | • | | • | • | • |
| 1.2 Developing capability and confidence in listening | • | • | • | • | • | • | | | |
| 1.3 Being sensitive to the spoken word | • | • | • | • | • | • | | | |
| 1.4 Talking together | • | • | | • | • | • | • | • | • |
| 1.5 Presenting and narrating | • | • | | | | • | • | • | |
| **Reading and writing** | | | | | | | | | |
| 2.1 Understanding and responding to the written word | • | | • | • | • | • | | • | |
| 2.2 Developing capability and confidence in reading | • | • | • | | • | • | • | • | • |
| 2.3 Being sensitive to the written word | | • | | • | | | • | | • |
| 2.4 Adapting and building text | • | • | • | | • | | • | • | |
| 2.5 Writing to create meaning | | • | • | | | | • | | • |
| **Intercultural understanding** | | | | | | | | | |
| 3.1 Appreciating cultural diversity | • | | • | • | | • | | • | |
| 3.2 Recognising different ways of seeing the world | • | | | • | | • | | | |
| **Knowledge about language** | | | | | | | | | |
| 4.1 Letters and sounds | • | • | • | • | • | • | • | • | • |
| 4.2 Words | • | | | • | | • | • | | |
| 4.3 Gender, number and other inflections | | • | | • | | | | | • |
| 4.4 Sentence structure | | • | • | | • | • | | | • |
| 4.5 Verbs and tenses | | • | • | | • | • | • | • | • |
| 4.6 Questions and negatives | • | • | | | | • | • | • | • |
| **Language learning strategies** | | | | | | | | | |
| 5.1 Identifying patterns in the target language | | • | • | | • | • | | • | |
| 5.2 Memorising | • | • | | • | | • | • | • | • |
| 5.3 Using knowledge of English or another language | | • | | | | | | • | |
| 5.4 Working out meaning | | | | | • | | • | • | • |
| 5.5 Using reference materials | • | • | • | • | • | • | | • | • |
| 5.6 Reading aloud | • | • | • | | • | • | | | • |
| 5.7 Planning and preparing | | | • | • | • | | | | • |
| 5.8 Evaluating and improving | • | • | • | • | • | • | • | • | • |

# Introduction

## The course

Welcome to *Clic! Access*!

*Clic!* is a broad-ability course for 11–14 year olds with two levels of coursebook (*Star* and *Plus*) for each part of the three-stage course as well as a separate strand for reluctant learners. The course has been written in response to an ever-growing need for greater flexibility and relevance in the early stages of teaching and learning French.

### How does *Clic!* differ from other courses on the market?

*Clic!* has been designed to take account of:
* greater diversity in Year 7 due to language learning in many primary schools
* raised expectations in learners, regarding the range and differing formats of content
* the renewed Key Stage 3 Framework for Languages (September 2009)
* the revised KS3 Programme of Study
* alternative styles of learning and assessment
* increased demands on teacher time in terms of planning, presentation and assessment
* greater variations in timetabling for Modern Foreign Languages.

To achieve this, *Clic!* offers:
* full differentiation using alternative pathways to teach the whole ability range and *Access* course for reluctant leaners
* structured grammar and skills practice at the right level.

### How does *Clic!* make it easier for you to meet the needs of your students?

Firstly, *Clic!* provides *clarity*:
* **a clear structure**
  - There are nine units per part, which makes it easy to teach one unit per half-term.
  - Each unit has three core spreads, plus vocabulary and test pages.
  - Additional (optional) spreads provide further practice and video pages.
* **clear presentation**
  - Activities are colour-coded by skill so that students can find their way easily around a spread.
  - Key language is highlighted, and core grammar and skills are presented in context.
* **clear progression**
  - Clear teaching and learning objectives show students exactly what they will learn.
  - Key grammar and skills are presented and practised carefully and systematically.

- Students are able to check their progress and identify areas for improvement via each unit's *I can…* statements on each unit's vocabulary page.

## The components of *Clic! Access*

### Students' Books

Both Students' Books consist of nine main units.

The units are set in different contexts. Each unit has been planned to be interesting and motivating, as well as to provide a coherent and systematic approach to language development in terms of grammar and study skills. An outline of the content of each unit is given on pages 4–5 of this book.

#### Core spreads
There are three core spreads per unit, via which the key language is presented and practised. Each double-page spread includes:
* a clear statement of the themes of the spread, given in English
* activities in all four skills to practise the key language of the spread
* colour-coding to identify each skill (listening, speaking, reading, writing)
* clearly identified key language panels, providing support and reference for students
* clearly presented grammar boxes to introduce and recap on grammar points
* language learning skills

For most units, there is a video clip on the topic(s) covered in that unit. In Book 2 these focus on the activities of three teenagers in Paris: Joe is an English boy visiting his French penfriend Max, and Nina is one of Max's friends. The video clips provide cultural information and highlight cultural differences and similarities between France and the UK. Activities to help students access the clips are provided in the Students' Book (*Blog-notes* and *Clic-vidéo*).

#### À moi!
This page provides additional practice material. It can be used in class, or as homework.

#### Grammaire
A grasp of grammar and structure lies at the heart of language learning. Grammatical items are incorporated into the regular sequence of activities running through the units, so that they are seen as an integral part of language practice.

An overview of the grammar points and language learning strategies covered in each unit is provided on pages 4–5 of this book.

*Vocabulaire*

This theme-based summary of the key language of the unit can be used by students as a reference or as an aid to learning.

*Clic-test*

This revision page recaps on the language and structures of the unit, and can also be used as a quick formative test of all four skills. The page is divided into four sections: listening, speaking, reading and writing.

*Blog-notes/Clic-vidéo*

This regular feature summarises the main points of the unit in context in the form of a video – a format that students should find fun, familiar and motivating.

*Glossaire*

A French–English glossary contains the words in the Students' Books for students' reference.

## Teacher's Book

Each unit contains the following detailed teaching notes:
- a Unit Overview Grid, providing a summary of the unit
- a Medium Term Plan, showing coverage of the teaching materials per week
- a Planner section for each core teaching spread for ease of lesson planning, including suggestions for starter and plenary activities
- ideas for presenting and practising new language
- detailed notes on all the Students' Book material, including answers to all activities
- suggestions for further activities to reinforce and extend the content of the Students' Book
- cross-references to other course components, e.g. margin icons indicate where corresponding resources are available on the *Clic! Interactif OxBox CD-ROMs*, or in Copymasters
- transcripts for all listening material and video clips.

## Audio CDs

The CDs provide the listening material to accompany the Students' Books. The listening material was recorded by native French speakers. The material is scripted and contains a range of text types, including monologues, short dialogues and longer conversations. All recorded material may be copied within the purchasing institution for use by teachers and students.

### CD contents

| | |
|---|---|
| CD 1 | Book 1, Units 1–6 |
| CD 2 | Book 1, Units 7–9 |
| | Book 2, Units 1–3 |
| CD 3 | Book 2, Units 4–9 |

## Copymasters

The Copymasters provide opportunities for extension of the language of the unit. They are cross-referenced in appropriate units of the teaching notes. They provide extended speaking, listening, reading and writing practice, allowing students access to more challenging activities.

## OxBox CD-ROMs

OxBox is a 'toolkit' of electronic resources provided for the main *Clic!* course. Some of the interactive activities are suitable for this *Access* course and these have been flagged up in appropriate units of the teaching notes. These activities provide further opportunities to either present the main language (in the electronic flashcard presentations) or to practise the key language (in the interactive activities). The interactive activities include sequencing, linking lines, drag and drop, fill the gap and multiple-choice activities.

# Course progression

## Teaching *Clic! Access* at Key Stage 3

*Clic! Access* has been designed so that it is possible to complete six units in a year. It is estimated that each unit will cover approximately half a term's work.

If your students have been set in year 8 and you have a class of least able students at the start of year 8, you can use Part 1 in year 8 and Part 2 in year 9, concentrating on the core spreads and using the additional material selectively.

## *Clic!* and the renewed Key Stage 3 Framework for Languages (2009)

The renewed Key Stage 3 Framework for Languages is effective as of the 1st September 2009. The new Framework has been created to improve alignment with other key initiatives such as the new secondary curriculum and the Key Stage 2 Framework for Languages. One of the main changes is that the focus is on the students' learning, so objectives in each strand are no longer called 'teaching objectives' but 'learning objectives'. *Clic!* has been fully updated in light of the new Key Stage 3 Framework.

## Review of the Key Stage 3 Programme of Study

The Modern Languages Key Stage 3 Programme of Study has been revised following consultations to increase curriculum flexibility and improve coherence and progression across Key Stages 2 to 4. The review reorganises the Programme of Study to match a common format. It also aims to align level descriptions with Languages Ladder statements.

The new Programme of Study identifies a number of *key concepts* – linguistic competence, knowledge about language, creativity, and intercultural understanding – that students need to deepen and broaden their skills and knowledge. It also identifies *key processes*, in the form of language learning strategies – identifying patterns, memorising techniques, applying knowledge of English, etc. – and specific language skills, for example listening for gist, initiating and sustaining conversations, re-using language in new contexts, etc. Many of these will be familiar to language teachers, but in the writing of *Clic!* we have taken care to ensure that the development of strategies and skills is specifically addressed and practised throughout the course.

## Presentation and practice of new language

*Clic! Access* provides extensive visual and audio-visual support for presentation and practice of new vocabulary.

In the Students' Book, new language is presented via the core spreads in a variety of ways, through photos, illustrations and different types of text. Recorded material is provided on CD and may be used for repetition by students in order to ensure the best possible pronunciation and intonation.

Once presented, the key language of each unit is developed through a wide variety of mixed-skill practice, with activities to ensure language development from supported/guided to more open-ended. *Clic!* intends each activity to have a purpose for students, and to be interesting and motivating as well as promoting linguistic development. Students should be encouraged to learn by heart on a regular basis, not only items of vocabulary but also short conversations. This promotes good language learning habits and ensures that students are able to transfer language learned to new contexts.

Additional reinforcement and extension activities are provided in the end sections of each unit (*À moi!;  Blog-notes/Clic-vidéo*).

## Target language in the classroom

*Clic!* aims to maximise the use of French as the means of communication in the classroom by providing rubrics in French wherever appropriate. It is worth spending time on a regular basis revising classroom language, so that students are reminded of the key phrases and encouraged to use them as much as possible.

## Differentiation

*Clic! Access* is specifically aimed at the least able (NC levels 1–2/3). The worksheets in Copymasters, OxBox activities and videos provide additional differentiation.

## Independent learning

In the early stages of learning a new language, students are reasonably dependent on their teacher for presentation of new language. However, the following features of *Clic! Access* are designed to encourage learner independence:
- The end sections of each unit (e.g. *À moi!, Blog-notes/ Clic-vidéo*) are ideal for independent work.
- Each unit's *I can...* statements on the vocabulary page encourages students to take responsibility for their own learning by providing opportunities to review their progress and reflect on areas for improvement.
- The *Vocabulaire* pages at the end of each unit can be used independently by students as a reference source or as an aid to learning.
- Language learning strategies throughout (*Top tips!*) encourage students to progress as independent learners.

## Thinking skills and creativity

One of the key aims of *Clic!*, and of the new KS3 MFL Framework as a whole, is that students should be able to learn in a meaningful way. This means, for example, thinking flexibly, analysing language and problem-solving, justifying answers, and making predictions based on previous knowledge. It encourages students to move towards becoming independent learners. Once students take a more active role in their language learning, they make quicker progress and the thinking skills learned can be applied to other curriculum areas.

Creativity in language learning is not simply imaginative use of language, such as poetry, creative writing, etc. It also refers to resourcefulness, e.g. finding ways to express oneself using only a limited range of language, taking risks and experimenting with language.

See previous paragraph on **Independent learning** on this page for examples of features of *Clic! Access* that encourage students to take a more active role in their learning. In addition, the following types of activity used in *Clic!* help to promote thinking skills and creativity:
- Encourage students to deduce new language for themselves (e.g. verb endings, adjective endings) by working from what they already know.
- Ask students to spot the odd-one-out in a group of words/phrases, giving a reason. All appropriate answers should be accepted, provided that students can justify them, e.g. answers may be based on meaning, grammar, pronunciation, etc.
- Encourage students to apply previously learned language in different contexts.
- Provide opportunities for students to use language spontaneously. This promotes the development of coping strategies, since students need to find ways of communicating when they don't know the word for something, dealing with unpredictable situations, etc.
- Provide opportunities for students to share their knowledge in pairs/groups or during whole-class feedback.

## Assessment

### Assessment of learning
Regular assessment of student progress is an integral part of the learning process. *Clic! Access* offers an approach to assessment in line with the National Curriculum and the 5–14 National Guidelines.

*Clic! Access* provides the following assessment opportunities:
- The *Clic-test* page at the end of each unit in the Students' Book can be used either as a revision page or as a quick formative test of all four skills.
- In the Planner boxes in this book, activities that may be suitable for formative assessment have been suggested for each double page spread.

### Assessment for Learning
Assessment for Learning (AfL) helps students to know and understand the standard they are aiming for, and also to understand what they need to do in order to achieve their objectives. It involves not only sharing learning goals with students, but also involving them in both peer- and self-assessment. AfL stresses the importance of ensuring that the information gained about students' progress is used, by both teachers and learners, to identify the next steps for learning.

This might involve giving students opportunities to talk about what they have learned and what they have found difficult.

Each unit's *I can...* checklist in the Students' Book is specifically designed to encourage students to review their progress and reflect on areas for improvement.

Further guidance on AfL can be found in *Training Materials for the Foundation Subjects* (Module 1 "Assessment for learning in everyday lessons"), which is available to download from The Standards Site (managed by the Department for Children, Schools and Families) (www.standards.dfes.gov.uk). For further guidance on AfL, see also the website of the Qualifications and Curriculum Authority (QCA) (www.qca.org.uk).

# How to teach the renewed KS3 MFL Framework with *Clic!*

## Long Term Plans and Medium Term Plans

- Long Term Plan (LTP)
  This provides an overview of objectives covered in *Clic! Access*. See pages 6–7 of this book for the *Clic! Access* Long Term Plans.
- Medium Term Plans (MTPs)
  These relate to individual units within the course and aim to cover six weeks' work. The MTPs provide a clear picture of the context for learning. See the beginning of each unit's teaching notes in this book for a copy of the MTP for each unit.

## Key areas of teaching and learning

*Clic! Access* reflects the focus of the MFL Framework on key areas of teaching and learning. These include:

- **Starters**
  – Suggestions for starter activities for each core spread are given in the Planner sections in this Teacher's Book.
- **Setting lesson objectives**
  – The Planner sections provide a clear list of objectives for each spread in terms of contexts and grammar. These can easily be adapted into individual lesson objectives.
- **Modelling**
  – *Clic! Access* provides clear examples for all activities, where appropriate, so that students have a visual demonstration of how to complete the activity.
  – Specific guidance is also given in the teacher's notes.
- **Questioning**
- **Practice**
- **Plenaries**
  – Suggestions for plenary activities for each core spread are given in the Planner sections in this Teacher's Book.

# La France et le français

| Unité 1: La France et le français Overview grid | | | | | | |
|---|---|---|---|---|---|---|
| Page reference | Contexts and objectives | Grammar | Language strategies and pronunciation | Key language | Framework | AT level |
| 4–5<br>**1.1 Vive la France!** | • Talk about France<br>• Recognise words in French | | | *Bonjour!* | 3.1, 5.3 | |
| 6–7<br>**1.2 Bonjour!** | • Say your name<br>• Say what nationality you are | • *je suis, tu es*<br>• Masculine and feminine adjectives | Listening to word endings | *Bonjour!*<br>*Je m'appelle …*<br>*Je suis français(e), sénégalais(e), britannique.* | 1.1, 1.4, 5.1 | 1.1<br>2.1<br>4.1 |
| 8–9<br>**1.3 En français!** | • Use French in class<br>• Spell words in French | • *tu, vous* | Using the alphabet<br>Pronunciation of accents | *Je ne comprends pas.*<br>*s'il te plaît*<br>*s'il vous plaît*<br>*Tu as un stylo?*<br>*Les toilettes, s'il vous plaît?* | 1.4, 2.1, 4.1, 5.4 | 1.1–2<br>2.1<br>3.1–2 |
| 10<br>**1.4 Vocabulaire** | • Practise pronunciation | | Not pronouncing the final *s*<br>*se* ending sounding like *z* | | 4.1, 5.5 | |
| 11<br>**1.4 Clic-test!** | • Recap on the language and structures of the unit<br>• Provide an opportunity for quick testing of all four skills | | | | 5.7 | 1.1–2<br>2.1–2<br>3.1–2<br>4.1–2 |
| 76<br>**À moi** | • Provide reinforcement activities for self-access work | | | | 2.1, 2.3, 2.4 | 3.2<br>4.2 |

| | | |
|---|---|---|
| **MEDIUM TERM GRID Week-by-week overview (assuming six weeks' work or approximately 10–12.5 hours)** | | |

**About Unit 1, *La France et le français***

In this unit, students are introduced to France, speaking a different language and recognising the French language. They are also introduced to adjectives of nationality (both masculine and feminine), the difference between *tu* and *vous*, using the alphabet to spell out words and listening carefully to word endings (masculine and feminine). Vocabulary introduced includes simple greetings, name, nationalities and phrases students need to use and understand in the classroom.

Reading, listening and comprehension skills are developed through a variety of texts, audio and video materials.

| Week | Resources | Objectives |
|---|---|---|
| 1 | 1.1 Vive la France! | Introduction to France and the French language<br>Talking about France including geography and general cultural information<br>Speaking in different languages<br>Recognising words in French<br>Saying hello |
| 2 | 1.2 Bonjour! | Saying your name and saying hello<br>Saying your nationality<br>French-speaking countries<br>Masculine and feminine adjectives |
| 3 | 1.3 En français! | Using French in the classroom<br>Asking for things in French<br>Using *tu* and *vous*<br>Saying the alphabet and spelling names out<br>French accents |
| 4 | Sound French! (p10)<br>À moi (p76)<br>Copymasters,<br>OxBox | Practising pronunciation (not sounding the final *s* and pronunciation of *se* at the end of a word)<br>Additional reading and writing practice<br>Using additional resources, such as Copymasters and OxBox activities, to reinforce and extend language met |
| 5 | 1.4 Vocabulaire<br>Clic-test! | Learning vocabulary<br>Recapping on vocabulary of unit<br>Preparing and carrying out of assessment in all four skills<br>Reviewing progress |
| 6 | Copymasters<br>(*Feuilles*)<br>OxBox | Reinforcement and extension of the language of the unit using extra resources<br>Reviewing progress via the Checklist on page 10, *Vocabulaire*<br>Going back over aspects of the unit which need reviewing after *Clic-test!* |

# 1.1 Vive la France

## *Planner*

> ### Objectives
> - Talk about France
> - Recognise words in French

> ### Resources
> Students' Book, pages 4–5
> CD 1, tracks 2–3

> ### Key language
> *Bonjour!*

> ### Framework reference
> 3.1, 5.3

> ### Starters
> - In English, students name as many foreign languages as they can in 30 seconds.
> - Name a country and students tell you which languages they think are spoken there.

> ### Plenaries
> - Discuss which languages students have experience of. Do they speak another language at home? Have they heard any other languages on holiday, on television or in their town/school? Why is it important to be able to speak different languages?
> - Each student says hello in French to create a Mexican Wave around the class

> ### Assessment opportunities
> - Reading: Students' Book page 5, exercise 5

### 1 Discute

- Students look at the map and the photos. Discuss with them what they already know about France and then explain details about the photos. Talk about the fact that not only people in France speak French, but that French is also the main language of many other countries too.

### 2 Lis.

- Students read the information about France and then discuss it as a class. Did they know that French is spoken in many African countries?

### 3 Écoute.

- Students listen to snippets of four different languages: English, French, German and Chinese. They identify in which order they hear them.
- In English, discuss the general sound of the languages: are they hard, soft, flowing, choppy?

*Answers*: a, c, d, b

 **CD 1, track 2**      page 5, activité 3

- *[Extract in English]*
- *[Extract in German]*
- *[Extract in Chinese]*
- *[Extract in French]*

### 4 Écoute.

- Students hear four people saying the greeting in the bubbles and note the order in which they hear them.

*Answers*: 1 d; 2 c; 3 a; 4 b

 **CD 1, track 3**      page 5, activité 4

1 Guten Morgen.
2 Good morning.
3 *[Hello in Chinese]*
4 Bonjour!

### 5 Lis.

- Students read and match each of the bubbles, which all mean 'hello'.
- Do students know any other languages (apart from Chinese) which use different letters or scripts?
- Do students see any similarities between English and German?

*Answers*: a Chinese; b French; c English; d German

# 1.2 Bonjour!

## *Planner*

> ### Objectives
> - Say your name
> - Say what nationality you are

> ### Resources
> Students' Book, pages 4–7
> CD 1, tracks 4–7
> OxBox *Clic! 1 Star, Unité 0 Départ, Bonjour!*

> ### Key language
> *Bonjour!*
> *Je m'appelle …*
> *Je suis français(e), sénégalais(e), britannique.*

> ### Grammar
> *je suis, tu es*
> Masculine and feminine adjectives

> ### Framework reference
> 1.1, 1.4, 5.1

> ### Starters
> - Focus on the two Senegalese teenagers on page 6 and point out that French is the official language of Senegal. Can students remember any other countries where French is spoken?
> - Bring in some photos of celebrities from magazines or the internet. Hold each one up, slowly revealing the image. Students say a greeting followed by the person's name in French: *Bonjour! Je m'appelle …*

> ### Plenaries
> - Display some French/British celebrity photos and the nationalities, *français, française, britannique*. Students match each photo to a nationality.
> - In pairs or groups, students discuss why it is important to use French as much as possible in the classroom. Suggestions could include: it's fun, it helps you learn quicker, etc.

> ### Assessment opportunities
> - Writing: Students' Book page 7, exercise 8

---

**AT 1.1** **1 Écoute, lis et répète.**

- Students listen while following the captions in the book and repeat. This is to give them a clear model of correct pronunciation and intonation. It introduces how to give your name in French.

*Answers:* 1 e; 2 b; 3 g; 4 f

 **CD 1, track 4**       page 6, activité 1

1  – Bonjour! Je m'appelle Thomas.
2  – Je m'appelle Manon.
3  – Je m'appelle Kouakou.
4  – Bonjour! Je m'appelle Adama!

**AT 1.1** **2 Écoute (1–4). Qui parle?**

- Students listen to the four teenagers giving a greeting and note in which order they speak.

*Answers:* 1 Adama; 2 Thomas; 3 Manon; 4 Kouakou

 **CD 1, track 5**       page 6, activités 2 et 3

1  – Bonjour! Je m'appelle Adama!
2  – Bonjour! Je m'appelle Thomas.
3  – Je m'appelle Manon.
4  – Je m'appelle Kouakou.

**AT 1.1** **3 Réécoute**

- Students listen again and put up their hand when they hear the word for 'hello'. They have met this in the previous spread. Students are also asked to pick out the specific phrase for 'my name is'.

*Answers:* a Bonjour!; b Je m'appelle.

**AT 2.1** **4 Parle et écris.**

- Students work in pairs. They each pretend to be a celebrity and introduce themselves to their partner. This could also work as a group activity.
- As follow-up, students write down how they would introduce themselves as three different celebrities.
- You may like to point out that *Je m'appelle* actually means 'I call myself'.

**AT 1.1** **5 Écoute et lis.**

- Students listen and follow the captions of six young people giving their nationality. They are asked questions on differences in the pronunciation of masculine and feminine nationalities.

*Answers:* a silent 's' when it is the final letter; b silent 's' when it is the final letter; c no

**CD 1, track 6**         page 7, activité 5

1 – Je m'appelle Thomas. Je suis français.
2 – Je m'appelle Manon. Je suis française.
3 – Je m'appelle Kouakou. Je suis sénégalais.
4 – Je suis sénégalaise. Je m'appelle Adama.
5 – Je m'appelle Harry. Je suis britannique.
6 – Je m'appelle Emily. Je suis britannique.

## Grammaire

- Discuss why pronunciation and spelling change when using masculine and feminine nationalities. Explain in as much detail as your students can cope with.
- Ask students to say what nationality they are. You may need to introduce new nationalities appropriate to your class.

 **6 Écoute (1–6). Qui parle?**

- Students listen and say which of the people from exercise 5 is speaking each time.

*Answers*: 1 Harry; 2 Emily; 3 Thomas; 4 Adama; 5 Kouakou; 6 Manon.

 **CD 1, track 7**         page 7, activité 6

| | |
|---|---|
| 1 | – Tu es britannique? |
| | – Oui, je suis britannique. |
| 2 | – Tu es britannique? |
| | – Oui, je suis britannique |
| 3 | – Tu es britannique? |
| | – Non, je suis français. |
| 4 | – Tu es britannique? |
| | – Non, je suis sénégalaise. |
| 5 | – Tu es français? |
| | – Non, je suis sénégalais. |
| 6 | – Tu es française? |
| | – Oui, je suis française. |

 **7 À deux.**

- Students work in pairs and interview each other, pretending to be people from this spread. This would also work as a group or whole class activity. The key language box provides support for this activity.

 **8 Écris.**

- Students find a photo of a famous British or French person from a magazine or the internet and write a speech bubble containing their name and nationality.

### Follow-up

- Throw a soft ball to someone in the class. They introduce themselves by saying *Bonjour!* followed by *Je m'appelle* + name and *Je suis* + nationality, before throwing the ball to someone else. Continue around the class making sure no one is left out.
- At this point you could use the interactive activity in OxBox, *Bonjour!* Students listen to nationalities and match them to the correct pictures. They identify meaning and gender.

# 1.3 En français!

## *Planner*

> **Objectives**
> - Use French in class
> - Spell words in French

> **Resources**
> Students' Book, pages 8–9
> CD 1, tracks 8–10
> OxBox *Clic! 1 Star, Unité 1, L'alphabet*

> **Key language**
> *Je ne comprends pas.*
> *s'il te plaît*
> *s'il vous plaît*
> *Tu as un stylo?*
> *Les toilettes, s'il vous plaît.*

> **Grammar**
> *tu, vous*

> **Framework reference**
> 1.4, 2.1, 4.1, 5.4

> **Starters**
> - Write six letters on the board and give students 30 seconds to put them into alphabetical order. If they already know the French alphabet (from primary school), ask them to read the letters out loud. Repeat this with other sets of letters.
> - Play Hangman using students' names.

> **Plenaries**
> - Spell out the names of nationalities or countries students have met so far. Students note down the letters and work out what the words spell.
> - Students say the alphabet as a whole class, in a Mexican Wave, with each student saying one letter each.

> **Assessment opportunities**
> - Writing: Student Book page 9, exercise 6

---

 **1 Écoute et lis.**

- Students listen to the cartoon while following it in their books. Can they guess the meanings of the phrases from the pictures? Explain any words they can't guess.

 **CD 1, track 8** — page 8, activité 1

1 – Bonjour, la classe!
2 – Bonjour!
3 – Faites l'activité trois!
4 – Je ne comprends pas.
5 – Tu as un stylo, s'il te plaît?
6 – Silence!
7 – Madame, les toilettes, s'il vous plaît!
8 – Fais vite!

 **2 Relie.**

- Students match the English phrases to the French phrases in the cartoon.
- As follow-up, students could read the cartoon out loud in pairs to practise pronunciation.

*Answers*: a 6; b 4; c 1; d 7; e 5; f 8; g 3; h 2

**Follow-up**

- Discuss strategies for practising and remembering classroom language. You could display a phrase of the week somewhere in class and encourage students to use it as often as possible during that week.

 **3 Écoute, lis et répète.**

- This activity asks students to repeat the letters of the alphabet, firstly just read out simply and then in a rap format.

**CD 1, track 9** — page 9, activité 3

A B C D E F G H I J K L M N O P Q R S T U V W X Y Z
On chante l'alphabet
L'ABC en français!
On chante l'alphabet en rap.
ABC
DEF
GHI
JKL
MNO
PQR
STU
VWX
YZ
[repeated]

**Follow-up**

- Students could make up their own alphabet raps by clicking fingers, clapping, etc.

 **4 Écoute, répète et continue. (1–6)**

- Students listen, repeat and say the next letter in the sequence.

*Answers*: 1 p; 2 t; 3 h; 4 d; 5 x; 6 j

**CD 1, track 10**   page 9, activité 4

1  m, n, o … p
2  q, r, s …
3  e, f, g …
4  a, b, c …
5  u, v, w …
6  g, h, i …

AT 2.1  **5 À deux.**

* Students work in pairs. One of them spells out the name of one of the famous French people listed. The other indicates who it is.

 **Follow-up**

* Students could work in pairs and spell out the name of somebody else in the class for a partner to write down.

* At this point you could use the interactive activity in OxBox, *L'alphabet*. Students listen to and practise the French alphabet.

AT 2.1  **6 Écris.**

* Students work in pairs. One spells out the name of a celebrity. The other writes the name down

# 1.4   Vocabulaire

page 10

## *Planner*

> **Resources**
Students' Book, page 10

> **Objectives**
* *Vocabulaire*: to provide a theme-based summary of the key language of the unit, which students can use as a reference or as an aid to learning
* To practise pronunciation

> **Framework reference**
4.1, 5.5

### Using the vocabulary page

* Encourage students to use the *Vocabulaire* page as a reference point throughout the unit. It can also serve as a useful revision tool before students do the *Clic-test*!
* Vocabulary is listed spread-by-spread and you could either ask students to learn each section for homework after each spread is completed, or set the whole page as a homework task before starting work on the test. Most students learn shorter sections best, so often it is better to give them manageable chunks to learn at a time.
* Encourage students to use different techniques to help them learn the vocabulary:
  – Cover up the English and see what they can remember; write down any words they can't remember and test themselves again on those words.
  – Cover up the French and see if they can remember the words or phrases this way round.
  – Make word cards with English on one side and French on the other. Students can then test themselves to see what they can remember. Put any cards they can't remember on one side and go over those again at the end.
  – Work in pairs to test each other, either using the vocabulary list or the word cards.
  – Record themselves saying the words both in English and French. Saying words and phrases out loud can often help with memorising them.

### Sound French!

* *Aim*: To practise pronunciation
* The points practised here are: not pronouncing the final *s* in French words and the ending *se* sounding like a *z*.
* Ask students to find examples of these in the vocabulary list and practise saying them out loud.

# 1.4 Clic-test!

page 11

## Planner

The page is divided into four sections: listening, speaking, reading and writing.

➤ **Objectives**
- To enable students to recap on the language and structures of the unit
- To provide an opportunity for quick testing of all four skills

➤ **Resources**
Students' Book, page 11
CD 1, track 11

➤ **Framework reference**
5.7

---

 **1 Écoute! (1–6)**
- Students listen and match each of the sentences to one of the English summaries.

*Answers*: 1 b; 2 a; 3 f; 4 e; 5 d; 6 c

**CD 1, track 11**  page 11, activité 1

1 Je m'appelle Jonathan.
2 Jonathan, c'est j-o-n-a-t-h-a-n.
3 Je suis français.
4 Bonjour, Susie!
5 S'il vous plaît! S'il vous plaît? Un stylo, s'il vous plaît!
6 Susie! Un stylo, s'il te plaît … Super, merci!

 **2 Lis!**
- Students read and complete the sentences with the correct words from the box.

*Answers*: a Amélie; b brittanique; c française; d m'appelle; e suis

 **3 Parle!**
- Students work with a partner and say six things in French from the list, in less than two minutes.

 **4 Écris!**
- Students write a speech bubble for each of the people listed, giving their name and nationality.

*Answers*: a Bonjour! Je m'appelle Thierry Henri. Je suis français. Bonjour! Je m'appelle Audrey Tautou. Je suis française. Bonjour! Je m'appelle Lewis Hamilton. Je suis britannique. Bonjour! Je m'appelle Lily Allen. Je suis britannique.

# À moi

page 76

## Planner

➤ **Objectives**
- To provide reinforcement activities for quiet work
- To provide alternative class and homework material for students who finish other activities quickly

➤ **Resources**
Students' Book, page 76

➤ **Framework reference**
2.1, 2.3, 2.4

---

### Les célébrités

 **1 Read the speech bubbles. Who's speaking? Write the correct name.**
- Students work out who is speaking each time from the clues given in the bubbles.

*Answers*: 1 David Beckham; 2 Paula Radcliffe; 3 Audrey Tautou; 4 Patrick Vieira; 5 Youssou N'Dour; 6 Dji Dieng

### Top Tips!

- Talk about the strategies students used when doing exercise 1, such as looking for masculine and feminine adjective endings to help work out the answers.

 **2 Adapt one of the bubbles to write about a footballer, an athlete, a musician, an actress or a top model you like.**

- Demonstrate how to adapt the sentences on the whiteboard, if necessary. Ask students to bring in photos from magazines or the internet.

# C'est la France!

| Unité 2: C'est la France! Overview grid | | | | | | |
|---|---|---|---|---|---|---|
| Page reference | Contexts and objectives | Grammar | Language strategies and pronunciation | Key language | Framework | AT level |
| 12–13 **2.1 1, 2, 3 … en France** | • Use numbers 1–10 • Name French things | • *le, la, les* • *c'est* | Thinking of words that help you remember | Numbers 1–10 *C'est quoi?* *C'est le vélo, le football, le parfum.* *C'est la baguette, la Tour Eiffel, la pétanque.* *C'est les gâteaux, les bandes dessinées, les Carambars.* | 3.2, 4.2, 4.3 | 1.1 2.1–3 3.1 4.1 |
| 14–15 **2.2 Bienvenue en France!** | • Name places in town • Say what there is or isn't | • *un, une, des* • *il y a, il n'y a pas de* | | *Dans ma rue, il y a un restaurant, un café, un supermarché, un cinéma, une poste, une pharmacie, des toilettes, des magasins.* *Il n'y a pas de …* *aussi* | 4.3, 4.6, 5.2, 5.5 | 1.1–2 2.1–2 3.2 4.1–2 |
| 16–17 **2.3 Mon pays, c'est la France** | • Name some countries where French is spoken • Name the colours on flags | • *c'est le, la, l'* • *l'* before vowels | Asking and answering questions | *Ton pays, c'est quoi?* *Mon pays, c'est le Canada, le Sénégal, la Belgique, la France, la Suisse, l'Algérie.* *blanc, bleu, jaune, noir, rouge, orange, vert* | 2.2, 3.1, 4.6 | 1.1–3 2.1–2 3.1 4.1 |
| 18 **2.4 Vocabulaire** | • Practise pronunciation | | Making your voice go up when asking a question | | 4.6 | |
| 19 **2.4 Clic-test!** | • Recap on the language structures of the unit • Provide an opportunity for quick testing of all four skills | | | | 5.7 | 1.1–2 2.1–2 3.1–2 4.1–2 |
| 77 **À moi** | • Provide reinforcement activities for self-access work | | | | 2.1, 2.4 | 3.2 4.2 |
| 85 **Blog-notes** | • Provide extended listening practice recycling the language of the whole unit | | | | 1.2, 1.3, 5.7 | 1.2–3 2.2–3 4.2 |

| MEDIUM TERM GRID Week-by-week overview (assuming six weeks' work or approximately 10–12.5 hours) |
|---|

**About Unit 2, *C'est la France!***

In this unit, students discover more about France and French-speaking countries, nouns and gender, (*le, la, l', les and un, une, des*, negatives, asking questions and ways of remembering words.

New vocabulary includes numbers 1–10, French things, places in a town, countries where French is spoken and colours.

Reading, listening and comprehension skills are developed through a variety of texts, audio and video materials.

| Week | Resources | Objectives |
|---|---|---|
| 1 | 2.1 1, 2, 3 … en France | Using numbers 1–10 and naming typical French things<br>Using *c'est le, la, les*<br>Masculine, feminine and plural nouns<br>Thinking of ways that help you remember vocabulary |
| 2 | 2.2 Bienvenue en France! | Naming places in a town<br>Saying what there is and isn't in a town<br>Using *un, une, des*<br>Using *il y a* and *il n'y a pas de* … |
| 3 | 2.3 Mon pays, c'est la France | Naming some countries where French is spoken<br>Understanding that French is spoken throughout the world<br>Naming colours on flags<br>Using *l'* before a vowel<br>Asking and answering questions |
| 4 | **Sound French!** (p18)<br>**À moi** (p77)<br>**Blog-notes** (p85) | Practising pronunciation (making your voice go up when asking a question)<br>Additional reading and writing practice<br>Using additional resources, such as Copymasters and OxBox activities, to reinforce and extend language met<br>Using the video for reinforcement, extension and follow-up work |
| 5 | **2.4 Vocabulaire**<br>Clic-test! | Learning vocabulary<br>Recapping on vocabulary of unit<br>Preparing and carrying out of assessment in all four skills<br>Reviewing progress |
| 6 | Copymasters (*Feuilles*)<br>OxBox | Reinforcement and extension of the language of the unit using extra resources<br>Reviewing progress via the Checklist on page 18, *Vocabulaire*<br>Going back over aspects of the unit which need reviewing after *Clic-test!* |

# 2.1   1, 2, 3 … en France

## *Planner*

> ### Objectives
> - Use numbers 1–10
> - Name French things

> ### Resources
> Students' Book, pages 12–13
> CD 1, tracks 12–15
> Video clip 7, *Clic! 1 Star*
> OxBox *Clic! 1 Star, Unité 1, un, deux, trois; La France; Nouns and gender*
> Copymasters 3, 12, *Clic! 1 Star*

> ### Key language
> Numbers 1–10
> *C'est quoi?*
> *C'est le vélo, le football, le parfum.*
> *C'est la baguette, la Tour Eiffel, la pétanque.*
> *C'est les gâteaux, les bandes dessinées, les Carambars.*

> ### Grammar
> *le, la, les*
> *c'est*

> ### Framework reference
> 3.2, 4.2, 4.3

> ### Starters
> - Students suggest places or items, such as types of food, which make them think of France.
> - Students do number bonds in pairs where one student says a number between one and ten, and the other student gives the number needed to make it up to ten:
>   A: *six*
>   B: *quatre! … un*
>   A: *neuf! …*

> ### Plenaries
> - In groups, students take turns to count from one to ten and then backwards from ten to one. The aim is to do this as quickly as possible, but accurately and with good pronunciation. Students time/ assess each other.
> - Students tell a partner three things which they have learned about France during this lesson and from the Unit 1 opening spread. Allow time for pairs to report back to the whole class.

> ### Assessment opportunities
> - Listening: Students' Book page 13, exercise 8

### Preparation
- Look at the photo of the French football team. Do students recognise any of the payers? What numbers can they see? Explain that they are going to learn numbers 1–10 on this spread.
- Students can complete exercise 1 *À tes marques!* from Copymaster 3.

*Answers*: 1a neuf, quatre, huit, un, six, trois; 1b deux, cinq, sept, dix

 **1 Écoute, lis et répète.**

- Students listen to the numbers 1–10 and repeat each one, imitating the pronunciation as closely as possible.

**CD 1, track 12**          page 12, activité 1

un, deux,
trois, quatre,
cinq, six,
sept, huit,
neuf, dix.

### Top Tips!
- Work together as a class, or ask students to work in pairs, to think of words in English that may help them remember the numbers 1–10 in French: *un* 'uh'; *deux* 'der'; *trois* 'trwa'; *quatre* 'cat'; *cinq* 'sank'; *six* 'sis'; *sept* 'set'; *huit* 'wheat'; *neuf* 'nuff'; *dix* 'diss'..

 **2 Écoute et continue.**

- Students listen to a series of two numbers and say the next number in each sequence.

*Answers*: 1 trois; cinq; sept; neuf; 2 quatre; six; huit; dix

**CD 1, track 13**          page 12, activité 2

| 1 | 2 |
|---|---|
| – un, deux | – un! |
| – trois, quatre | – deux, trois |
| – cinq, six | – quatre, cinq |
| – sept, huit | – six, sept |
| – dix! | – huit, neuf |

**Follow-up**

- Students could work in pairs doing similar sequences as exercise 2. Student A says two numbers and student B says the next number.

 **3 Dictée de chiffres.**

- Say numbers 1–10 in a random order in French. Students note the numbers in figures in the order you say them. Repeat with students acting as the teacher.

 **4 Lis et écris les nombres.**

- Students separate the written French numbers in the word scarf. They should also write the numbers in figures to show understanding.

*Answers*: deux 2; dix 10; trois 3; six 6; neuf 9; un 1; quatre 4; sept 7; cinq 5; huit 8

**Follow-up**

- Interactive matching activities on numbers 1–10 are available on OxBox, *un*, *deux*, *trois* and one on France, *La France*.
- Do further practice of numbers together. One student says a number and another says the number which comes before.
  A: *deux*.
  B: *un*.
- Extend this by asking for numbers before and after the given number.
- The next part of the spread concentrates on things that are typically French. If you have not already done so as a Starter activity, ask students for any places, people or items that come to mind when they think of France. Pool ideas and discuss as a class. If possible, bring in some items in advance, such as French cheese and pictures of French footballers, the Eiffel Tower, Mediterranean beaches, etc.

 **5 Écoute, lis et répète.**

- Students listen to the nine typically French items and repeat the answers. Point out the meaning of *C'est quoi?* before listening.
- Discuss the photos of the various items as a class. Which items would best represent their countries?

**CD 1, track 14**          page 13, activité 5

– Numéro 1, c'est quoi?
– C'est la baguette.
– Numéro 2, c'est quoi?
– C'est le football.
– Numéro 3, c'est quoi?
– C'est les bandes dessinées.
– Numéro 4, c'est quoi?
– C'est les Carambars.
– Numéro 5, c'est quoi?

– C'est la Tour Eiffel.
– Numéro 6, c'est quoi?
– C'est le vélo.
– Numéro 7, c'est quoi?
– C'est le parfum.
– Numéro 8, c'est quoi?
– C'est les gâteaux.
– Numéro 9, c'est quoi?
– C'est la pétanque.

## Grammaire

- The grammar box explains how there are three words for 'the' in French. Explain the concept of masculine, feminine and plural to the class, and use the captions from the photos to illustrate.

- Further practice of nouns and gender is provided by a grammar presentation on OxBox, Nouns and gender.

 **6 À deux.**

- Students work in pairs. One student says a number in French and the other student names the corresponding object on the page.

 **7 Recopie et complète le sudoku.**

- This activity practises thinking skills. Sudoku rules should be followed, meaning there must be three different words for 'the' horizontally and vertically. Students complete the nine boxes according to this rule.

*Answers*:

| le | les | la |
|----|-----|-----|
| les | la | le |
| la | le | les |

**Follow-up**

- Students could make more sudoku grids, using objects representative of their country. They could look up masculine and feminine words in a dictionary.

 **8 Regarde. Tu reconnais?**

- Students watch the video clip of teenagers saying what is typically French in their eyes. Can they recognise the items mentioned? Ask students to put up their hand when they recognise an item.
- Play the clip again and pause it when an unknown item is mentioned. Discuss the item.
- Ask students to identify the picture which isn't mentioned: picture 8 *les gâteaux*.

*Answers*: 1 la baguette; 3 les bandes dessinées; 7 le parfum; 2 le football; 6 le vélo; 5 la Tour Eiffel; 4 les Carambars; 9 le pétanque

**Video clip 7**  page 13, activité 8

**CD 1, track 15**

- Bonjour! Je m'appelle Julien. Je suis français. Aujourd'hui on va parler de la France. C'est quoi, la France? Regardez. C'est quoi pour toi la France?
- La France, c'est la baguette.
- La France, c'est Astérix.
- La France, c'est le parfum.
- La France, c'est quoi? ... C'est le football!
- C'est quoi la France pour toi? C'est le football?
- Le football? Non ... c'est le vélo.
- C'est quoi la France?
- C'est la Tour Eiffel.

- La France, c'est quoi? ... C'est la FNAC, non?
- La France pour moi, c'est le jean.
- C'est quoi pour toi la France?
- La France, c'est les Carambars.
- La France pour moi, c'est le TGV.
- La France, c'est la pétanque. C'est typiquement français, ça!

**C12 Follow-up**

- Copymaster 12 provides more work on typically French items. Students match the pictures representing various symbols of France to the corresponding words.

*Answers:* 1 h; 2 e; 3 b; 4 i; 5 g; 6 d; 7 a; 8 c; 9 f

# 2.2  Bienvenue en France! pages 14–15

## *Planner*

> **Objectives**
  - Name places in town
  - Say what there is and isn't

> **Resources**
  Students' Book, pages 14–15
  CD 1, tracks 16–18

> **Key language**
  *Dans ma rue, il y a un restaurant, un café, un supermarché, un cinéma, une poste, une pharmacie, des toilettes, des magasins.*
  *Il n'y a pas de ...*
  *aussi*

> **Grammar**
  *un, une, des*
  *il y a*
  *il n'y a pas de*

> **Framework reference**
  4.3, 4.6, 5.2, 5.5

> **Starters**
  - To revise numbers 1–10 (introduced in spread 2.1) set some simple sums for students to do against the clock. Alternatively, students could make up sums for a partner to solve:
  *quatre – trois = ...*
  *cinq + ... = sept*
  - Display photos of places in a town, but just reveal a small part of the picture. Students write the French words for the places in the order you show the photos.

> **Plenaries**
  - Call out a word from the lesson, such as *cinéma!* Students supply the correct indefinite article, *un cinéma*, or put the word into a sentence: *Il y a un cinéma.*
  - Give students two minutes to make as many different sentences as they can from the key language box on page 15.

> **Assessment opportunities**
  - Writing: Students' Book page 15, exercise 7

**AT 1.1**
**AT 2.1**
**1 Écoute, lis et répète.**
- Students listen to the places in a town and repeat each one, copying the pronunciation as closely as possible.

 **CD 1, track 16** page 14, activité 1

Dans ma rue, il y a ...
1 un restaurant
2 un café
3 un supermarché
4 un cinéma
5 une poste
6 une pharmacie
7 des toilettes
8 des magasins

**2 À deux!**

- This is a memory game. Student A says a number and student B names the matching place without looking back at the book.

 **3 Écoute. Oui ✓ ou non ✗ (1–8).**

- Before doing the activity, point out the small box which explains the negative. Give students a few sentences with *Il n'y'a pas de* and explain what it means. Say a few more sentences with *Il y a* and *Il n'y a pas de*. Ask students to respond with a thumbs-up for *Il y a* and a thumbs-down for *Il n'y a pas de*.
- Students jot down the numbers of the eight places from exercise 1. They then listen to Amélie and note with a tick or a cross whether the places are on her street or not.

*Answers*: 1 un restaurant ✓; 2 un café ✓; 3 un supermarché ✗; 4 un cinéma ✗; 5 une poste ✓; 6 une pharmacie ✗; 7 des toilettes ✓; 8 des magasins ✓

**CD 1, track 17**　　　　　　page 14, activité 3

**1**
– Il y a un restaurant?
– Oui, il y a un restaurant.

**2**
– Il y a un café?
– Oui, il y a un café.

**3**
– Il y a un supermarché?
– Non, il n'y a pas de supermarché.

**4**
– Il y a un cinéma?
– Non, il n'y a pas de cinéma.

**5**
– Il y a une poste?
– Oui, il y a une poste.

**6**
– Il y a une pharmacie?
– Non, il n'y a pas de pharmacie.

**7**
– Il y a des toilettes?
– Oui, il y a des toilettes.

**8**
– Il y a des magasins?
– Oui, il y a des magasins.

 **4 Trouve des photos. Écris.**

- Ask students to find photos of places in their town from a brochure, local paper or on the internet. They can use a dictionary to look up any new words for places.

## Grammaire

- Explain the words for 'a' and 'some' in French. Stress the fact that all places are either masculine or feminine. Ask students to look at the list of places and tell you which are masculine and which are feminine.

 **5 Écoute et lis. C'est Lola ou Lucas?**

- Students listen and follow the text of Lola and Lucas saying what there is and isn't on their street. They decide who the poster belongs to.

*Answer*: Lucas

**CD 1, track 18**　　　　　　page 15, activité 5

– Bienvenue dans ma rue.
Il y a un restaurant.
Il y a aussi des magasins.
Dans ma rue, il n'y a pas de cinéma.

– Bienvenue dans ma rue.
Il y a une pharmacie.
Il y a aussi des toilettes.
Dans ma rue, il n'y a pas de poste.

 **6 À deux!**

- Students work in pairs using the poster from exercise 5. Student A asks questions about places and student B responds with either a positive or negative answer.

 **7 Imagine une rue et écris!**

- Students make a poster of their ideal street. They draw symbols or find photos to accompany their sentences explaining what there is and isn't on their street.

# 2.3 Mon pays, c'est la France

## *Planner*

> ### Objectives
> * Name some countries where French is spoken
> * Name the colours in flags

> ### Resources
> Students' Book, pages 16–17
> CD 1, tracks 19–23
> OxBox *Clic! 1 Star, Unité 1, C'est quel drapeau?*
> Copymaster 5, *Clic! 1 Star*
> CD 3, track 53

> ### Key language
> *Ton pays, c'est quoi?*
> *Mon pays, c'est le Canada, le Sénégal, la Belgique, la France, la Suisse, l'Algérie.*
> *blanc, bleu, jaune, noir, rouge, orange, vert*

> ### Grammar
> *c'est le, la, l'*
> *l'* before vowels

> ### Framework reference
> 2.2, 3.1, 4.6

> ### Starters
> * Ask students if they can name any countries or regions (apart from France) where French is spoken. They should remember some from Unit 1.
> * If students already know the colours (from primary school perhaps), point at items in the classroom and ask them to name the colours. Alternatively, call out colours in French and ask students to point to something of the corresponding colour in the classroom.
> * For a competitive game, divide the class into approximately four teams. Each team appoints a 'runner' and when you call out a colour in French, the team members find an item of the appropriate colour (someone's pencil case, pen, bag, etc.) and give it to the runner, who brings it out to you. The first runner to hand you an item of the correct colour, wins a point for his/her team.

> ### Plenaries
> * Play Noughts and Crosses using colours. Prepare a three-by-three grid for use on the whiteboard, with a different colour in each square. In addition to the seven colours presented here, *gris, rose* and *violet* are introduced in OxBox, *C'est quel drapeau?* This then gives you enough colours to fill the nine squares. Divide the class into two teams. Team members name colours in an attempt to win three squares in a row.
> *  Display some groups of words from the spread and ask students to choose an odd-one-out in each: *la Belgique, la France, le Sénégal.* Accept *le Sénégal* because it isn't in Europe, or any other sensible answer. Explain there is no single correct answer for any of these, but students must be able to justify their choice.

> ### Assessment opportunities
> * Listening: Students' Book page 17, exercise 7

---

### 1 Écoute, lis et répète.

* Students listen to six teenagers introducing themselves and saying whey they live. They could listen first and then repeat, taking care with pronunciation.
* Explain that *mon pays* means 'my country'.

**CD 1, track 19**                    page 16, activité 1

**A**
Salut! Je m'appelle Nico.
Mon pays, c'est la France.
**B**
Salut! Je m'appelle Ana.
Mon pays, c'est le Sénégal.
**C**
Salut! Je m'appelle Samuel.
Mon pays, c'est le Canada.
**D**
Salut! Je m'appelle Omar.
Mon pays, c'est l'Algérie.
**E**
Salut! Je m'appelle Laura.
Mon pays, c'est la Belgique.
**F**
Salut! Je m'appelle Christophe.
Mon pays, c'est la Suisse.

### 2 Trouve le français.

* Students find the French names in exercise 1 for the English countries listed.
* Explain that French is spoken in all these countries.

*Answers*: a Canada/le Canada; b Senegal/le Sénégal; c Algeria/l'Algérie; d Belgium/la Belgique; e Switzerland/la Suisse; f France/la France

**3 Écoute et note l'ordre (A–F de l'activité 1).**

- Students listen and note the order of the countries mentioned from exercise 1.

*Answers*: F, C, E, B, A, D

  **CD 1, track 20**    page 16, activité 3

- – C'est quoi, ton pays?
- – Mon pays, c'est la Suisse. Et toi?
- – Mon pays, c'est le Canada.

- – Salut! C'est quoi, ton pays?
- – Mon pays, c'est la Belgique. Et toi?
- – Mon pays, c'est le Sénégal.

- – Salut! C'est quoi, ton pays?
- – Mon pays, c'est la France. Et toi?
- – Mon pays, c'est l'Algérie.

 **4 À deux.**

- Students interview each other, pretending they are the people in exercise 1, giving their name and saying where they are from.

**Follow-up**

- Explain that mon and ton mean 'my' and 'your'. If students can cope, you could also explain *ma* and *ta*.

 **5 Écoute, lis et répète.**

- Students look at the colours, listen and repeat each one.
- In addition to the colours introduced here, the digital flashcards on OxBox, *C'est quel drapeau?* include three extra colours, if required: *gris*, *rose* and *violet*.

**CD 1, track 21**    page 17, activité 5

bleu
jaune
rouge
vert
orange
noir
blanc

 **6 Complète.**

- Students list the colours on each national flag.

*Answers*: a bleu, blanc, rouge; b vert, jaune, rouge; c noir, jaune, rouge

 **7 Écoute. C'est quel pays? (1–5)**

- Students listen and say which of the flags pictured is being described.

*Answers*: 1 le Canada; 2 la France; 3 l'Algérie; 4; le Sénégal 5 la Belgique

  **CD 1, track 22**    page 17, activité 7

- – Numéro un: le drapeau est rouge et blanc.
- – Numéro deux: le drapeau est bleu, blanc, et rouge.
- – Numéro trois: le drapeau est vert, rouge, blanc.
- – Numéro quatre: le drapeau est vert, jeune, rouge.
- – Numéro cinq: le drapeau est noir, jaune, rouge.

 **8 À deux.**

- Students work in pairs. One student names the colours on one of the flags and the other student names the country.

**9 Écoute la chanson «Vive les couleurs!» C'est quel pays?**

- Play the song for students to listen to. Ask them to note which colours and countries are mentioned.
- Hand out colour cards to students. They hold them up when the colour on their card is mentioned.
- Students could write different verses for other flags, such as China (*rouge*, *jaune*) or Brazil (*vert*, *jaune*, *bleu*).

 **CD 1, track 23**    page 17, activité 9

**Vive les couleurs!**

Vive les couleurs! Vive les couleurs!
Bleu, blanc, rouge,
Noir, jaune, vert.

Vive la France! Vive la France!
Bleu, blanc, rougo,
Bleu, blanc, rouge.

Vive les couleurs! Vive les couleurs! ...

Vive la Belgique! Vive la Belgique!
Noir, jaune, rouge,
Noir, jaune, rouge.

Vive les couleurs! Vive les couleurs! ...

**Follow-up**

- An interactive matching activity on flags and colours is provided on OxBox, *C'est quel drapeau?*
- Students could research flags from other French-speaking countries. They could draw them and label the colours in French.

- Further activities to practise colours, countries and flags are provided on Copymaster 5, exercise 3 (listening). Students listen and note down the letter of each country's flag. This sheet also contains activities on numbers and the alphabet.

*Answers*: 1 b; 2 e; 3 a; 4 f; 5 d; 6 c

**CD 3, track 53** Feuille 5, *Clic! 1 Star*, activité 3

1 Mon pays, c'est le pays de Galles.
2 Mon pays, c'est la France.
3 Mon pays, c'est l'Algérie.
4 Mon pays, c'est la Suisse.
5 Mon pays, c'est le Sénégal.
6 Mon pays, c'est le Canada.

# 2.4 Vocabulaire
page 18

## *Planner*

> **Objectives**
  - *Vocabulaire*: to provide a theme-based summary of the key language of the unit, which students can use as a reference or as an aid to learning
  - To practise pronunciation and intonation

> **Resources**
Students' Book, page 18
Copymaster 10, *Clic! 1 Star*

> **Framework reference**
4.6

### Using the vocabulary page

- Encourage students to use the Vocabulaire page as a reference point throughout the unit. It can also serve as a useful revision tool before students do the Clic-test!
- Vocabulary is listed spread-by-spread and you could either ask students to learn each section for homework after each spread is completed, or set the whole page as a homework task before starting work on the test. Most students learn shorter sections best, so often it is better to give them manageable chunks to learn at a time.
- Encourage students to use different techniques to help them learn the vocabulary:
  - Cover up the English and see what they can remember; write down any words they can't remember and test themselves again on those words.
  - Cover up the French and see if they can remember the words or phrases this way round.
  - Make word cards with English on one side and French on the other. Students can then test themselves to see what they can remember. Put any cards they can't remember on one side and go over those again at the end.
  - Work in pairs to test each other, either using the vocabulary list or the word cards.
  - Record themselves saying the words both in English and French. Saying words and phrases out loud can often help with memorising them.

### Learning vocabulary

C10

- For general support in learning vocabulary, use Copymaster 10 which provides some activities to help students think of different ways of learning vocabulary.

*Answers*: 1a/1b

| c'est | *it is* |
|---|---|
| elle | *she* |
| la France | *France* |
| gallois | *Welsh* |
| il y a | *there is/are* |
| noir | *black* |
| oui | *yes* |
| le parfum | *perfume* |
| le pays | *country* |
| la pharmacie | *chemist* |
| quoi | *what* |
| sept | *seven* |
| le sportif | *sportsman* |
| les toilettes (f) | *toilets* |

*Possible answers*: 2
les pays: Algérie, Belgique, pays de Galles, Suisse
les nationalités et les adjectifs: allemand, anglaise, flamand, japonais, étrangère
les couleurs: blanc, brun, rouge, violet
les symboles de la France: Carambars, vélo
les numéros: dix, huit, trois
les prénoms: Nicole, Patrice
les expressions pour s'introduire: je m'appelle
autres expressions: c'est, elle est, il y a

### Sound French!

- *Aim*: To practise intonation in questions
- Point out that when you ask a question in French, you can make a sentence into a question simply by making your voice go up at the end. Give students a few examples, then make a statement and ask them to turn it into a question, just by changing the intonation of their voice.

## 2.4    Clic-test!

page 19

---

### *Planner*

The page is divided into four sections: listening, speaking, reading and writing.

➢ **Objectives**
  - To enable students to recap on the language and structures of the unit

- To provide an opportunity for quick testing of all four skills

➢ **Resources**
  Students' Book, page 19
  CD 1, track 24

➢ **Framework reference**
  5.7

---

 **1 Écoute!  (1–6)**

- Students listen and match each of the extracts to one of the summaries.

*Answers*: 1 b; 2 f; 3 a; 4 e; 5 d; 6 c

 **CD 1, track 24**          page 19, activité 1

**1**
– C'est quoi?
– C'est la Tour Eiffel!

**2**
– Alors, il y a une poste, un supermarché et une pharmacie.

**3**
– C'est bleu et rouge?
– Non, c'est vert et jaune.

**4**
– Alors, il y a un, deux, trois, quatre gâteaux.
– Non, il y a cinq gâteaux.

**5**
– Mon pays, c'est le Canada. Et toi?
– Moi, mon pays, c'est la Belgique.

**6**
– Il y a un cinéma?
– Euh non, il n'y a pas de cinéma.

 **2 Lis!**

- Students find the correct French sentences to match the English statements.

*Answers*: a 5; b 6; c 3; d 4; e 1; f 2

 **3 Parle!**

- Students play a memory game in pairs. They take turns asking each other whether their town has a certain place or not. They answer according to the pictures which they must remember from the book.

 **4 Écris.**

- Students write answers to five questions about themselves.

*Answers*: a Salut!/Bonjour!; b Je m'appelle ...; c Mon pays, c'est ...; d Dans ma rue, il y a ...; e C'est ...

# À moi

## *Planner*

> **Objectives**
> • To provide reinforcement activities for quiet work
> • To provide alternative class and homework material for students who finish other activities quickly

> **Resources**
> Students' Book, page 77

> **Framework reference**
> 2.1, 2.4

### Les mascottes!

**1 Read the descriptions of the World Cup mascots. Match each one to its photo.**

• From their understanding of colours and countries, students should be able to match each mascot to the correct short text.

*Answers*: 1 B; 2 D; 3 A; 4 C

AT 4.2 | **2 Read the details for 2010 in the blue box. Write the description for this mascot.**

• Using the details given and the other texts as a model, students write a similar text for the 2010 mascot.

*Answers*: Je m'appelle Zakumi. Mon pays, c'est l'Afrique du Sud. Mes couleurs, c'est vert, jaune et blanc.

AT 4.2 | **3 Design your own World Cup mascot! Draw it and write its description in French.**

• Students can now use their creativity to design their own mascot and write about it.

# Blog-notes

## *Planner*

> **Objectives**
> • To summarise the main points of the unit in context, in a format that is fun and familiar to students, i.e. a video blog
> • To provide a model enabling students to personalise the language of the unit
> • To provide opportunities for students to ask as well as answer questions
> • To provide extended listening practice recycling the language of the whole unit

> **Resources**
> Students' Book, page 85
> Video clip 3, *Clic! 1 Star*
> CD 1, track 25
> Copymaster 2, *Clic! 1 Star*

> **Framework reference**
> 1.2, 1.3, 5.7

### Preparation

• Discuss with students how to plan and prepare for the activities on this page.
• Encourage them to prepare for watching the video clip by reading through the questions and checking they understand them. Can they predict any of the answers before watching the video, e.g. by looking at the photos and ID card?
• Point out that the answers are likely to come up on the video in the same sequence as the questions are listed in the book, so students can focus on each question in order.
• It is worth spending time at this early stage focusing on how to plan and prepare for a piece of work, because this is a skill that students will find useful throughout their learning.

**1 Watch Thomas' video diary. Choose a or b to complete each sentence.**

- Students watch the video diary which Thomas has recorded and choose a or b to complete each statement correctly. Pause the video after each section to allow students time to answer.

*Answers*: 1 b; 2 b; 3 b; 4 a; 5 a

 **Video clip 3**        page 85, activités 1 et 2

**CD 1, track 25**

10, 9, 8, 7, 6, 5, 4, 3, 2, 1 … Salut! Bienvenue sur mon vidéo-blog!
Je m'appelle Thomas, Thomas Garnier!
G – A – R – N – I – E – R. Et toi, tu t'appelles comment? Voilà … ça, c'est moi – magnifique, hein!
Mon pays, c'est la France. Tu vois, là, c'est écrit R – F, République française. Et toi, c'est quoi, ton pays?
Moi, je suis français. Tu vois, c'est écrit là: nationalité française. Et toi, c'est quoi, ta nationalité?
Je parle français et je parle aussi anglais … *a little bit English, not a big bit!* Et toi, tu parles quelles langues? Pour moi, les langues, c'est très important pour la communication, pour les voyages et aussi pour son travail! Surtout pour les pilotes, comme Sébastien Bourdais et Fernando Alonso.
Sébastien Bourdais, c'est mon idole! Il est super super super super!
Il est pilote de course. C'est un pilote super. Ton idole, c'est qui? Il ou elle est quoi?
Magnifique, la photo, non! Ma couleur préférée, c'est le bleu! Le bleu, c'est super! C'est aussi la couleur des footballeurs français! Et c'est la couleur de cette belle voiture Renault! Magnifique, non!
Pour moi, la France, c'est les voitures Renault. Elles sont super, les voitures Renault, hein! Et pour toi, c'est quoi, la France? Les voitures? Le parfum? Le fromage? Allez, ciao, à bientôt!

 **2 Watch again. Can you work out …?**

- Students watch again and answer three further questions about the video clip.

*Answers*: 1 a; 2 b; 3 a

 **3 Copy and complete sentences 1–5 in activity 1 with your own details.**

- Students use the sentence structures from exercise 1 and add details about themselves.

 **Follow-up**

- Students interview each other to find out five pieces of personal information.
- Students write their own blog, based on their interviews.
- If the appropriate technology is available, allow students to record their video blogs and play them to the class.

- Use the checklist on Copymaster 2 which provides an opportunity for students to review what they have learned and reflect on areas for improvement.

# Le weekend

| Unité 3: Le weekend  Overview grid | | | | | | |
|---|---|---|---|---|---|---|
| Page reference | Contexts and objectives | Grammar | Language strategies and pronunciation | Key language | Framework | AT level |
| 20–21<br>**3.1 Tu aimes …?** | • Talk about things you like and don't like | • *j'aime, je n'aime pas, tu aimes …?* (verb patterns) | *et, mais* | *J'aime … Je n'aime pas … Tu aimes …?*<br>*le sport, la musique, les ordinateurs, les films d'action, les jeux vidéo, les animaux*<br>*ça*<br>*et, mais* | 1.2, 4.4, 4.5 | 1.1–3<br>2.1–2<br>3.1–2<br>4.2 |
| 22–23<br>**3.2 Tu as …?** | • Say what you have and don't have | • *j'ai, je n'ai pas de*<br>• *avoir (je/tu)* | | *J'ai un animal, un ordinateur, un portable, une console de jeux*<br>*Je n'ai pas de …* | 4.6, 5.1, 5.3 | 1.1–2<br>2.2<br>3.2–3<br>4.1–2 |
| 24–25<br>**3.3 J'adore le weekend!** | • Say what you like and dislike doing at the weekend | • *j'aime, je n'aime pas, j'adore, je déteste* + infinitive | Checking spelling and accents | *J'aime, Je n'aime pas, J'adore, Je déteste …*<br>*faire du sport, jouer sur l'ordinateur, visiter un musée, regarder la télé, écouter de la musique, aider à la maison*<br>*J'aime ça.* | 4.1, 5.4, 5.6 | 1.1–2<br>2.1–2<br>3.2–3<br>4.1–3 |
| 26<br>**3.4 Vocabulaire** | • Practise pronunciation | | Accents change pronunciation of vowels | | 4.1 | |
| 27<br>**3.4 Clic-test!** | • Recap on the language and structures of the unit<br>• Provide an opportunity for quick testing of all four skills | | | | 5.8 | 1.1<br>2.1–2<br>3.2<br>4.1–2 |
| 78<br>**À moi** | • Provide reinforcement activities for self-access work | | | | 2.1, 2.2 | 1.2<br>3.2 |

| MEDIUM TERM GRID Week-by-week overview (assuming six weeks' work or approximately 10–12.5 hours) | |
|---|---|

**About Unit 3, *Le weekend***

In this unit, students talk about free-time activities and use *j'aime* and *je n'aime pas* + nouns and verbs. They also learn to use connectives *et* and *mais* to make longer sentences and to check their spelling and accents.

New vocabulary includes talking about things you like and don't like, things you have and don't have and weekend activities.

Reading, listening and comprehension skills are developed through a variety of texts, audio and video materials.

| Week | Resources | Objectives |
|---|---|---|
| 1 | 3.1 Tu aimes …? | Using *j'aime* and *je n'aime pas* + noun to talk about things you like and don't like<br>Asking questions with *Tu aimes* …?<br>Looking at *je* and *tu* verb endings<br>Using *et* and *mais* to make longer sentences |
| 2 | 3.2 Tu as …? | Using *j'ai* + noun to say what you have<br>Using the negative *je n'ai pas de* + noun to say what you don't have<br>Using *je* and *tu* forms of *avoir* |
| 3 | 3.3 J'adore le weekend! | Using *j'aime, je n'aime pas, j'adore* and *je déteste* + infinitive to say what you like and don't like doing at the weekend<br>Checking spelling and accents<br>Using *j'aime ça* |
| 4 | **Sound French!** (p26)<br>**À moi** (p78)<br>**Copymasters (*Feuilles*)**<br>**OxBox** | Practising pronunciation (accents changing the pronunciation of vowels)<br>Additional reading and writing practice<br>Using additional resources, such as Copymasters and OxBox activities, to reinforce and extend language met |
| 5 | **3.4 Vocabulaire**<br>**Clic-test!** | Learning vocabulary<br>Recapping on vocabulary of unit<br>Preparing and carrying out of assessment in all four skills<br>Reviewing progress |
| 6 | **Copymasters (*Feuilles*)**<br>**OxBox** | Reinforcement and extension of the language of the unit using extra resources<br>Reviewing progress via the Checklist on page 26, *Vocabulaire*<br>Going back over aspects of the unit which need reviewing after *Clic-test!* |

# 3.1 Tu aimes ...?

## *Planner*

> ### Objectives
> * Talk about things you like and don't like

> ### Resources
> Students' Book, pages 20–21
> CD 1, tracks 26–28
> Video clip 4, *Clic! 1 Star*
> OxBox *Clic! 1 Star*, Unité 2, *Qu'est-ce que tu aimes faire?*
> Copymaster 23, *Clic! 1 Star*
> CD 3, tracks 54–55

> ### Key language
> *J'aime ... Je n'aime pas ... Tu aimes ...?*
> *le sport, la musique, les ordinateurs, les films d'action, les jeux vidéo, les animaux*
> *ça*
> *et, mais*

> ### Grammar
> *j'aime, je n'aime pas, tu aimes ...?*
> (verb patterns)

> ### Framework reference 1.2, 4.4, 4.5

> ### Starters
> * Before starting work on the vocabulary, ask students to look at the photos in exercise 2 and guess which topic is going to be covered. Read out the French words and see if students can work out which photo you are referring to, using those which sound like their English equivalents as support.
> * Students compete to solve anagrams of the key leisure activities that have been introduced.

> ### Plenaries
> * Students choose the odd-one-out from sets of words/phrases covered on the spread, giving a reason for each one: *j'aime la musique, j'aime le sport, je n'aime pas les animaux*
> * *Je n'aime pas* could be the odd-one-out here because it says you don't like something, or accept any other good reason!
> * Students have 30 seconds to list from memory as many words from the spread as they can. They then check their lists with a partner for spellings.

> ### Assessment opportunities
> * Writing: Students' Book page 21, exercise 7
> * Listening: Students' Book page 21, exercise 8

## Preparation

* If you have not already done so in the Starter, look at the photos in exercise 2 and introduce the topic you are going to cover. Talk in English about which leisure activities students like and don't like doing.

### 1 Écoute, lis et répète (1–6).

* Students listen to the new vocabulary while reading the words in their books and repeat, trying to sound as French as possible. Point out that the final *s* in *les films* and *les ordinateurs* is not pronounced.

**CD 1, track 26**    page 20, activité 1

1 la musique
2 le sport
3 les films d'action
4 les ordinateurs
5 les jeux vidéo
6 les animaux

## Follow-up

* To reinforce the new vocabulary, you could use the flashcard presentation from OxBox *Qu'est-ce que tu aimes faire?* Included in this presentation are more sports which you may like to introduce to extend students' vocabulary.
* For more detailed work on not pronouncing final letters, Copymaster 23 can be used at this point.

*Answers*: 1a all the final letters are silent apart from: 2 un cheval; 6 un animal; 8 le cinéma; 9 le rap

**CD 3, track 54** Feuille 23, *Clic! 1 Star*, activité 1b

1 le sport
2 un cheval
3 chocolat
4 les jeux
5 j'aime
6 un animal
7 les films
8 le cinéma
9 le rap
10 un rat

Le weekend ③

 **CD 3, track 55** Feuille 23, *Clic! 1 Star,* activité 2b

1 J'aime le chocolat.
2 J'ai un animal.
3 Je fais du sport.
4 Je n'aime pas les films.

 **2 Relie.**

AT 3.1

- Students match photos a–f with words 1–6, using strategies such as similarity to English words, sensible guesses, etc. When going over the answers, extend students' French, if possible, by modelling a longer answer: *Photo a, c'est quatre, les ordinateurs.*

*Answers*: a 4; b 1; c 6; d 2; e 3; f 5

 **3 À deux.**

AT 2.1

- Students play Read My Lips with a partner. One partner mouths one of the words silently and the other student works out which word it is.
- To reinforce the alphabet, you could ask students to spell out the new words to each other.
- Students could also spell out a word by drawing with a finger on a partner's back.

**4 Écoute (1–8). C'est quelle photo?**

AT 1.1

- Students listen and say which photo from exercise 2 is referred to in each of the eight statements.
- This listening activity also starts to familiarise students with the new expressions *J'aime* and *Je n'aime pas*. Introduce these expressions on the whiteboard, using a heart shape and a crossed out heart or use thumbs-up and thumbs-down gestures. Then ask students to listen again and make a thumbs-up or thumbs-down gesture, as appropriate, for each statement.

*Answers*: 1 d; 2 a; 3 c; 4 b; 5 e; 6 c; 7 f; 8 a

 **CD 1, track 27**                page 20, activité 4

1 J'aime le sport.
2 J'aime les ordinateurs.
3 Je n'aime pas les animaux.
4 J'aime la musique.
5 Les films d'action? Non, je n'aime pas ça.
6 J'aime bien les animaux.
7 J'aime les jeux vidéo.
8 Je n'aime pas les ordinateurs

**5 Lis et réponds.**

AT 3.2

- Students now see *J'aime* and *Je n'aime pas* in a reading activity. Read the speech bubbles together, before asking students to work quietly for a few minutes to answer the questions.

- Go over the meaning of *mais* and *et* and explain how they are very useful little words which can make sentences longer. Say two sentences and ask students to join them together using *mais* or *et*.
- Students could work together in pairs to read the bubbles out loud, trying to sound as French as possible.

*Answers*: a Alex; b Yasmina; c Alex; d Thomas; e no; f yes; g karate and skiing; h and, but

 **6 À deux.**

AT 2.2

- In pairs, students guess each other's favourite things, practising the question *Tu aimes …?* and the response *J'aime …* or *Je n'aime pas …*
- If appropriate, explain at this stage that *je* becomes *j'* when used before a word beginning with a vowel.

**Follow-up**

- Draw attention to the spelling of *aimes* after *tu*. Explain, if appropriate, that verbs change in French, as in English, depending on the person doing the verb: I like/he likes, etc. English often adds 's' for the he/she form. French usually adds *s* for the *tu* form of the verb. Explain that *s* on the end of a verb is not pronounced in French.

 **7 Écris ta bulle.**

AT 4.2

- Students write a speech bubble saying if they like or don't like the items pictured. Encourage them to use *et* and *mais* in their sentences.

 **8 Regarde le clip et décide.**

AT 1.2–3

- Show the video clip with young people talking about what they like and don't like. Ask students to note what each person is talking about and whether they like or don't like it by putting a tick or a cross.
- Watch again and ask what other cultural things students notice from the video. How are the people and places different from their own country?

*Answers*: 1 computers ✓ animals ✗; 2 music ✓ computers ✗; 3 films ✓ music/rap ✗; 4 computer games ✓ (action) films ✗; 5 animals (horses) ✓ computer games ✗; 6 sport (tennis, badminton, judo, rugby, football, judo) ✓

                 **page 21, activité 8**

– Aujourd'hui, on parle de vos passions! Quelles sont tes passions? Tu aimes quoi? Tu aimes les ordinateurs?
– Oui, j'aime les ordinateurs.
– Et les animaux, tu aimes les animaux?
– Les animaux, non, je n'aime pas les animaux!

**2** – Salut! Tu aimes la musique?
 – Comment?
 – Tu aimes la musique?
 – Ah oui, j'aime la musique.
 – Et les ordinateurs? Tu aimes les ordinateurs?

**3** – Salut! Tu aimes les films?
 – Oui, j'aime les films d'action ... Jackie Chan!
 – Et la musique, tu aimes la musique? Comme le rap?
 – Euh. Non! Je n'aime pas trop le rap.

**4** – Ah! Salut! Tu as une console?
 – Oui, j'aime les jeux vidéo!
 – Et les films, tu aimes les films d'action?
 – Les films d'action? Non, je n'aime pas ça!

 – Salut! Tu aimes les animaux?
 – Oui, j'aime bien les animaux, surtout les chevaux!
 – Et les jeux vidéo, tu aimes?
 – Non, je n'aime pas ça.
 – Salut! Tu aimes le sport?
 – Ah le sport, j'aime ça! J'adore le sport! J'aime le tennis, le badminton, le judo.
 – Bien, mais le cricket, tu aimes le cricket?
 – Le cricket? Je ne connais pas! On ne joue pas au cricket en France.
   Moi j'aime le rugby, le football, le basket...
 – Bon, très bien, merci ...!

# 3.2    Tu as ...?

pages 22–23

## *Planner*

### ➤ Objectives
- Say what you have and don't have

### ➤ Resources
Students' Book, pages 22–23
CD 1, tracks 29–32

### ➤ Key language
*J'ai un animal, un ordinateur, un portable, une console de jeux*
*Je n'ai pas de ...*

### ➤ Grammar
*j'ai, je n'ai pas de*
*avoir (je/tu)*

### ➤ Framework reference
4.6, 5.1, 5.3

### ➤ Starters
- Allow students one minute to work in pairs to prepare as many sentences as they can about what they like and don't like. Who can make the most sentences?
- Say 10–20 sentences in quick succession, all starting with *J'ai /Je n'ai pas*. Students respond with a thumbs-up to the positive sentences and a thumbs-down to the negative ones.

### ➤ Plenaries
- Discuss good ways of remembering and learning vocabulary from the last two spreads. Ideas might include using mime, testing each other, using a 'write, cover, check' system, etc. Pool other ideas.
- To make sure students can discriminate between *j'ai/je n'ai pas* and *j'aime/je n'aime pas*, say several sentences using one of these four structures. Students note which one you are using in each sentence. Use ticks, crosses, hearts, hearts crossed out or any other easy way of noting.

### ➤ Assessment opportunities
- Reading: Students' Book page 23, exercise 5

---

**AT 1.1–2**

**1 Écoute, lis et répète.**
- Students listen while following the captions in their books and repeat.
- This activity introduces *j'ai* and *je n'ai pas*. Make it clear that it means 'I have' and 'I don't have'.
- Make sure students have accurate pronunciation from the beginning and differentiate from *j'aime* and *je n'aime pas* from the previous spread.
- You could write *j'aime* and *j'ai* in one column on the whiteboard and *je n'aime pas* and *je n'ai pas* in another. See if students can deduce a pattern, for example *n' ... pas* is added to both to make a negative sentence.

 **CD 1, track 29**          page 22, activité 1

1 J'ai un animal.
2 J'ai un ordinateur.
3 J'ai un portable.
4 J'ai une console de jeux.

5 Je n'ai pas d'animal.
6 Je n'ai pas d'ordinateur.
7 Je n'ai pas de portable.
8 Je n'ai pas de console de jeux.

**2 Écoute (1–10). Trouve les phrases négatives.**

- Students listen to ten sentences and put up their hand when someone does not have something, thus showing they have identified a negative sentence. This helps students listen for detail. Warn students they will hear other things on the audio too, but they should just concentrate on listening for *je n'ai pas*.

*Answers*: 3, 4, 5, 8

 **CD 1, track 30**     page 22, activité 2

1  Moi, j'ai un chien. Il s'appelle Gréco.
2  J'ai une Nintendo DS. C'est super!
3  Je n'ai pas de console. Je n'aime pas ça.
4  Je n'ai pas d'animal. Maman n'aime pas les animaux!
5  Je n'ai pas d'ordinateur. Je n'aime pas beaucoup ça!
6  Moi, j'ai un portable! Il est génial!
7  J'ai un lapin et un poisson. J'adore les animaux.
8  Non, moi, je n'ai pas de portable. Papa n'aime pas ça.
9  Moi, j'ai un ordinateur. J'adore communiquer avec mes amis par MSN!
10  Moi, j'ai trois oiseaux, Tic, Tac et Toc. J'adore les oiseaux!

 **3 À deux.**

- Students work in pairs. One student chooses to be one of the five people pictured. The other asks what items they have and then works out who they are. Practise the activity with volunteers first to model the pattern.
- This also practises the *tu* form of *avoir*, *tu as*.
- Remind students that their voice must go up at the end of a sentence when asking a question.

 **4 Écris.**

- Students write sentences using *je n'ai pas de* to explain what the people pictured don't have.
- If appropriate, you may want to point out that after a negative, such as *je n'ai pas*, *un* and *une* change to *de* (or *d'* before a vowel). However, use your discretion if this would confuse students.

*Answers*: a Luc: Je n'ai pas d'ordinateur. b Julie: Je n'ai pas d'animal. c Marc: Je n'ai pas de portable. e Laura: Je n'ai pas de console de jeux. f Ali: Je n'ai pas d'ordinateur.

**Grammaire**

- Explain, if you have not done so already, the two parts of the verb *avoir* seen on this spread: *j'ai* and *tu as*. How many sentences and questions can students make using each one?

**5 Lis et écoute. Trouve l'équivalent en français.**

- Students read through the survey in their books while listening along to it. The text contains some unknown words. Tell students not to worry and give them a few minutes to work on the questions, either on their own or in pairs. Students should look for similarities with English to help them understand any unfamiliar vocabulary and expressions.
- Students match the seven English phrases with their French equivalents from the text.

*Answers*: a Tu as; b J'ai; c animaux; d C'est pratique; e Ce n'est pas moderne; f Sondage

 **CD 1, track 31**     page 23, activité 5

- J'ai une PSP. Ce n'est pas moderne, mais j'aime ça. Le plus important pour moi, c'est la PSP.
- J'ai un portable. C'est pratique. Le plus important pour moi, c'est le portable.
- J'ai un chat et c'est le plus important pour moi. J'aime les animaux.
- J'ai un ordinateur. J'aime l'Internet. L'ordinateur, c'est le plus important pour moi.

**6 Relis et relie.**

- Students read the survey again and match each question to the person who answers it. Go over the question first with students to clarify meaning.

*Answers*: A Manon; B Thomas; C Mehdi; D Diane

**7 Écoute (1–5). C'est quelle question?**

- Students listen to five people saying what they have or have not got. They note which question from the survey (A–D) each person is answering.

*Answers*: 1 C; 2 B; 3 D; 4 D; 5 B

 **CD 1, track 32**     page 23, activité 7

1  Je n'ai pas de console. Je n'aime pas ça.
2  Je n'ai pas d'ordinateur. Je n'aime pas beaucoup ça!
3  Moi, j'ai un portable! Il est génial!
4  Non, moi, je n'ai pas de portable. Papa n'aime pas ça.
5  Moi, j'ai un ordinateur. J'adore communiquer avec mes amis par MSN!

# 3.3 J'adore le weekend!

## *Planner*

> **Objectives**
- Say what you like and dislike doing at the weekend

> **Resources**
Students' Book, pages 24–25
CD 1, tracks 33–34
OxBox *Clic! 1 Star, Unité 2, Qu'est-ce que tu aimes faire?*

> **Key language**
*J'aime, Je n'aime pas, J'adore, Je déteste …
faire du sport, jouer sur l'ordinateur, visiter un musée, regarder la télé, écouter de la musique, aider à la maison
J'aime ça.*

> **Grammar**
*j'aime, je n'aime pas, j'adore, je déteste* + infinitive

> **Framework reference**
4.1, 5.4, 5.6

> **Starters**
- Before beginning work on this spread, recap quickly on likes and dislikes. Call out the names of some celebrities (or hold up photos of them)

and ask students to invent appropriate sentences about their likes and dislikes, such as Bill Gates: *J'aime les ordinateurs*; George Clooney: *J'aime les films*. Students should also imagine things that the celebrities don't like, such as Thierry Henri: *Je n'aime pas le cricket*.
- Use a variety of props (magazine pictures, advertisements, CDs, tennis ball/football, etc.) to prompt students to form sentences using the phrases you have introduced: *J'aime faire du sport. J'aime regarder la télé. Je n'aime pas aider à la maison.*

> **Plenaries**
- In pairs, groups or as a whole class, students play Word Tennis to practise likes and dislikes.
  A: *J'aime*
  B: *faire*
  A: *du sport.*
- Call out an infinitive from the spread. Students complete the expression and then say whether they like, love, don't like or hate doing it.
  Teacher: *visiter*
  Student A: *visiter un musée*
  Student B: *Je n'aime pas visiter un musée.*

> **Assessment opportunities**
- Reading: Students' Book page 25, exercise 6
- Writing: Students' Book page 25, exercise 7

---

 **1 Écoute, lis et répète.**

- Students listen and repeat the phrases while following in their books. This is an introduction to infinitive expressions before they are used with likes and dislikes.
- Which phrases can students guess the meaning of? Students should use the pictures and similarities with English to help them. Go over any phrases students can't guess.

 **CD 1, track 33**        page 24, activité 1

Qu'est-ce que tu aimes faire le weekend?
1 faire du sport
2 jouer sur l'ordinateur
3 visiter un musée
4 regarder la télé
5 écouter de la musique
6 aider à la maison

AT 2.1 **2 À deux: jeu de mime.**

- Students work in pairs to mime one of the activities from exercise 1 for a partner to guess.

### Preparation

- Use the symbols in the book or thumbs-up/thumbs down signs to revise *j'aime* and *je n'aime pas*. Use a double thumbs-up to introduce *j'adore* and a double thumbs-down for *je déteste*.

AT 1.2 **3 Écoute. (1–8)**

- Students listen to eight messages left for a radio programme on the subject of weekend activities. They choose a symbol (a–d) for each speaker to identify the level of like or dislike. This activity practises recognition of the four phrases for likes and dislikes.

*Answers:* 1 a; 2 b; 3 d; 4 a; 5 a; 6 c; 7 b; 8 d

**CD 1, track 34**    page 24, activité 3

Bienvenue sur Clic! Radio. Le sondage
aujourd'hui, c'est "Qu'est-ce que tu aimes faire le
week-end?" Alors, on écoute les messages …
1 Le weekend, j'aime faire du sport.
2 Le weekend, j'adore regarder la télé.
3 Le weekend, je déteste aider à la maison.
4 Moi, j'aime jouer sur l'ordinateur.
5 J'aime visiter un musée.
6 Moi, je n'aime pas faire du sport.
7 Le weekend, j'adore écouter de la musique!
C'est relaxant.
8 Le weekend, moi, je déteste regarder la télé.

 **4 Complète pour toi.**

- To reinforce the like and dislike expressions,
students write four sentences about themselves,
to express what they like, love, dislike and hate
doing at the weekend. A key language box is
provided for support.

**AT 2.2**

**5 À deux.**

- Students interview each other about whether they
like or dislike doing the various activities from
the spread. They answer using *J'aime/Je n'aime
pas/J'adore/Je déteste ça*. Explain that *ça* means
'that/it' and it avoids repeating the whole phrase
again.

 **6 Lis et décide: vrai ou faux?**

- Students read the texts and say if the English
statements are true or false.
- If necessary, read aloud together the texts first to
familiarise students with the language. They can
also practise reading aloud in pairs.

*Answers*: a true; b true; c false; d true; e false; f true

 **7 Écris ton message.**

- Students use the messages from exercise 6 as
models to help them write their own message.
Prepare one together first on the whiteboard.
Some students could use a dictionary to find other
vocabulary for activities they do and don't like
doing.
- Put all their messages in a hat. You or a volunteer
picks one out to read aloud and the class guesses
who wrote it.

**Follow-up**

- As an extension task for students who would
like to use alternative infinitive phrases, use the
flashcard presentation from OxBox, *Qu'est-ce que
tu aimes faire?*

**Top Tips!**

- Encourage students to check spellings in their
written work. Have they remembered to put
accents on words where necessary? You could
also encourage them to check each other's work.

# 3.4   Vocabulaire                    page 26

---

## *Planner*

> **Objectives**
- *Vocabulaire*: to provide a theme-based summary
of the key language of the unit, which students
can use as a reference or as an aid to learning
- To practise pronunciation

> **Resources**
Students' Book, page 26

> **Framework reference**
4.1

---

## Using the vocabulary page

- Encourage students to use the *Vocabulaire* page as
a reference point throughout the unit. It can also
serve as a useful revision tool before students do
the *Clic-test!*
- Vocabulary is listed spread-by-spread and you
could either ask students to learn each section for
homework after each spread is completed, or set
the whole page as a homework task before starting
work on the test. Most students learn shorter
sections best, so often it is better to give them
manageable chunks to learn at a time.

- Encourage students to use different techniques to
help them learn the vocabulary:
  - Cover up the English and see what they can
remember; write down any words they can't
remember and test themselves again on those
words.
  - Cover up the French and see if they can
remember the words or phrases this way round.
  - Make word cards with English on one side
and French on the other. Students can then test
themselves to see what they can remember. Put
any cards they can't remember on one side and
go over those again at the end.

- Work in pairs to test each other, either using the vocabulary list or the word cards.
- Record themselves saying the words both in English and French. Saying words and phrases out loud can often help with memorising them.

## Sound French!

- *Aim:* To practise pronunciation
- The point practised here is that accents can change the sound of a vowel. The focus is *é*. Ask students to practise saying the words listed out loud. Practise them together before students work in pairs.
- Ask students to spend two minutes finding more words in the units they have covered so far which use the 'e' acute accent.

# 3.4   Clic-test

page 27

## *Planner*

The page is divided into four sections: listening, speaking, reading and writing.

> ## Objectives
- To enable students to recap on the language and structures of the unit

- To provide an opportunity for quick testing of all four skills

> ## Resources
Students' Book, page 27
CD 1, track 35

> ## Framework reference
5.8

---

**AT 1.1**

### 1 Écoute!  (1–6)

- Students listen to six statements about Laura's likes and dislikes and note the pictures in the order she mentions them.

*Answers*: 1 c; 2 a; 3 e; 4 b; 5 f; 6 d

**CD 1, track 35**   page 27, activité 1

1 Je n'aime pas les films d'action.
2 J'aime la musique.
3 J'adore les jeux vidéo.
4 Je déteste le sport.
5 J'aime les animaux.
6 Et j'aime aussi les ordinateurs.

**AT 3.2**

### 2 Lis!

- Students read the short French texts and answer the English questions.

*Answers*: a Lisa; b Lisa; c pets; d music; e sport, help at home; f computers, video games

**AT 2.1–2**

### 3 Parle!

- Students work with a partner to ask and answer the questions. Practise first with a volunteer to model, if more support is needed.

**AT 4.1–2**

### 4 Écris!

- Students copy the sentence starters and write their own ending to each.

# À moi

---

## *Planner*

> **Objectives**
> * To provide reinforcement activities for quiet work
> * To provide alternative class and homework material for students who finish other activities quickly

> **Resources**
> Students' Book, page 78
> CD 1, track 36

> **Framework reference**
> 2.1, 2.2

---

| AT 3.2 | **1 Read the song lyrics. Choose a photo to go with each verse.** |

* Students may not understand every word in the song but they should be able to pick out enough to match each verse with a picture. Tell them not to worry about what they don't understand.
* Before students do the activities, play the recording of the song for them to listen to.

*Answers*: 1 c; 2 e; 3 d; 4 b; 5 a

| AT 3.2 | **2 Choose a verse and write it out in English.** |

* Students translate a verse of their choice.

| AT 1.2 | **3 Listen to the song. Read the lyrics in your head as you listen.** |

* When students have finished the activities, play the song again and ask them to follow the text. They can start to join in as they become more familiar with it, if they wish.

 **CD 1, track 36**  page 78, activité 3

**Yo, je kiffe!**
- Yo! Qu'est-ce que tu aimes faire?
- J'aime faire du sport.
- Le sport, super! J'adore le sport!

- Yo! Qu'est-ce que tu aimes faire?
- J'aime faire du ski.
- Le ski, youpi! J'adore le ski!

- Yo! Qu'est-ce que tu aimes faire?
- J'aime faire du cheval!
- Le cheval, génial! J'adore le cheval!

- Yo! Qu'est-ce que tu aimes faire?
- Moi, j'aime danser!
- Danser, le pied! J'adore danser!

- Yo! Qu'est-ce que tu aimes faire?
- J'aime faire du rap!
- Le rap, c'est cool! Moi, je kiffe le rap!

# 4 Bonne année!

| Page reference | Contexts and objectives | Grammar | Language strategies and pronunciation | Key language | Framework | AT level |
|---|---|---|---|---|---|---|
| **Unité 4: Bonne Année! Overview grid** | | | | | | |
| 28–29<br>**4.1 Le premier janvier** | • Say numbers 1–31<br>• Name months of the year and say dates | | | Numbers 1–31<br>*janvier, février, mars, avril, mais, juin, juillet, août, septembre, octobre, novembre, décembre*<br>*C'est le deux janvier.*<br>*C'est le premier mars.* | 1.4, 3.1, 4.2 | 1.1–2<br>2.1<br>3.1<br>4.1 |
| 30–31<br>**4.2 J'ai onze ans** | • Say how old you are<br>• Talk about birthdays | • *mon/ton*<br>• *j'ai* + age | Asking and answering more questions<br>Question words | *Tu as quel âge?*<br>*J'ai (12) ans.*<br>*C'est quand ton anniversaire? Mon anniversaire, c'est le deux mars.* | 1.1, 4.3, 4.6 | 1.1–2<br>2.1–2<br>3.2<br>4.1–2 |
| 32–33<br>**4.3 Noël: super ou nul?** | • Say what you do on special occasions<br>• Give opinions | • *c'est* + adjective<br>• Verb patterns for *-er* verbs (*je/tu*) | | *C'est super! C'est nul! Bof ... C'est génial.*<br>*Je joue avec mes copains/sur la PlayStation.*<br>*Je regarde des films/ la télé.*<br>*Je mange un gâteau /des chocolats.*<br>*J'ai des cadeaux/des cartes.* | 2.5, 4.4, 4.5 | 1.2<br>2.2–3<br>3.2<br>4.2 |
| 34<br>**4.4 Vocabulaire** | • Practise pronunciation | | Nasal sounds in French | | 4.1, 5.7, 5.8 | |
| 35<br>**4.4 Clic-test!** | • Recap on the language and structures of the unit<br>• Provide an opportunity for quick testing of all four skills | | | | 5.8 | 1.2<br>2.1–3<br>3.2<br>4.1–2 |
| 79<br>**À moi** | • Provide reinforcement activities for self-access work | | | | 2.1, 2.3, 2.4 | 3.2–3<br>4.2 |
| 86<br>**Blog-notes** | • Provide extended listening practice recycling the language of the whole unit through a video | | | | 1.2, 1.3, 1.5 | 1.2–3<br>2.2–3<br>4.2–3 |

| MEDIUM TERM GRID Week-by-week overview (assuming six weeks' work or approximately 10–12.5 hours) | | |
|---|---|---|

**About Unit 4, *Bonne année!***

In this unit, students learn about dates, age and special occasions. They also learn how to ask and answer questions using more question words. They give their opinion using *c'est* + adjective and look at the patterns of *-er* verbs. New vocabulary includes numbers 10–31, months, dates, *j'ai* + age, activities for special occasions and adjectives. Reading, listening and comprehension skills are developed through a variety of texts, audio and video materials.

| Week | Resources | Objectives |
|---|---|---|
| 1 | 4.1 Le premier janvier | Using numbers 10–31<br>Naming months of the year and saying dates<br>Using *le premier* for dates |
| 2 | 4.2 J'ai onze ans | Saying how old you are<br>Saying when your birthday is<br>Asking and answering more questions<br>Using more question words |
| 3 | 4.3 Noël: super ou nul? | Saying what you do on special occasions<br>Using *c'est* + adjective to express your opinion<br>Looking at patterns for *je* and *tu* forms of *-er* verbs |
| 4 | **Sound French!** (p34)<br>**À moi** (p79)<br>**Blog-notes** (p86) | Practising pronunciation (nasal sounds)<br>Additional reading and writing practice<br>Using the video for reinforcement, extension and follow-up work |
| 5 | 4.4 Vocabulaire<br>Clic-test! | Learning vocabulary<br>Recapping on vocabulary of unit<br>Preparing and carrying out of assessment in all four skills<br>Reviewing progress |
| 6 | **Copymasters** (*Feuilles*)<br>**OxBox** | Reinforcement and extension of the language of the unit using extra resources<br>Reviewing progress via the Checklist on page 34, *Vocabulaire*<br>Going back over aspects of the unit which need reviewing after *Clic-test!* |

# 4.1 Le premier janvier

## *Planner*

> **Objectives**
> * Say numbers 1–31
> * Say months of the year and say dates

> **Resources**
> Students' Book, pages 28–29
> CD 1, tracks 37–40
> OxBox *Clic! 1 Star, Unité 2, Les nombres 11– 31; Les mois et les fêtes*

> **Key language**
> Numbers 1– 31
> *janvier, février, mars, avril, mais, juin, juillet, août, septembre, octobre, novembre, décembre*
> *C'est le deux janvier. C'est le premier mars.*

> **Framework reference**
> 1.4, 3.1, 4.2

> **Starters**
> * To revise numbers one to ten (introduced in Unit 1), set some simple sums for students to do against the clock. Alternatively, students can make up sums for a partner to solve:
> *quatre – trois = …*
> *cinq + … = sept*
> * In pairs or groups, students play a version of Fizz Buzz, counting from one to 31 and replacing every multiple of a certain number (e.g. two, five) with an agreed word or phrase in French (e.g. *Au revoir!*).

> **Plenaries**
> * *Contre la montre: du plus vieux au plus jeune!* Working as a class or in groups, students say the date of their birthday (the number, not the month) and organise themselves into order, ranging from smallest numbers to highest. When they are standing in line, they each say their birthday number again, to check whether they are in the correct order or not.
> * Using the OHP or whiteboard, display the twelve months of the year in a jumbled order, with all the vowels missing: *j _ _ l l _ t, j _ n v _ _ r*, etc. Students compete to fill in the missing letters and rearrange the months into the correct sequence.

> **Assessment opportunities**
> * Writing: Students' Book page 29, exercise 8

## Preparation

* To introduce numbers 11–31, use the flashcard presentation from OxBox, *Les nombres 11–31*.

 **1 Écoute, lis et répète.**
* Students listen to the recording and repeat numbers 11–31, copying the pronunciation as accurately as possible.

 **CD 1, track 37**  page 28, activité 1

– onzzze, douzzze, treizzze, quatorzzze, quinzzze, seizzzze
– onze, douze, treize quatorze, quinze, seize
– dix-sept, dix-huit, dix-neuf
– vingt
– vingt et un, vingt-deux, vingt-trois, vingt-quatre, vingt-cinq, vingt-six, vingt-sept, vingt-huit, vingt-neuf
– trente
– trente et un!

**AT 1.1**
**AT 2.1**
**2 Écoute et continue.**
* Students listen to a series of two numbers being spoken in a sequence and they provide the next number. They then hear the numbers repeated with the correct answer added.

 **CD 1, track 38**  page 28, activité 2

onze, douze
onze, douze, treize
onze, douze, treize, quatorze
onze, douze, treize, quatorze, quinze
seize, dix-sept
seize, dix-sept, dix-huit
vingt, vingt et un, vingt-deux
vingt-trois, vingt-quatre, vingt-cinq
vingt-six, vingt-sept, vingt-huit, vingt-neuf
vingt-neuf, trente

 **Follow-up**
* Students could work in pairs in a similar way to the audio from exercise 2, with one student saying two numbers and the other providing the third in the sequence.

**3 Lis et complète.**

- Students read the sums and fill in the missing number in figures.
- For further practice in listening to numbers, call out some numbers for students to write down in figures. Get a little faster as you say more. How many can they manage?

*Answers*: a 13; b 16; c 31; d 33; e 25; f 39

 **4 À deux.**

- Students work in pairs to play Number Ping-pong. One student says a number between one and 31 in English. The other student says it in French as quickly as possible. How many can they do in one minute?

 **5 Écoute, lis et répète.**

- Students listen to and read the names of the months. They then repeat them as accurately as possible, using clapping as per the audio, if it helps.
- To help introduce months further, use the flashcard presentation in OxBox, *Les mois et les fêtes*. The second box on each screen presents a festival, but at this stage just introduce the months – you can use the festivals later, if you wish.

 **CD 1, track 39**         page 29, activité 5

janvier
février
mars
avril
mai
juin
juillet
août
septembre
octobre
novembre
décembre

 **6 Lis et réponds.**

- Students match the dates on the French calendar to the dates in English. Point out that dates are written in the following format: *le 25 avril* and that *le premier* is used for the first of any month.

- This activity also provides the opportunity to discuss some key festivals, if you wish. You could go back to use the presentation from exercise 5 and introduce more festivals, if appropriate.

*Answers*: 1 B; 2 A; 3 D; 4 C

 **7 Écoute et écris la date.**

- Students listen to various dates and note them in English.
- Provide more oral practice of dates, if necessary, by reading out further sequences of dates for students to note.

*Answers*: 11 Jan, 17 May, 30 Oct; 12 Aug, 14 Nov, 22 Jul, 31 Mar; 13 Feb, 15 Dec, 16 Apr, 18 Jun

 **CD 1, track 40**         page 29, activité 7

- Quelle est la date aujourd'hui?
- le onze janvier
- le dix-sept mai
- le trente octobre
- Quelle est la date aujourd'hui?
- le douze août
- le quatorze novembre
- le vingt-deux juillet
- le trente et un mars
- Quelle est la date aujourd'hui?
- le treize février
- le quinze décembre
- le seize avril
- le dix-huit juin

 **8 Écris la date.**

- Students write the dates in full in French, using the key language box as support.

*Answers*: a C'est le 22 septembre. b C'est le 11 mars. c C'est le 19 janvier. d C'est le 21 juillet. e C'est le 5 avril. f C'est le 18 juin.

**Follow-up**

- For further practice of dates, use the interactive matching activity from OxBox, *Les mois et les fêtes*.

# 4.2   J'ai onze ans

## *Planner*

> **Objectives**
>   • Say how old you are
>   • Talk about birthdays

> **Resources**
> Students' Book, pages 30–31
> CD 1, tracks 41–43
> OxBox *Clic! 1 Star, Unité 2, Interview Express*
> Copymasters 15, 16, 17, 19, *Clic! 1 Star*
> CD 3, track 56

> **Key language**
> *Tu as quel âge?*
> *J'ai (12) ans.*
> *C'est quand ton anniversaire?*
> *Mon anniversaire, c'est le deux mars.*

> **Grammar**
> *mon/ton*
> *j'ai* + age

> **Framework reference**
> 1.1, 4.3, 4.6

> **Starters**
> | C15 |   • Students complete Copymaster 15 *À tes marques!* exercise 1 and 2.

*Answers*: 1

| U | O | C | I | U | S | E | J | J |
|---|---|---|---|---|---|---|---|---|
| J | A | N | V | I | E | R | U | U |
| H | V | S | L | E | P | T | I | G |
| N | R | E | Y | U | T | M | L | A |
| T | I | B | K | S | E | E | L | O |
| G | L | P | A | L | M | D | E | U |
| Q | F | E | I | V | B | E | T | T |
| O | C | T | O | B | R | E | L | W |
| J | R | H | E | F | E | O | R | E |

*Answers*: 2 quatorze; b vingt-trois; c trente et un; d vingt-deux; e dix; f dix-neuf

   • Carry out a quick survey on birthdays: *C'est quand ton anniversaire?* Find out which is the most and least common month for birthdays in the class.

> **Plenaries**
>   • To practise asking and saying ages, set up a Mexican Wave around the class, encouraging students to go faster and faster.
> Teacher: *Tu as quel âge?*
> Student A: *J'ai douze ans. Tu as quel âge?*
> Student B: *J'ai onze ans. Tu as quel âge?*
> Student C: *J'ai …*
> | C16 |   • Students can complete Copymaster 16 *Bilan de leçon* exercise 1 and 2.
>
> *Answers 1*: a quinze (15); b vingt (20); c vingt-quatre (24); d quatorze (14); e douze (12); f trente et un (31)
>
> *Answers 2*: 1 e; 2 f; 3 d; 4 a; 5 c; 6 b

> **Assessment opportunities**
>   • Speaking: Students' Book page 31, exercise 6
>   • Writing: Students' Book page 31, exercise 7

---

| AT 1.1 | **1 Lis et écoute. Qui parle?**
  • Revise numbers by asking students to count forwards and backwards quickly from one to 31 before doing this exercise.
  • Students can then listen and read the bubbles of four people giving their age. They match each bubble with the correct picture.
  • Point out that to say their age in French, students need to use *J'ai* 'I have'.

*Answers*: 1 b; 2 d; 3 a; 4 c

 **CD 1, track 41**          page 30, activité 1

**1**
– Tu as quel âge?
– J'ai seize ans.
**2**
– Tu as quel âge?
– J'ai trente ans.
**3**
– Tu as quel âge?
– J'ai dix ans.
**4**
– Tu as quel âge?
– J'ai vingt ans.

## 2 Écoute (1–5). Note l'âge.

- Students listen and note the age of each person speaking. Point out the question form: *Tu as quel âge?*

*Answers*: 1 12; 2 17; 3 21; 4 9; 5 14

 **CD 1, track 42**                page 30, activité 2

**1**
- – Tu as quel âge?
- – J'ai douze ans.

**2**
- – Tu as quel âge?
- – J'ai dix-sept ans.

**3**
- – Tu as quel âge?
- – J'ai vingt et un ans.

**4**
- – Tu as quel âge?
- – J'ai neuf ans.

**5**
- – Tu as quel âge?
- – J'ai quatorze ans.

## 3 À deux.

- Students practise asking and answering questions on age, pretending to be the people in exercise 1.

## 4 Écris des bulles. (1–4)

- Students look at the dates of birth, work out the current age of each person and write a bubble.

*Answers*: Depends on year

## 5a Lis et écoute.

- Students read four speech bubbles, then listen to the four boys giving their birthdays and identify the order in which they hear them.

*Answers*: 1 Omar; 2 Nico; 3 Louis; 4 Samuel

**CD 1, track 43**          page 31, activité 5a et 5b

- – C'est quand, ton anniversaire?
- – Mon anniversaire, c'est le 20 décembre.

- – C'est quand, ton anniversaire?
- – Mon anniversaire, c'est le premier septembre.

- – C'est quand, ton anniversaire?
- – Mon anniversaire, c'est le 21 septembre.

- – C'est quand, ton anniversaire?
- – Mon anniversaire, c'est le 11 novembre.

## 5b Réécoute et note.

- Students listen again and note the birthdays in the order they hear them.

*Answers*: 1 20 Dec; 2 1 Sep; 3 21 Sep; 4 11 Nov

## 6 À deux.

- Students interview each other, pretending they are the people in exercise 5. They ask and answer questions about birthdays. Before they do the activity, practise asking the question: *C'est quand ton anniversaire?*

## Top Tips!

- The tip box lists some useful question words. Go over the meaning of *quoi*, *quand*, *comment* and *quel* and practise asking and answering questions with these words around the class.
- Further practice of question words is provided in *À moi* on page 79.
-  To further practise questions and answers, an interactive sequencing activity is provided in OxBox, *Interview Express*.

## 7 Écris une bulle pour une célébrité.

- Students find a picture of a celebrity they like in a magazine or on the internet and write a speech bubble for him/her, including name, age and birthday.

## Follow-up

- Exercise 1 on Copymaster 17 provides an additional listening activity on birthdays.
- Students listen while reading statements a–f giving the dates of six people's birthdays.
- They note whether each statement is true or false, and correct the false statements.

*Answers*: a vrai; b faux (le 23 mai); c faux (le 17 août); d vrai; e faux (le 30 octobre); f vrai

 **CD 3, track 56** Feuille 17, *Clic! 1 Star*, activité 1

- **a** Laurent: Mon anniversaire, c'est le neuf janvier.
- **b** Aimée: Mon anniversaire, c'est le vingt-trois mai.
- **c** Noémie: Mon anniversaire, c'est le dix-sept août.
- **d** Benoît: Mon anniversaire, c'est le quinze juillet.
- **e** Élise: Mon anniversaire, c'est le trente octobre.
- **f** Léo: Mon anniversaire, c'est le seize mars.

- Copymaster 19 provides reading and writing activities on age and birthday.

*Answers*: 1

b Je m'appelle Lucas. J'ai douze ans. Mon anniversaire, c'est le premier mai.

c Je m'appelle Thomas. J'ai treize ans. Mon anniversaire, c'est le vingt-trois décembre.

# 4.3 Noël: super ou nul?

## Planner

> ### Objectives
> - Say what you do on special occasions
> - Give opinions

> ### Resources
> Students' Book, pages 32–33
> CD 1, track 44

> ### Key language
> *C'est super! C'est nul! Bof ... C'est génial.*
> *Je joue avec mes copains/sur la PlayStation.*
> *Je regarde des films/la télé.*
> *Je mange un gâteau/des chocolats.*
> *J'ai des cadeaux/des cartes.*

> ### Grammar
> *c'est* + adjective
> Verb patterns for *-er* verbs *(je/tu)*

> ### Framework reference
> 2.5, 4.4, 4.5

> ### Starters
> - Call out one of the festivals from spread 4.2. Can anyone remember the key dates?
>   Teacher: *noël*
>   Student: *le 25 décembre*
> - Provide the eight sentences from exercise 1 with the words from each sentence in a jumbled order. See how many sentences students can unjumble in two minutes.

> ### Plenaries
> - Call out a verb from one of the expressions from the spread and ask students to provide the ending.
>   Teacher: *Je mange ...*
>   Students: *des chocolats!*
> - As a class, play I Went To Market. One student says an activity; a second student adds an opinion; a third student repeats those two sentences and adds another activity; the next student adds another opinion, etc. Each subsequent student must say everything that has been said before and add a further activity or opinion. How long can the class keep going?

> ### Assessment opportunities
> - Speaking: Students' Book page 33, exercise 5
> - Writing: Students' Book page 33, exercise 6

---

- The aim of this spread is to introduce key verbs in the first person and to show that verbs can be used with different endings to form a variety of sentences.

### 1 Lis et relie.

- Students read eight sentences and match each one to the appropriate picture. Encourage students to tackle this on their own or in pairs, using strategies such as: looking at the pictures for clues; looking for individual words they may already understand; working out words which look like English words, etc. Go through the answers together and explain the meaning of any sentences which were unclear.

*Answers*: 1 a; 2 f; 3 b; 4 d; 5 g; 6 e; 7 c; 8 h

### 2 Relis. Trouve le français.

- This activity concentrates on establishing the meaning of the four verbs used in the sentences. Students find the French for the English verbs listed. They should be able to do this from understanding the meaning of the rest of the sentences.

*Answers*: I play je joue; I watch je regarde; I eat je mange; I have j'ai

### 3 Écoute Alex et Yasmina. Qui fait quoi?

- Students listen and note the correct pictures for each person.

*Answers*: a Alex; b Yasmina; c Yasmina; d Alex; e Yasmina; f Yasmina; g Alex; h Alex

**CD 1, track 44**  page 32, activité 3

**1**
Tu aimes bien Noël, Alex?
Oui, Noël, c'est super!
Je joue avec des copains. Génial!
Je regarde des films. Génial!
Je mange des chocolats. Génial!
Et j'ai des cadeaux! Génial!
Noël, c'est super!

**2**
Tu aimes bien Noël, Yasmina?
Non, Noël, c'est nul!
Je joue à la PlayStation. Bof ...
Je regarde la télé. Bof ...
Je mange un gâteau. Bof ...
Et j'ai des cartes. Bof ...
Noël, c'est nul!

**4 Écris les activités a–h (page 32). Ajoute ton opinion.**

- To reinforce the activities, students write out the activities and add their opinion.

 **5 À deux.**

- Students work in pairs to ask and answer questions about how they celebrate their birthday. They also express an opinion.

## Grammaire

- Look at the grammar box with the class and ask them to look at patterns with verbs in the *je* form. Then do the same for the *tu* form. Hopefully they will be able to deduce that the *je* form ends in *e* and the *tu* form ends in *es*. Explain that the final *s* is not pronounced.

- Give students some more *-er* verbs they have already met and practise forming the *je* and *tu* forms: *aimer, adorer, détester, écouter, visiter*.

**AT 4.2** **6 Décris une fête.**

- Students choose a special occasion and write down four sentences to explain what they do on that occasion, including one sentence which is false. They then show their sentences to a partner who guesses which sentence is false.
- Demonstrate the activity with the class first to clarify, if necessary.
- Challenge students to find different endings to the verbs covered, using a dictionary if possible, to include in their writing.

# 4.4    Vocabulaire                                                        page 34

## *Planner*

> **Objectives**
> - *Vocabulaire*: to provide a theme-based summary of the key language of the unit, which students can use as a reference or as an aid to learning
> - To practise pronunciation

> **Resources**
> Students' Book, page 34
> Copymaster 11, *Clic! 1 Star*
> CD 3, tracks 57–59

> **Framework reference**
> 4.1, 5.7, 5.8

## Using the vocabulary page

- Encourage students to use the *Vocabulaire* page as a reference point throughout the unit. It can also serve as a useful revision tool before students do the *Clic-test!*
- Vocabulary is listed spread-by-spread and you could either ask students to learn each section for homework after each spread is completed, or set the whole page as a homework task before starting work on the test. Most students learn shorter sections best, so often it is better to give them manageable chunks to learn at a time.
- Encourage students to use different techniques to help them learn the vocabulary:
  - Cover up the English and see what they can remember; write down any words they can't remember and test themselves again on those words.
  - Cover up the French and see if they can remember the words or phrases this way round.
  - Make word cards with English on one side and French on the other. Students can then test themselves to see what they can remember. Put any cards they can't remember on one side and go over those again at the end.

- Work in pairs to test each other, either using the vocabulary list or the word cards.
- Record themselves saying the words both in English and French. Saying words and phrases out loud can often help with memorising them.

## Sound French!

- *Aim:* To practise pronunciation
- The points practised here are the nasal sounds *an*, *en* and *em*.
- Demonstrate and practise the sounds with the words listed.
- Ask students to find examples of these in any of the vocabulary lists and practise saying them out loud.
- **C11** Copymaster 11 provides further activities in practising nasal sounds.

*Answers:* 1c a un; b parfum; c ton; d un; e vin; f canadien; g grand; h ange

**CD 3, track 57** Feuille 11, *Clic! 1 Star,* activité 1

- **a** une … un
- **b** parfum … parfumerie
- **c** tonique … ton
- **d** un … unité
- **e** vin … vinaigre
- **f** canadien … canadienne
- **g** granite … grand
- **h** âne … ange

**CD 3, track 58** Feuille 11, *Clic! 1 Star,* activité 2

1 un
2 bonjour
3 français
4 comment?
5 cinq
6 non
7 important
8 parfum
9 restaurant
10 canadien

 **CD 3, track 59** Feuille 11, *Clic! 1 Star,* activité 3

- Son chat chante sa chanson.
- Dans ta tente, ta tante t'attend.
- Combien sont ces six saucissons?

# 4.4   Clic-test!

## *Planner*

The page is divided into four sections: listening, speaking, reading and writing.

➤ **Objectives**
- To enable students to recap on the language and structures of the unit

- To provide an opportunity for quick testing of all four skills

➤ **Resources**
Students' Book, page 35
CD 1, track 45

➤ **Framework reference**
5.8

---

**AT 1.2** | **1 Écoute! (1–6)**
- Students listen to the six extracts and match each one to its English equivalent.

*Answers:* 1 b; 2 d; 3 c; 4 a; 5 e; 6 f

 **CD 1, track 45**          page 35, activité 1

**1**
- Tu as quel âge?
- J'ai treize ans.

**2**
- Quelle est la date aujourd'hui?
- Aujourd'hui? C'est le 21 octobre.

**3**
- Halloween, c'est en novembre?
- Non, Halloween, c'est en octobre.

**4**
- Tu joues à la PlayStation?
- Oui, je joue à la PlayStation. Et toi?
- Oui, oui.

**5**
- C'est génial!
- Ah non, c'est nul!

**6**
- C'est quand, ton anniversaire?
- C'est le 8 janvier.

**AT 3.2** | **2 Lis!**
- Students read the sentences and match each one to a picture.

*Answers:* 1 d; 2 a; 3 f; 4 e; 5 b; 6 c

**AT 4.1–2** | **3 Écris!**
- Students adapt sentences to describe themselves and give their own opinions.

**AT 2.1–3** | **4 Parle!**

- Students work in pairs. They look at the photo and ask and answer questions as they think the person pictured would do.

# À moi
page 79

## *Planner*

> **Objectives**
> - To provide reinforcement activities for quiet work
> - To provide alternative class and homework material for students who finish other activities quickly

> **Resources**
> Students' Book, page 79

> **Framework reference**
> 2.1, 2.3, 2.4

### Interviews express

**1 Read the interviews and find the correct person.**

- These interviews provide further practice of questions and answers as introduced in the main unit. If necessary, read through the interviews first. Students then answer the questions in English.

*Answers:* a Shivani; b Shivani; c Ahmed; d Ahmed; e Shivani; f Ahmed

AT 4.2 **2 Copy and adapt this paragraph. Fill in your own details.**

- Students adapt the paragraph so that it reflects themselves.
- As follow-up they could write their answers in an interview format.

# Blog-notes
page 86

## *Planner*

> **Objectives**
> - To summarise the main points of the unit in context, in a format that is fun and familiar to students, i.e. a video blog
> - To provide a model enabling students to personalise the language of the unit
> - To provide opportunities for students to ask as well as answer questions

- To provide extended listening practice recycling the language of the whole unit

> **Resources**
> Students' Book, page 86
> Video clip 5, *Clic! 1 Star*
> CD 1, track 46

> **Framework reference**
> 1.2, 1.3, 1.5

**1 Watch Alex's video diary. Choose a or b to complete each sentence.**

- Students watch Alex's video diary and choose a or b in answer to each question. Pause the clip after each section to allow students time to answer.

*Answers*: 1 b; 2 a; 3 b; 4 b; 5 b; 6 b

 **Video clip 5**　　　　page 86, activités 1 et 2

 **CD 1, track 46**

Salut! Bienvenue sur mon vidéo-blog!
Je m'appelle Alex! Je suis français. Je suis à Nantes.

**a** J'ai 12 ans. Et toi, tu as quel âge?

**b** Mon anniversaire, c'est le 31 mars …

**c** Euh… Quel jour sommes nous aujourd'hui? Nous sommes le 21 septembre …, octobre, novembre, décembre, janvier, février, mars … Encore six mois attendre! Et toi? C'est quand ton anniversaire?

**d** Moi, ma passion, c'est la Chine! Mon rêve, ce serait de visiter la Chine! Moi, ma fête préférée, c'est le Nouvel An chinois. C'est génial! Et toi, c'est quoi, ta fête préférée? Mon signe du calendrier chinois, c'est le rat! Je déteste les rats! Beurk!

**e** Moi, mon animal préféré, c'est le panda. J'adore les pandas! Il y a des pandas en Chine! Et toi, c'est quoi, ton animal préféré?

**f** Tu as un animal? Moi, j'ai un chat! Le voilà Il s'appelle Jet! J'aime beaucoup Jet! Il a deux ans. Il est super!

**g** Qu'est-ce que tu aimes faire, le weekend? Moi, je n'aime pas beaucoup le sport, mais j'aime bien l'aïkido. Regarde.

**h** Moi, le weekend, je retrouve mes copains. Ma copine idéale déteste faire du shopping et adore le foot! Euh … je n'ai pas de copine! Et toi, comment est ton copain idéal? Comme moi? Allez, salut! Zài jiàn.

 **2 Watch again. Can you work out …?**

- Students watch the clip again and choose a or b to answer the questions correctly.

*Answers*: 1 b; 2 b; 3 a; 4 b

 **3 Copy and complete sentences 1–6 in activity 1 with your own details.**

- Students use the sentence beginnings from exercise 1 and complete them with their own details.

   **Follow-up**

- Students interview each other using their answers from exercise 3.
- Students write their own blog, based on their answers to the interview questions. Suggest a limit of 100 words.
- If the appropriate technology is available, allow students to record their video blogs and play them to the class.

# Le collège

| Unité 5: Le collège  Overview grid | | | | | | |
|---|---|---|---|---|---|---|
| Page reference | Contexts and objectives | Grammar | Language strategies and pronunciation | Key language | Framework | AT level |
| 36–37<br>**5.1 Les matières** | • Say what your favourite subject is<br>• Say which subjects you do and don't like | • Likes and dislikes | Working out meaning | *C'est quoi, ta matière préférée?*<br>*Ma matière préférée, c'est …*<br>*l'anglais, le dessin, le sport, le français, la géographie, l'histoire, les maths, la musique, les sciences, la technologie*<br>*J'adore, J'aime bien, Je n'aime pas beaucoup, Je déteste …* | 1.2, 1.3, 3.1, 5.4 | 1.1–3<br>2.1–2<br>3.2<br>4.1–2 |
| 38–39<br>**5.2 Quelle heure est-il?** | • Use numbers up to 60<br>• Say what time it is | • *il est* + time<br>• *tu/vous* | | Numbers 30–60<br>*Quelle heure est-il? Il est (sept) heures … quinze, trente, quarante-cinq*<br>*Il est midi/minuit.* | 2.1, 4.2 | 1.1–2<br>2.1<br>3.1–3<br>4.1 |
| 40–41<br>**5.3 Mon emploi du temps** | • Name days of the week<br>• Say what day you have a subject | • Using *on* | | *lundi, mardi, mercredi, jeudi, vendredi, samedi, dimanche*<br>*Le mercredi, on a français.* | 1.4, 4.4 | 1.1–3<br>2.1–2<br>3.1–2<br>4.2 |
| 42<br>**5.4 Vocabulaire** | • Practise pronunciation | | Difference in pronunciation between English and French words which are the same | | 4.1, 5.7 | |
| 43<br>**5.4 Clic-test!** | • Recap on the language and structures of the unit<br>• Provide an opportunity for quick testing of all four skills | | | | 5.8 | 1.2<br>2.1–2<br>3.2<br>4.1–2 |
| 80<br>**À moi** | • Provide reinforcement activities for self-access work | | | | 2.2, 2.3, 2.5 | 3.2–3<br>4.2–3 |
| 87<br>**Blog-notes** | • Provide extended listening practice recycling the language of the whole unit through a video | | | | 1.1, 1.2, 1.5 | 1.2–3<br>2.2–3<br>4.2–3 |

| MEDIUM TERM GRID Week-by-week overview (assuming six weeks' work or approximately 10–12.5 hours) | | |
|---|---|---|

**About Unit 5, *Le collège***

In this unit, students learn about school and expressing likes and dislikes. They learn numbers up to 60 and *il est +* time, when to use *tu, vous* and on and how to work out the meaning of new words.

New vocabulary includes school subjects, numbers 30-60; telling the time; days of the week.

Reading, listening and comprehension skills are developed through a variety of texts, audio and video materials.

| Week | Resources | Objectives |
|---|---|---|
| 1 | **5.1 Les matières** | Asking and saying what your favourite subject is<br>Saying which subjects you like and don't like<br>Working out the meaning of new words |
| 2 | **5.2 Quelle heure est-il?** | Using numbers up to 60<br>Asking for and saying the time<br>Using *tu* and *vous* |
| 3 | **5.3 Mon emploi du temps** | Naming days of the week<br>Saying on what day you have a particular subject<br>Using *on* to mean 'we' |
| 4 | **Sound French!** (p42)<br>**À moi** (p80)<br>**Blog-notes** (p87) | Practising pronunciation (difference in pronunciation between French and English words which look the same)<br>Additional reading and writing practice<br>Using the video for reinforcement, extension and follow-up work |
| 5 | **5.4 Vocabulaire**<br>**Clic-test!** | Learning vocabulary<br>Recapping on vocabulary of unit<br>Preparing and carrying out assessment in all four skills<br>Reviewing progress |
| 6 | **Copymasters (*Feuilles*)**<br>**OxBox** | Reinforcement and extension of the language of the unit using extra resources<br>Reviewing progress via the Checklist on page 42, *Vocabulaire*<br>Going back over aspects of the unit which need reviewing after *Clic-test!* |

# 5.1 Les matières

## *Planner*

> ### Objectives
> - Say what your favourite subject is
> - Say which subjects you like and don't like

> ### Resources
> Students' Book, pages 36–37
> CD 1, tracks 47–49
> Video clip 6, *Clic! 1 Star*
> OxBox *Clic! 1 Star*, Unité 3, *Les matières; Mon opinion*
> Copymaster 36, *Clic! 1 Star*

> ### Key language
> *C'est quoi, ta matière préférée?*
> *Ma matière préférée, c'est …*
> *l'anglais, le dessin, le sport, le français, la géographie, l'histoire, les maths, la musique, les sciences, la technologie*
> *J'adore, J'aime bien, Je n'aime pas beaucoup, Je déteste …*

> ### Grammar
> Likes and dislikes

> ### Framework reference
> 1.2, 1.3, 5.4, 3.1

> ### Starters
> - To revise *j'aime, je n'aime pas, j'adore* and *je déteste*, hold a quick question and answer session about students' likes and dislikes of the following items from Unit 3: *le sport, la musique, les ordinateurs, les films, les jeux vidéo, les animaux*.
> - Display groups of three subjects on the board. Students identify the odd-one-out in each. For example, in the group *le français, l'anglais, la musique* the answer could be *la musique* because it is feminine or because it doesn't end *-ais*.

> ### Plenaries
> - Students organise the school subjects into different groups to try to make learning them easier. Students decide on how to form the groups, such as masculine and feminine groups, or by type of subject (science and maths subjects together, languages together, practical subjects together). Discuss students' ideas as a whole class.
> - Students have 30 seconds to list from memory as many subjects as they can. They then check their lists with a partner for spellings and genders.

> ### Assessment opportunities
> - Listening: Students' Book page 37, exercise 5
> - Reading: Students' Book page 37, exercise 6

 **Preparation**
- Present and practise the school subjects using the visuals on OxBox, *Les matières*.

 **1 Écoute, lis et répète.**
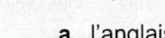
- Students listen to the school subjects, following the words in their books and repeat each one as accurately as possible.

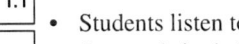 **2 Écoute et note l'ordre.**
- Students listen to people saying what their favourite subjects are and note the order of the subjects mentioned.
- Familiarise students with the question and answer: *C'est quoi, ta matière préférée? Ma matière préférée, c'est …* Practise around the class.

*Answers*: c, h, g, j, d, f, e, b, i, a

 **CD 1, track 47**       page 36, activité 1

  a  l'anglais
  b  le dessin
  c  le sport
  d  le français
  e  la géographie
  f  l'histoire
  g  les maths
  h  la musique
  i  les sciences
  j  la technologie

**CD 1, track 48**       page 36, activité 2

  – C'est quoi, ta matière préférée?
  – Le sport.
  – La musique.
  – Les maths.
  – C'est la technologie.
  – C'est le français.
  – C'est l'histoire.
  – C'est la géographie.
  – Ma matière préférée, c'est le dessin.
  – Ma matière préférée, c'est les sciences.
  – Ma matière préférée, c'est l'anglais.

### 3 À deux.

- Students work in pairs. One chooses a person from the five pictures and says what their favourite subject is. Their partner works out who they are from the pictures.

### 4 Écris.

- To practise writing the subjects, students compile a list of their top ten school subjects, starting with the one they like best.
- Collate results afterwards to find out what the most popular subjects in the class are.

## Preparation

- Before watching the video clip, revise *j'aime, je n'aime pas, j'adore* and *je déteste* if you have not already done so in the Starter.

### 5 Regarde le clip.

- Students watch the video clip where French students are talking about their school subjects. Firstly, they note the subjects in the order mentioned (they can just write abbreviations in English) and then they watch again and draw a symbol by each subject to show what the speaker thinks of it.
- Point out that an alternative word for sport, *EPS*, is used in the video.
- On completion of the task, students could listen to the final four speakers and note their favourite subjects in English (1 geography, 2 maths, 3 sport, 4 science).

*Answers*: a geo, his, mat, l'ang, EPS, tech, sci, mus, dess, fran; b 1 la géographie ♥, l'histoire ♥; 2 les maths ♥, l'anglais ♥ ♥; 3 EPS/le sport ♥ ♥, la technologie ✖; 4 les sciences ♥, la musique ✖; 5 le dessin ♥, le français ♥ ♥

**Video clip 6**                    page 37, activité 5

**CD 1, track 49**

- Aujourd'hui on parle du collège. Le collège, c'est super ... non? Et toi, tu aimes quelles matières?
1  – Au collège, j'aime la géographie et l'histoire.
2  – J'aime les maths ... et l'anglais ... j'adore l'anglais.
3  – Et toi? Au collège, tu aimes quelles matières?
   – J'aime l'EPS, mais je n'aime pas la technologie.
   – L'EPS, c'est quoi ça?
   – Ah, c'est l'éducation physique et sportive. J'adore le sport.

4  – J'aime les sciences ... mais je n'aime pas beaucoup la musique.
5  – Tu aimes quelles matières?
   – J'aime le dessin et bien sûr, j'adore le français!
1  – Ta matière préférée, c'est quoi?
   – Ma matière préférée, c'est la géographie. La géo, c'est super!
2  – Ma matière préférée, c'est les mathématiques. Les maths, c'est intéressant.
3  – Qu'est-ce que c'est ta matière préférée?
   – Ma matière préférée, c'est l'EPS. C'est bien.
4  – Moi, ma matière préférée, c'est les sciences. J'adore ça.

### 6 Lis. C'est qui?

- Read the web messages with students, before giving them a few minutes to answer the questions in English. Refer to the *Top Tips!* box.
- In pairs, students read aloud the messages for further pronunciation practice.

*Answers*: a Ali; b Emma; c Louis; d Emma; e Ali; f Louis

## Top Tips!

- This box gives advice on reading strategies. Students are encouraged to work out or guess the meaning of unknown words. They can often guess from the rest of the sentence or from the similarity with an English word. If students are really stuck, encourage them to use the glossary at the back of the book or a dictionary.

### 7 Sondage.

- Students carry out a survey in groups to find out the three most popular subjects in the class.
- Provide dictionaries or a list of any extra subjects students might need, such as *l'informatique* (ICT), *l'instruction religieuse* (RE), *l'art dramatique* (drama).
- Students feed back the results of their group survey to the class. Record the results for the whole class on the whiteboard or OHP. Collating the findings provides an opportunity to revise numbers.
- Students present their results graphically and compare them with the French results on
- page 36 *Matières top en France*.

### 8 Écris.

- Students write their own messages for the internet forum. They give their opinion of each of their school subjects, using the key language grid for support.

**Follow-up**

C36

- An interactive activity on school subjects and opinions is provided in OxBox, *Mon opinion*.
- For general cultural work on French schools, use Copymaster 36.

*Answers*: 1 <u>south-west</u>: Spanish; <u>north-east</u>: German; <u>south-east</u>: Italian

*Answers*: 2 1 no; 2 yes; 3 no; 4 yes; 5 yes; 6 sometimes; 7 sometimes; 8 no; 9 sometimes; 10 students' own answers

# 5.2   Quelle heure est-il?

pages 38–39

## *Planner*

> ### Objectives
> - Use numbers up to 60
> - Say what time it is

> ### Resources
> Students' Book, pages 38–39
> CD 1, tracks 50–52
> OxBox *Clic! 1 Star, Unité 3, Les nombres 20–60*

> ### Key language
> Numbers 30–60
> *Quelle heure est-il? Il est (sept) heures …*
> *quinze, trente, quarante-cinq*
> *Il est midi/minuit.*

> ### Grammar
> *il est* + time
> *tu/vous*

> ### Framework reference
> 2.1, 4.2

> ### Starters
> - Before introducing numbers up to 60, play Number Shoot-Out to revise numbers up to 20. Two students stand up, you call out a number in French and the pair compete to tell you the number required to add up to 20.

Teacher: *onze*
Student: *neuf*
- The first student to give you the correct number is the winner. The other student sits down and is replaced by a new challenger.
- Using a clockface with movable hands (either a real clock or a clock on the OHP or whiteboard), say some times and ask students to come out and move the hands to give the correct time. Alternatively, students take turns to move the clock hands themselves and ask *Quelle heure est-il?*

> ### Plenaries
> - Play games to reinforce the numbers:
>   - counting in pairs, with students saying alternate numbers
>   - Mexican Wave around the class.
> - For a variation on the Starter clockface activity, ask a volunteer to come out and set the clock hands to a time but keep it hidden from the class. Students take turns to try to guess the time. The student who guesses correctly, comes out and takes over. Students inevitably have to use a wide range of time phrases before they guess the correct one, so this activity is particularly good for confirming what has been learned.

> ### Assessment opportunities
> - Speaking: Students' Book page 39, exercise 7

---

 AT 1.1
AT 2.1

**1 Écoute, lis et répète.**

- This activity introduces numbers 30, 40, 50 and 60 (not the numbers in between). Students listen and repeat. Ask them if they notice a pattern in the spelling of the numbers (all end *-nte* and three of them end *-ante*).

- To introduce the numbers in between you could use OxBox, *Les nombres 20–60*.
- Play games to reinforce the numbers, such as Fizz Buzz, where you count around the class and replace multiples of a given number (two, five) with a French word or phrase (*Au revoir! Salut!* or the name of a school subject).

 **CD 1, track 50**          page 38, activité 1

Trente
Quarante
Cinquante
Soixante

 AT 1.1
AT 2.1

**2 Écoute, répète et continue.  (1–10)**

- Students listen to the starts of number sequences, repeat them and then say the next number in the sequence before they hear the answer given.

**CD 1, track 51**    page 38, activité 2

1 – vingt ... vingt et un ...
   – vingt-deux
2 – trente ... trente et un ...
   – trente-deux
3 – quarante-quatre ... quarante-cinq ...
   – quarante-six
4 – cinquante-cinq ... cinquante-six ...
   – cinquante-sept
5 – trente-trois ... trente-quatre ...
   – trente-cinq
6 – vingt-huit ... vingt-neuf ...
   – trente
7 – trente ... trente et un ...
   – trente-deux
8 – quarante-huit ... quarante-neuf ...
   – cinquante
9 – cinquante-huit ... cinquante-neuf...
   – soixante
10 – quarante et un ... quarante-deux...
   – quarante-trois

 **Follow-up**

• Students could play their own version of the audio in exercise 2. One partner gives two consecutive numbers and the other provides the third in the sequence.

 **3 À deux.**

• Students work in pairs to read each line of numbers as quickly as possible. They time each other, if possible, to see how quickly they can do each line.

 **4 Lis et réponds.**

• Students read the sums and choose the correct number from the box as the answer to each one. Students should also write the numbers as figures to show understanding.

*Answers*: a 60 soixante; b 33 trente-trois; c 59 cinquante-neuf; d 58 cinquante-huit; e 47 quarante-sept; f 21 vingt et un; g 29 vingt-neuf; h 56 cinquante-six

 **5 À deux.**

• Students write similar sums for each other to solve.

## Preparation

• The second page of this spread concentrates on telling the time on the hour, half hour and quarter hour.
• Use the panel at the top of the page and a clockface, if you have one, to present simple time orally.

 **6 Écoute (1–6). C'est quelle montre?**

• Students listen to the times and note the watch which matches each one. If necessary, go through the watch times first to make sure students are clear what time each one is showing.

*Answers*: 1 b; 2 a; 3 e; 4 c; 5 f; 6 d

 **CD 1, track 52**    page 39, activité 6

1
– Quelle heure est-il?
– Il est deux heures trente.
2
– Quelle heure est-il?
– Il est sept heures.
3
– Quelle heure est-il?
– Il est dix heures trente.
4
– Quelle heure est-il?
– Il est dix heures quinze.
5
– Quelle heure est-il?
– Il est trois heures.
6
– Quelle heure est-il?
– Il est huit heures quarante-cinq.

 **7 À deux.**

• Students work in pairs to say the times showing on the watches. Their partner identifies the correct watch.

**8 Lis et réponds.**

• Students read the cartoon about Toto being late for school and answer the questions in English. Read the cartoon first with students.
• Point out to students that French has two words for 'you': *tu* – for a friend or family member, *vous* – to be polite.

*Answers*: a because Toto is late; b What's the time?; c asks the teacher if he has forgotten when lessons start; d vous

**Follow-up**

• Ask students if they would use *tu* or *vous* to address the person sitting next to them in class, a sibling, parent, their head teacher, a shopkeeper, their dog and the mother of their best friend.

# 5.3 Mon emploi du temps

## *Planner*

> **Objectives**
- Name days of the week
- Say what day you have a subject

> **Resources**
Students' Book, pages 40–41
CD 1, tracks 53–54
Copymaster 27, *Clic! 1 Star*

> **Key language**
*lundi, mardi, mercredi, jeudi, vendredi, samedi, dimanche*
*Le mercredi, on a français.*

> **Grammar**
Using *on*

> **Framework reference**
1.4, 4.4

> **Starters**
- Ask students to look at the French school timetable on page 40 and to spot any differences between school routine in France and the UK (lunch lasts for two hours, school day is longer). Talk about other features of French school routine:
  - some French schools have a half day on Wednesdays, with lessons in the morning only
  - lessons can start as early as eight a.m. and may not start at the same time each day.
- To recap on school subjects, call out a subject in English and ask students to either give you the French word or to tell you whether they like or dislike the subject
Teacher: science
Student A: *les sciences*
Student B: *J'aime les sciences.*

C27
- Students can complete Copymaster 27 *À vos marques!* exercise 1 for practice of the days of the week.

*Answers*: 1 jeudi; 2 dimanche; 3 lundi; 4 mercredi; 5 vendredi; 6 mardi; 7 samedi

> **Plenaries**
- Students work in pairs and write the days of the week from memory with accurate spelling. The first pair who finishes with accurate spelling wins.
- Students write sentences for a partner to fill in about their own timetable:
*Le lundi, on a …*
*Le mardi, on a …*
- They check each other's sentences for accuracy, not only in terms of spellings but also to make sure they have correctly described their timetable.

> **Assessment opportunities**
- Speaking: Students' Book page 41, exercise 5
- Writing: Students' Book page 41, exercise 6

---

AT 1.1
**1 Écoute, lis et répète.**

AT 2.1
- Students listen to and repeat the days of the week.
- Ask students what pattern they notice in the words: they all end in *-di* apart from *dimanche* which starts with *di-*. Point out that capital letters are not usually used for days of the week in French.

**CD 1, track 53**      page 40, activité 1

Les jours de la semaine …
lundi
mardi
mercredi
jeudi
vendredi
samedi
dimanche

AT 2.1

**2 À deux: ping-pong.**
- Students play Verbal Ping-pong. One says the day of the week in French and the other says the English equivalent.

AT 3.1
**3 Lis et réponds.**
- Students look again at the timetable and complete the sentences in English.

*Answers*: a music; b English; c French; d maths; e geography; f art

AT 3.2
**4 Lis. Vrai ou faux?**
- Students read the speech bubbles and refer back to the timetable to see if the sentences are true or false.
- These bubbles introduce the use of *on* to talk about 'we'. Point out to students the meaning and explain that *on* is very often used in French. If appropriate, mention that *on* can also be used to mean 'they'.

*Answers*: Manon true; Thomas true; Alex false; Yasmina false

AT 2.2

### 5 À deux.

- Students work in pairs to make up sentences about the timetable. Their partner says if their sentences are true or false. The key language box can be used for support.
- Model this with a volunteer first and practise the structure: *Le* (day), *on a* (subject).

 AT 4.2

### 6 Écris.

- Students write ten sentences about their own timetable using the structures covered earlier. Again, the key language is provided for support.

 AT 1.2–3

### 7 Écoute la chanson.

- Students listen to the song and note down the days of the week on a first hearing and then the four subjects mentioned on a second hearing.
- If students enjoy the song, display the words on the whiteboard and gradually encourage them to join in.
- You could also provide a gapped version of one of the verses for students to complete:
  *Aujourd'hui, c'est* [1]
  *Le vendredi, on a* [2]
  *J'aime, j'aime, j'aime*
  *J'aime* [3] *le français.*
  *En français,* [4] *suis parfait!*

*Answers*: lundi, mercredi; jeudi; vendredi. géo; dessin; musique; français

---

 **CD 1, track 54**  page 41, activité 7

**Une semaine au collège**

Aujourd'hui, c'est lundi
Le lundi, on a géo
J'aime, j'aime, j'aime
J'aime bien la géo
La géo, c'est rigolo.

Aujourd'hui, c'est mercredi
Le mercredi, on a dessin
J'aime, j'aime, j'aime
J'aime bien le dessin
Le dessin, c'est super bien.

Aujourd'hui, c'est jeudi
Le jeudi, on a musique
J'aime, j'aime, j'aime
J'aime bien la musique
La musique, c'est fantastique.

Aujourd'hui, c'est vendredi
Le vendredi, on a français
J'aime, j'aime, j'aime
J'aime bien le français
En français, je suis parfait!

---

# 5.4  Vocabulaire  page 42

---

## *Planner*

> **Objectives**
> - *Vocabulaire*: to provide a theme-based summary of the key language of the unit, which students can use as a reference or as an aid to learning
> - To practise pronunciation

> **Resources**
> Students' Book, page 42

> **Framework reference**
> 4.1, 5.7

---

### Using the vocabulary page

- Encourage students to use the *Vocabulaire* page as a reference point throughout the unit. It can also serve as a useful revision tool before students do the *Clic-test!*
- Vocabulary is listed spread-by-spread and you could either ask students to learn each section for homework after each spread is completed, or set the whole page as a homework task before starting work on the test. Most students learn shorter sections best, so often it is better to give them manageable chunks to learn at a time.
- Encourage students to use different techniques to help them learn the vocabulary:

  – Cover up the English and see what they can remember; write down any words they can't remember and test themselves again on those words.
  – Cover up the French and see if they can remember the words or phrases this way round.
  – Make word cards with English on one side and French on the other. Students can then test themselves to see what they can remember. Put any cards they can't remember on one side and go over those again at the end.
  – Work in pairs to test each other, either using the vocabulary list or the word cards.
  – Record themselves saying the words both in English and French. Saying words and phrases out loud can often help with memorising them.

### Sound French!

- *Aim*: To practise pronunciation
- The point practised here is the difference in pronunciation between French and English words which look the same.

- Look at the examples together and ask students to look for vocabulary from previous units which looks the same as English. Practise pronouncing the words and collate results with the class.

# 5.4 Clic-test! page 43

---

## *Planner*

The page is divided into four sections: listening, speaking, reading and writing.

> **Objectives**
- To enable students to recap on the language and structures of the unit

- To provide an opportunity for quick testing of all four skills

> **Resources**
Students' Book, page 43
CD 1, track 55

> **Framework reference**
5.8

---

**AT 1.2** **1 Écoute. (1–6)**

- Students listen to the six extracts and say whether answer a or b is correct for each.

*Answers*: 1 b; 2 a; 3 b; 4 a; 5 a; 6 b

 **CD 1, track 55**  page 43, activité 1

**1**
– Quelle heure est-il?
– Il est dix heures trente … Dépêche-toi!

**2**
– Le jeudi à neuf heures, on a maths … non?
– Oui! À neuf heures, on a maths.

**3**
– Tu aimes les sciences ?
– Pff … c'est nul! Je n'aime pas les sciences.

**4**
– C'est quoi, ta matière préférée?
– Ma matière préférée, c'est le français.
– Moi aussi, ma matière préférée, c'est le français!

**5**
– On a musique?
– Oui, on a musique à onze heures trente.
– Ah oui, c'est à onze heures trente.

**6**
– Le mardi, on a géographie, non?
– Oui, on a géographie le mardi et le jeudi.

**AT 3.2** **2 Lis!**

- Students read Lola's message and answer the questions in English.

*Answers*: a French, history, art; b science, maths, technology

**AT 2.1–2** **3a Parle!**

- Students work in pairs and say the times on the clockfaces.

*Answers*: a Il est neuf heures. b Il est trois heures. c Il est sept heures. d Il est onze heures quinze. e Il est deux heures trente. f Il est quatre heures quarante-cinq.

**3b Parle!**

- Students then choose two different subjects and explain which day they have them.

**AT 4.1–2** **4 Écris!**

- Students copy and complete the sentences about school.

# À moi

---

## *Planner*

> **Objectives**
> - To provide reinforcement activities for quiet work
> - To provide alternative class and homework material for students who finish other activities quickly

> **Resources**
> Students' Book, page 80

> **Framework reference**
> 2.2, 2.3, 2.5

---

### Au collège

 **1 Read and answer in English.**

- Students read the cartoon strip and answer the question.
- Read the text together first with students, if necessary, and encourage them to read out loud in pairs.

*Answers:* a Séb; b Émilie; c it's his favourite subject; d maths; e she likes it; f Wednesday, 3 p.m.; g she has maths then

 **2 What would you do if you were Émilie? Turn the page round and read what she does.**

- Students read the answer and think about what they would do in Emily's situation.

 **3 Write your own cartoon strip. Adapt the one above and change the subjects and opinions.**

- Demonstrate how students might adapt the cartoon. Ask them to write their own version, changing the subjects and opinions.

# Blog-notes

---

## *Planner*

> **Objectives**
> - To summarise the main points of the unit in context, in a format that is fun and familiar to students, i.e. a video blog
> - To provide a model enabling students to personalise the language of the unit
> - To provide opportunities for students to ask as well as answer questions

- To provide extended listening practice recycling the language of the whole unit

> **Resources**
> Students' Book, page 87
> Video clip 7, *Clic! 1 Star*
> CD 1, track 56

> **Framework reference**
> 1.1, 1.2, 1.5

---

**1 Watch Yasmina's video diary. Choose a or b to complete each sentence.**

- Students watch Yasmina's video diary and choose a or b to answer each question. Pause the clip after each section to allow students time to answer.

*Answers*: 1 b; 2 a; 3 b; 4 b; 5 a; 6 a

 **Video clip 7**          page 87, activités 1 et 2

**CD 1, track 56**

Moteur! Action! Je m'appelle Yasmina, j'ai 13 ans. Je suis française et algérienne. J'adore le foot! Mon rêve c'est d'être une grande footballeuse.

a   Bon ... bref ... Aujourd'hui, c'est samedi ... Ah là là! Le samedi, c'est dur ... J'ai des cours le samedi matin. Moi, j'adore le college ... le mercredi et le dimanche! Pas le lundi, pas le mardi, pas le jeudi, pas le vendredi ... et pas le samedi matin...

b   Mon collège, c'est le collège Jean-Moulin.

c   Mon collège, il est nul, nous n'avons pas d'ordinateurs dans les classes! Pffff ... nul.

d   Bon. Quelle heure est-il? Oh là là ... il est huit heures ... Ahhhhhhh! Les cours commencent à huit heures trente!

e   Vite, vite, mes affaires ... mon cartable, ma trousse, mon emploi du temps ...

f   Alors le samedi, à huit heures trente, j'ai anglais! *I'm not very good at English ... but I like it!* Moi, j'aime bien l'anglais. C'est intéressant. Mon livre d'anglais, et hop! Et toi, tu aimes quelles matières?

g   Après, à neuf heures trente, j'ai maths ... oh, maths ... J'ai maths aussi le lundi à neuf heures trente. Je n'aime pas les maths, c'est nul! Mon classeur de maths ... et ma calculatrice, hi hi hi!

h   Après, à dix heures trente, on a deux heures d'EPS. Youpi! J'adore l'EPS! C'est super! C'est ma matière préférée! C'est quoi, ta matière préférée?
Voilà, je suis prête! Collège, j'arrive! Oh, pardon! Bonne journée!
Et à bientôt! Ciao!

 **2 Watch again. Can you work out...?**

- Students watch the clip again and choose a or b to answer each question.

*Answers*: 1 b; 2 b; 3 a; 4 a

 **3 Copy and complete sentences 1–6 in activity 1 with your own details.**

- Students write their own versions of the sentences.

 **Follow-up**

- Students use their answers from exercise 3 to help them write their own blog.
- If the appropriate technology is available, allow students to record a video blog to play to the class.

# 6 Chez moi

| Unité 6: Chez moi  Overview grid | | | | | | |
|---|---|---|---|---|---|---|
| Page reference | Contexts and objectives | Grammar | Language strategies and pronunciation | Key language | Framework | AT level |
| 44–45 **6.1 Quel temps fait-il?** | • Say what the weather is like <br> • Describe the weather in some French regions | • *il fait, il y a* + weather | | *Quel temps fait-il aujourd'hui?* <br> *Il pleut. Il neige. Il y a du soleil. Il y a du brouillard. Il fait froid. Il fait chaud. Il y a de l'orage. Il y a du vent. Ma région, c'est … le Poitou-Charentes, la Provence, la Picardie, l'Auvergne.* | 2.4, 3.1, 5.1 | 1.1–2 <br> 2.1–2 <br> 4.2 |
| 46–47 **6.2 Tu habites où?** | • Say where you live <br> • Give an opinion | • *c'est* + opinions | | *J'habite …* <br> *dans une petite ville, dans une grande ville, dans un village, à la campagne, à la montagne, au bord de la mer* <br> *Tu habites où?* <br> *C'est … super, génial, nul. Moi, j'adore! Bof! Moi, je n'aime pas.* | 1.4, 2.1 | 1.1–3 <br> 2.1–2 <br> 3.2 <br> 4.2–3 |
| 48–49 **6.3 Ma chambre** | • Say what there is in your bedroom <br> • Explain why you like or dislike it | • *il y a, il n'y a pas de* <br> • *c'est* + adjectives <br> • *et, mais, parce que* | Reading strategies: look for words that are similar in English Use the dictionary Making longer sentences | *Dans ma chambre, il y a … une chaise, une petite table, une lampe, une armoire, un lit, un bureau, un tapis, des étagères* <br> *Il n'y a pas de …* <br> *C'est … grand, petit, moderne, vieux, joli, moche.* <br> *J'aime ma chambre parce que c'est (joli).* | 4.4, 5.2, 5.3, 5.5 | 1.1–3 <br> 2.1 <br> 3.1–3 <br> 4.1–3 |
| 50 **6.4 Vocabulaire** | • Practise pronunciation | | Final *s, t* and *d* not pronounced | | 4.1 | |
| 51 **6.4 Clic-test!** | • Recap on the language and structures of the unit <br> • Provide an opportunity for quick testing of all four skills | | | | 5.8 | 1.2 <br> 2.1–2 <br> 3.2 <br> 4 1–2 |
| 81 **À moi** | • Provide reinforcement activities for self-access work | | | | 2.1, 2.2, 2.4 | 3.2–3 <br> 4.2–3 |
| 88 **Blog-notes** | • Provide extended listening practice recycling the language of the whole unit through a video | | | | 1.2, 1.3, 1.5 | 1.2–3 <br> 2.2–3 <br> 4.2–3 |

| MEDIUM TERM GRID Week-by-week overview (assuming six weeks' work or approximately 10–12.5 hours) |
| --- |

**About Unit 6, *Chez moi***

In this unit, students learn about home and local area, expressing opinions using *c'est* + adjective and giving reasons why they like or don't like something.

They use *il y a* and *il n'y a pas de* and *et, mais* and *parce que* to make longer sentences. They also learn about reading strategies and using the dictionary.

New vocabulary includes weather phrases, saying what sort of town or area you live in, items in a bedroom and adjectives to describe a room.

Reading, listening and comprehension skills are developed through a variety of texts, audio and video materials.

| Week | Resources | Objectives |
| --- | --- | --- |
| 1 | **6.1 Quel temps fait-il?** | Asking about the weather and saying what the weather is like<br>Naming some French regions and saying what the weather is like there<br>Saying what region you come from |
| 2 | **6.2 Tu habites où?** | Asking someone where they live<br>Saying what sort of village or town you live in<br>Saying what the area is like<br>Giving an opinion of your area<br>Using *c'est* + adjective to give your opinion |
| 3 | **6.3 Ma chambre** | Saying what there is and isn't in your bedroom<br>Giving an opinion of your bedroom<br>Saying why you like or don't like your bedroom<br>Looking for words in texts that are similar to English<br>Using a dictionary<br>Making longer sentences with connectives |
| 4 | **Sound French!** (p50)<br>**À moi** (p81)<br>**Blog-notes** (p88) | Practising pronunciation (not pronouncing the final letters *s, t, d*)<br>Additional reading and writing practice<br>Using the video for reinforcement, extension and follow-up work |
| 5 | **6.4 Vocabulaire**<br>**Clic-test!** | Learning vocabulary<br>Recapping on vocabulary of unit<br>Preparing and carrying out of assessment in all four skills<br>Reviewing progress |
| 6 | **Copymasters (*Feuilles*)**<br>**OxBox** | Reinforcement and extension of the language of the unit using extra resources<br>Reviewing progress via the Checklist on page 50, *Vocabulaire*<br>Going back over aspects of the unit which need reviewing after *Clic-test!* |

# 6.1 Quel temps fait-il?

## *Planner*

> ## Objectives
> - Say what the weather is like
> - Describe the weather in some French regions

> ## Resources
> Students' Book, pages 44–45
> CD 1, tracks 57–60

> ## Key language
> *Quel temps fait-il aujourd'hui?*
> *Il pleut. Il neige. Il y a du soleil. Il y a du brouillard.*
> *Il fait froid. Il fait chaud. Il y a de l'orage. Il y a du vent.*
> *Ma région, c'est … le Poitou-Charentes, la Provence, la Picardie, l'Auvergne.*

> ## Grammar
> *il fait, il y a* + weather

> ## Framework reference
> 2.4, 3.1, 5.1

> ## Starters
> - Refer students to the map on page 45 and ask them if they have visited any areas of France. What was the weather like? What was the weather like in any other countries they have visited?

- Help students become familiar with the pronunciation of areas on the map.
- Play Weather Bingo. Students copy down three or four weather symbols from page 45. Call out random weather phrases and students cross out the corresponding symbols as you mention them. The winner is the first student to cross out all the symbols. A confident student could take over as the bingo caller.

> ## Plenaries
> - In pairs, students invent and draw a new set of weather symbols, different from those in their books. They could use a melting ice cream for *il fait chaud*, sunglasses for *il y a du soleil*, an umbrella blown inside-out for *il y a du vent*, etc. They exchange their symbols with another pair of students, who label each one with the corresponding weather phrase. Pairs give each other feedback on the accuracy of the French and the clarity/effectiveness of the symbols.
> - List on the board a few areas of the UK and give brief details in English about the weather conditions, such as 'Sutherland: windy, snow'. Students choose a couple of areas and describe them to a partner. Provide a model on the board, if necessary: *Ma région, c'est le Sutherland. Il y a du vent et il neige.*

> ## Assessment opportunities
> - Writing: Students' Book page 45, exercise 7

---

AT 1.1
AT 2.1

**1 Écoute, lis et répète.**

- Students listen to the weather expressions while following them in their books. They repeat each one, following the pronunciation as closely as possible.
- Ask students if any of the expressions have anything in common. Look at the patterns: some start with *il fait* and some start with *il y a*. In order to learn the expressions better, it may be worth dividing them into small groups which have something in common.

 **CD 1, track 57**       page 44, activité 1

1 – Il pleut.
2 – Il neige.
3 – Il y a du soleil.
4 – Il y a du brouillard.
5 – Il fait froid.
6 – Il fait chaud.
7 – Il y a de l'orage.
8 – Il y a du vent.

AT 1.1

**2 Écoute et note l'ordre des images. (1–8)**

- Students hear the same weather expressions but in a different order. They note the order of the pictures mentioned.
- Point out the question, *Quel temps fait-il?* This is also the title of the spread. Help students pronounce it correctly.

*Answers:* 5, 1, 2, 7, 4, 6, 3, 8

 **CD 1, track 58**       page 44, activité 2

1 – Quel temps fait-il aujourd'hui?
  – Il fait froid.
2 – Quel temps fait-il aujourd'hui?
  – Il pleut.
3 – Quel temps fait-il aujourd'hui?
  – Il neige.
4 – Quel temps fait-il aujourd'hui?
  – Il y a de l'orage.
5 – Quel temps fait-il aujourd'hui?
  – Il y a du brouillard.
6 – Quel temps fait-il aujourd'hui?
  – Il fait chaud.

7 – Quel temps fait-il aujourd'hui?
  – Il y a du soleil.
8 – Quel temps fait-il aujourd'hui?
  – Il y a du vent.

### 3 Quel temps fait-il aujourd'hui? Écris des phrases.

- Students write sentences for each weather symbol, taking care with accurate spellings. Ask them to check each other's spelling.

*Answers:* Aujourd'hui, … a il fait froid; b il pleut; c il neige; d il y a de l'orage; e il y a du brouillard; f il fait chaud; g il y a du soleil; h il y a du vent

### 4 À deux.

- Students use the symbols from exercise 3 and ask and answer questions about the weather.

### 5 Écoute. Qui parle?

- Look at the map, if you have not already done so in the Starter, and familiarise students with the areas pictured as well as their correct pronunciation.
- Students listen and say who is speaking by looking at the map.

*Answers:* 1 Léo; 2 Anya; 3 Éric; 4 Suzie; 5 Simon

**CD 1, track 59**          page 45, activité 5

1  Ma région, c'est le Poitou-Charentes.
2  Ma région, c'est la Provence.
3  Ma région, c'est l'Alsace.
4  Ma région, c'est la Picardie.
5  Ma région, c'est l'Auvergne.

### 6 Écoute les jeunes (1–5). Quel temps fait-il?

- Students listen to the same young people answering questions about their weather. They note the letter of the symbol from exercise 3 that they mention.

*Answers:* 1 h; 2 f; 3 a; 4 e; 5 c

**CD 1, track 60**          page 45, activité 6

1
– Quel temps fait-il dans ta région aujourd'hui, Léo?
– Aujourd'hui, dans ma région, il y a du vent.
2
– Quel temps fait-il dans ta région aujourd'hui, Anya?
– Aujourd'hui, dans ma région, il fait chaud.
3
– Quel temps fait-il dans ta région aujourd'hui, Éric?
– Aujourd'hui, dans ma région, il fait froid.
4
– Quel temps fait-il dans ta région aujourd'hui, Suzie?
– Aujourd'hui, dans ma région, il y a du brouillard.
5
– Quel temps fait-il dans ta région aujourd'hui, Simon?
– Aujourd'hui, dans ma région, il y a de l'orage.

### 7 Écris une bulle pour chaque personne de l'activité 5.

- Students write a speech bubble for each person on the map saying where they live and what the weather is like there.

### Follow-up

- Students could write similar sentences about their own area and weather conditions.

# 6.2 Tu habites où?

## *Planner*

> **Objectives**
> * Say where you live
> * Give an opinion

> **Resources**
> Students' Book, pages 46–47
> CD 1, tracks 61–64
> Video clip 8, *Clic! 1 Star*

> **Key language**
> *J'habite …*
> *dans une petite ville, dans une grande ville, dans un village, à la campagne, à la montagne, au bord de la mer*
> *Tu habites où?*
> *C'est … super, génial, nul.*
> *Moi, j'adore! Bof! Moi, je n'aime pas.*

> **Grammar**
> *c'est* + opinions

> **Framework reference**
> 1.4, 2.1

> **Starters**
> * Students answer the register using sentences or phrases from the last spread: *Il fait froid. Ma région, c'est le Yorkshire.*

> * Call out letters between A and F, corresponding to the pictures in exercise 1 on page 46. Students respond with the place and an opinion:
> * Teacher: *E*
> * Student: *À la montagne! C'est super!*

> **Plenaries**
> * Say a word from the lesson and ask students to include it in a sentence:
>   Teacher: *mer*
>   Student: *J'habite au bord de la mer.*
> * In pairs or groups, students play Word Tennis to build sentences based on the language of the spread. Provide key words and phrases on the board for support. The aim is to keep the 'rally' going for as long as possible:
>   Student A: *J'habite …*
>   Student B: *dans une petite ville …*
>   Student A: *à la montagne.*
>   Student B: *C'est …*
>   Student A: *super.*

> **Assessment opportunities**
> * Listening: Students' Book page 47, exercise 7
> * Writing: Students' Book page 47, exercise 8

---

**AT 1.2**
**AT 2.1**

### 1 Écoute, lis et répète.

* Students listen, follow the captions in their books and repeat.
* Do further oral practice of the expressions by asking students, *Tu habites où?* Provide some pictures from magazines or the internet showing different places and ask students to pretend they live there and to reply to the question in French.

**CD 1, track 61**　　　　　page 46, activité 1

– J'habite dans une petite ville.
– J'habite dans une grande ville.
– J'habite dans un village.
– J'habite à la campagne.
– J'habite à la montagne.
– J'habite au bord de la mer.

**AT 1.2**

### 2 Écoute (1–6). Note les photos.

* Students listen and note the photos from exercise 1 in the order they hear them mentioned.

*Answers:* 1 E; 2 D; 3 C; 4 A; 5 F; 6 B

**CD 1, track 62**　　　　　page 46, activité 2

**1** – Tu habites où?
　　 – J'habite à la montagne.
**2** – Tu habites où?
　　 – J'habite à la campagne.
**3** – Tu habites où?
　　 – J'habite dans un village.
**4** – Tu habites où?
　　 – J'habite dans une petite ville.
**5** – Tu habites où?
　　 – J'habite au bord de la mer.
**6** – Tu habites où?
　　 – J'habite dans une grande ville.

**AT 2.2**

**3 À deux.**

- Students work in pairs. One student chooses a photo secretly. The other student asks questions to work out which it is. This also practises the *tu* form of the verb. Remind students that they use *tu* for someone they know, but *vous* to an adult they don't know so well.

**AT 4.2**

**4 Regarde les lettres et écris les phrases.**

- Students write sentences using the codes and the pictures from exercise 1. Ask them to check each other's work for spelling mistakes.

*Answers*: a J'habite (A) dans une petite ville (D) à la campagne. b J'habite (A) dans une petite ville (E) à la montagne. c J'habite (R) dans une grande ville (F) au bord de la mer. d J'habite (C) dans un village (D) à la campagne.

**AT 3.2**

**5 Lis et regarde les photos.**

- Students read the speech bubbles and match each one to the correct photo.
- If necessary, look at the photos first to establish what each one is depicting.

*Answers*: 1 Amiens; 2 Tusson; 3 Sanary; 4 Bellefontaine

**AT 1.2**

**6a Écoute et vérifie.**

- Students listen to check their answers to exercise 5.

 **CD 1, track 63**      page 47, activités 6a et 6b

- Salut! Je suis Suzie. J'habite à Amiens. Amiens, c'est une grande ville. Amiens, c'est super!

- Bonjour, moi, je suis Léo. J'habite à Tusson. Tusson, c'est un village à la campagne. Tusson, c'est nul!

- Salut. Je m'appelle Anya. J'habite à Sanary. C'est une petite ville au bord de la mer. Sanary, moi, j'adore!

- Bonjour! Moi, je m'appelle Éric. J'habite à Bellefontaine. C'est un village à la montagne. C'est génial!

**Preparation**

- Do a quick revision of *c'est* + adjectives and opinions which students meet again here. Write the following on the board and ask students to categorise them into positive and negative: *C'est super. Bof! C;est nul! C'est génial. Moi, je n'aime pas. Moi, j'adore.*

**AT 1.2**

**6b Réécoute. Note les opinions.**

- Students listen again and note if the people like where they live or not.

*Answers*: 1 ; 2 ; 3 ; 4

**AT 1.2–3**

**7 Regarde le clip. Note.**

- Students watch the video clip in which people give brief details about where they live. They note the order of the places A–F from exercise 1, as they are mentioned.
- On a second viewing, students note whether the teenagers like where they live or not.

*Answers*: 1 B ; 2 C, D ; 3 B, F ; 4 C, E ; 5 C, F

 **Video clip 8**      page 47, activité 7

 **CD 1, track 64**

- Bonjour! Aujourd'hui … on parle de là où tu habites … Tu habites où? En ville? À la campagne? Dans un village?
1 - Tu habites où?
- J'habite dans une grande ville. C'est super!
2 - Tu habites où?
- J'habite dans un village, à la campagne. C'est nul!
3 - J'habite dans une petite ville, au bord de la mer. J'aime bien.
4 - Tu habites où?
- J'habite dans un village, à la montagne. C'est génial!
5 - J'habite dans un petit village au bord de la mer. Moi, j'adore!

**Follow-up**

- Ask students to rate the places mentioned on the video on a scale of 1–6. Which would be their favourite place to live? And which their least favourite?

**AT 4.2–3**

**8 Sondage: «Ta ville, c'est super ou c'est nul?»**

- Students write answers for the survey, saying where they live and whether they like it or not. Show students how they might adapt the example, if more support is needed.

# 6.3    Ma chambre

---

## *Planner*

> ### Objectives
> - Say what there is in your bedroom
> - Explain why you like or dislike it

> ### Resources
> Students' Book, pages 48–49
> CD 1, tracks 65–67

> ### Key language
> *Dans ma chambre, il y a …*
> *une chaise, une petite table, une lampe, une armoire,*
> *un lit, un bureau, un tapis, des étagères*
> *Il n'y a pas de …*
> *C'est … grand, petit, moderne, vieux, joli, moche.*
> *J'aime ma chambre parce que c'est (joli).*

> ### Grammar
> *il y a, il n'y a pas de*
> *c'est + adjectives*
> *et, mais, parce que*

> ### Framework reference
> - 4.4, 5.2, 5.3, 5.5

> ### Starters
> - Students name the colours they see in the Van Gogh painting.
> - Play Hangman to practise furniture items.

> ### Plenaries
> - Give jumbled sentences using phrases from the spread. Students write them out in the right order as quickly as possible: *bureau. n'y a Il de pas*
> - In pairs or groups, students draw a mind map on the theme of *Chez moi*, summarising everything they have learned in Unit 6: *Ma région, Le temps, Ma ville/Mon village, Ma chambre, Opinions.* Students list as many words for each category as they can. Allow time for feedback with the whole class.

> ### Assessment opportunities
> - Reading: Students' Book page 49, exercise 6
> - Writing: Students' Book page 49, exercise 7

---

**AT 1.1**
**AT 2.1**

### 1 Écoute, lis et répète.

- Students listen, look at the picture in their books and repeat the items. Ask them to point at the item as they are repeating it.
- Do further oral practice, pointing to items in the classroom or bringing in pictures from magazines and encouraging students to say what items they can see.
- Students could also do this in pairs if you have enough pictures to go round.
- Give some background information on Van Gogh.

 **CD 1, track 65**　　　　page 48, activité 1

Dans ma chambre, il y a …
une chaise
une petite table
un lit
une lampe
une armoire
un bureau
un tapis
des étagères

**AT 2.1**

### 2 À deux.

- Students work in pairs. One of them names five of the eight items they have learned. The other student names the three missing items. Remind students to use *et* to join the last two words in a list.

**AT 1.2**

### 3 Écoute. Qui est Van Gogh?

- Students look at the painting and listen to find out which of the two people is the real Van Gogh who is describing the painting accurately.
- It may be easier to do this by pausing between each item and asking students to give a thumbs-up or thumbs-down for each item mentioned, according to whether they can see it in the painting or not.

*Answer:* Person 1

 **CD 1, track 66**　　　　page 48, activité 3

**1**
Dans ma chambre, il y a un lit. Il y a deux chaises et une table mais il n'y a pas de lampe. Il n'y a pas de tapis et il n'y a pas d'étagères.

**2**
Dans ma chambre, il y a un petit lit. Il y a une petite table avec une lampe. Il y a deux chaises et un bureau. Il y a des étagères mais il n'y a pas d'armoire.

**AT 4.2**

### 4 Décris la chambre de Van Gogh.

- Students write a description of the bedroom painted by Van Gogh. They should use the key language grid as support for this activity.
- Remind students of the structures *il y a* to mean

there is/are and *il n'y a pas de* to mean there isn't/
are not which they first met in Unit 2 with places
in a town.

- Remind students that after *il n'y a pas* they must
use *de* rather than *un/une*.

 **5 Relie.**

- Students match the French with the English
phrases using the strategies mentioned in *Top
Tips!*
- Students have already met other opinion adjectives
with *c'est* so this should be a familiar structure.

*Answers*: 1 d; 2 a; 3 e; 4 f; 5 c; 6 b

## Top Tips!

- Students should look for words which are similar
to English to help work out the meaning of new
words (as in exercise 5). Encourage them to first
look for words which are obviously similar to
English ones and only to look in the glossary or a
dictionary as a final resort.

 **6 Regarde la chambre de Khalida. Écoute
et lis.**

- Students listen to the text while following in
their books, then they close their books and try
to remember four things Khalida said about her
room. Compare with a partner.
- Students could then work in pairs to read
aloud Khalida's text, concentrating on good
pronunciation.

*Answers*: There is a bed. There is also a desk, a chair,
a wardrobe, shelves, a lamp and a chest of drawers.
There isn't a small table. My room is ugly but it is big. I
like my room because it is modern.

 **CD 1, track 67**          page 49, activité 6

Dans ma chambre, il y a un lit. Il y a aussi un
bureau, une chaise, une armoire, des étagères,
une lampe et une commode. Il n'y a pas de
petite table. Ma chambre, c'est moche mais c'est
grand. J'aime bien ma chambre parce que c'est
moderne!

## Top Tips!

- Encourage students to use the connectives *et, mais*
and *parce que* to make longer sentences in their
writing and speaking.
- Practise some opinion phrases orally using *parce
que* and the key language box as support. *J'aime
bien ma chambre parce que … c'est grand. Je
n'aime pas ma chambre parce que … c'est petit.*
Ask students to complete these sentences as
appropriate for themselves.

 **7 Dessine et décris ta chambre.**

- Students draw their bedroom and label it. They
write a short description and say why they like or
don't like it. Model this on the board first using
the example, if students need more support.
- If students can handle quantifiers, introduce *assez,
très* and *trop* and encourage students to use them
in their description.

# 6.4    Vocabulaire

## Planner

➤ **Objectives**
- *Vocabulaire:* to provide a theme-based summary of the key language of the unit, which students can use as a reference or as an aid to learning
- To practise pronunciation

➤ **Resources**
Students' Book, page 50

➤ **Framework reference**
4.1

### Using the vocabulary page

- Encourage students to use the *Vocabulaire* page as a reference point throughout the unit. It can also serve as a useful revision tool before students do the *Clic-test!*
- Vocabulary is listed spread-by-spread and you could either ask students to learn each section for homework after each spread is completed, or set the whole page as a homework task before starting work on the test. Most students learn shorter sections best, so often it is better to give them manageable chunks to learn at a time.
- Encourage students to use different techniques to help them learn the vocabulary:
  - Cover up the English and see what they can remember; write down any words they can't remember and test themselves again on those words.
  - Cover up the French and see if they can remember the words or phrases this way round.
  - Make word cards with English on one side and French on the other. Students can then test themselves to see what they can remember. Put any cards they can't remember on one side and go over those again at the end.
  - Work in pairs to test each other, either using the vocabulary list or the word cards.
  - Record themselves saying the words both in English and French. Saying words and phrases out loud can often help with memorising them.

### Sound French!

- *Aim:* To practise pronunciation
- The point practised here is that you don't pronounce the final *s, t* or *d* in French words.
- Practise the listed words, then ask students to find examples of these in the vocabulary list and practise saying them out loud.

# 6.4    Clic-test!

## Planner

The page is divided into four sections: listening, speaking, reading and writing.

➤ **Objectives**
- To enable students to recap on the language and structures of the unit

- To provide an opportunity for quick testing of all four skills

➤ **Resources**
Students' Book, page 51
CD 1, track 68

➤ **Framework reference**
5.8

**AT 1.2**  **1 Écoute! (1–6).**
- Students listen and match each listening extract to one of the English sentences.

*Answers:* 1 f; 2 d; 3 b; 4 e; 5 a; 6 c

 **CD 1, track 68**        page 51, activité 1

**1**
J'habite à Lyon. Lyon, c'est une grande ville en France.
**2**
Moi, j'habite dans un village au bord de la mer.
**3**
J'habite à Vannes. C'est une petite ville en France.

**4**
J'habite dans un village à la campagne.
**5**
J'habite dans une petite ville, au bord de la mer.
**6**
J'habite dans une petite ville, à la montagne.

| AT 3.2 | **2 Lis!** |

- Students read the descriptions and look at the picture to decide whether sentence a or b is correct each time.

*Answers*: 1 a; 2 a; 3 b; 4 a; 5 b; 6 a

| AT 4.1–2 | **3 Écris!** |

- Students write sentences for each of the weather symbols.

*Answers*: a Il fait froid. b Il neige. c Il y a du brouillard. d Il pleut. e Il y a du vent. f Il y a de l'orage.

| AT 2.1–2 | **4 Parle!** |

- Students complete the sentences to speak about themselves. Prepare with them first, if necessary.

# À moi

page 81

## Planner

> **Objectives**
- To provide reinforcement activities for quiet work
- To provide alternative class and homework material for students who finish other activities quickly

> **Resources**
Students' Book, page 81

> **Framework reference**
2.1, 2.2, 2.4

### La Camargue

| AT 3.2 | **1 Read about this French teenager from the south of France.** |

- Students read the text and identify the correct paragraph for three topics. Read through with students first, if necessary.

*Answers*: 1 a; 2 c; 3 b

| AT 3.3 | **2 Read again. Correct the mistake in each sentence.** |

- Students now look at the detail in the text and correct six sentences in English.

*Answers*: a in a small town; b loves his town; c hot, sunny and windy; d dislikes the wind; e bedroom is small; f because it's comfortable

| AT 4.2–3 | **3 Adapt the text to write about where you live. Find photos to illustrate your description.** |

- Provide support, if necessary, by showing students how they can adapt the text to talk about their own area. Model a description on the board.

# Blog-notes

## *Planner*

➢ **Objectives**
  - To summarise the main points of the unit in context, in a format that is fun and familiar to students, i.e. a video blog
  - To provide a model enabling students to personalise the language of the unit
  - To provide opportunities for students to ask as well as answer questions

  - To provide extended listening practice recycling the language of the whole unit

➢ **Resources**
Students' Book, page 88
Video clip 9, *Clic! 1 Star*
CD 1, track 69

➢ **Framework reference**
1.2, 1.3, 1.5

---

**1 Watch Manon's video diary. Choose a or b to complete each sentence.**

  - Students watch Manon's video diary and choose a or b in answer to questions about her home. Pause the clip after each section to allow students time to answer.

*Answers*: 1 b; 2 b; 3 b; 4 a; 5 b; 6 a

 **Video clip 9** page 88, activités 1 et 2

 **CD 1, track 69**

Salut! Bienvenue sur mon vidéo-blog! Et bienvenue chez moi!
Je m'appelle Manon! J'ai 12 ans et je suis française.
  a Mon pays, c'est la France. Ma région s'appelle les Pays de la Loire. Ici.
  b Et les Pays de la Loire, c'est ici... dans l'ouest de la France. Et toi? Comment s'appelle ta région? C'est où?
  c Bon, aujourd'hui, il fait très beau! Il n'y a pas de nuages, et il fait chaud. Quel temps fait-il chez toi?
  d Moi, j'habite en ville, à Pornichet. Pornichet, c'est une petite ville, au bord de la mer. Et toi, tu habites en ville ou à la campagne?
  e J'aime beaucoup habiter ici! C'est super! À côté de Pornichet, il y a une assez grande ville: c'est Nantes. J'adore Nantes! Oui, moi, j'aime beaucoup habiter ici. Et toi, tu aimes là où tu habites?
  f J'habite dans une maison au bord de la mer. Elle est assez grande et assez moderne. Au rez-de-chaussée, il y a une cuisine ... des toilettes ... un salon-salle à manger ... Au premier étage, il y a deux grandes chambres ... et deux petites chambres et une salle de bains. Il y a aussi un garage et un jardin, mais le jardin est assez petit. Et chez toi, c'est comment?

  g Comment est la maison de tes rêves? Moi, la maison de mes rêves, c'est une grande maison moderne, au bord de la mer. Il y a un grand jardin, et une piscine, bien sûr! Les chambres sont grandes, très grandes, et très confortables!
  h Regarde ma chambre! Elle est assez petite.
  i Qu'est-ce qu'il y a dans ma chambre? Et bien, il y a un lit bien sûr, un bureau, une chaise, des étagères. Qu'est-ce qu'il y a dans ta chambre, à toi?
    – Manon, tu es prête? Tu as rangé ta chambre? On t'attend!
  Oh là là! C'est maman! Bon, j'y vais... Je range ma chambre!! Salut!

 **2 Watch again. Can you work out ...?**
  - Students watch the clip again and choose a or b in answer to each question.

*Answers*: 1 a; 2 b; 3 b; 4 a

 **3 Copy and complete sentences 1–6 in activity 1 with your own details.**
  - Students write their own endings to sentences 1–6.

 **Follow-up**
  - Students use their answers from exercise 3 to help them write their own blog.
  - If the appropriate technology is available, allow students to record their video blogs and play them to the class.

# 7

# Ma famille

| Unité 7: Ma famille  Overview grid | | | | | | |
|---|---|---|---|---|---|---|
| Page reference | Contexts and objectives | Grammar | Language strategies and pronunciation | Key language | Framework | AT level |
| 52–53<br>**7.1 C'est ma famille** | • Introduce your family<br>• Say how many brothers and sisters you have | • *j'ai, je n'ai pas de*<br>• *mon, ma, mes* | Working out meaning using visual clues and logic | *C'est … mes grands-parents, mon grand-père, ma grand-mère, mes parents, ma mère, mon père, ma belle-mère, mon beau-père, mon frère, ma sœur.*<br>*J'ai un frère/deux frères.*<br>*J'ai une sœur/deux sœurs.*<br>*Je n'ai pas de frères et sœurs.* | 1.2, 4.6, 5.3, 5.4 | 1.1–3<br>2.1<br>3.1–2<br>4.1–2 |
| 54–55<br>**7.2 Il est comment?** | • Say what someone looks like | • *il/elle est*<br>• Adjective agreement | | *Il est … mince, brun, gros, petit, grand, blond, roux.*<br>*Elle est … mince, brune, grosse, petite, grande, blonde, rousse.* | 4.2, 4.3, 4.5 | 1.1–2<br>2.2<br>3.2–3<br>4.2–3 |
| 56–57<br>**7.3 Mon caractère** | • Describe your personality<br>• Describe someone else's personality | • *il/elle est*<br>+ adjective agreement | Remembering words and phrases using cards | *Je suis … Il/Elle est … bavard(e), drôle, égoïste, gentil(le), généreux/ généreuse, intelligent(e), sportif/sportive, timide très* | 1.4, 5.2, 5.6 | 1.1–2<br>2.1–2<br>3.1–2<br>4.1–3 |
| 58<br>**7.4 Vocabulaire** | • Practise pronunciation | | Pronouncing *r* | | 4.1, 5.5 | |
| 58<br>**7.4 Clic-test!** | • Recap on the language and structures of the unit<br>• Provide an opportunity for quick testing of all four skills | | | | 5.7, 5.8 | 1.2<br>2.1–2<br>3.2<br>4.1–2 |
| 82<br>**À moi** | • Provide reinforcement activities for self-access work | | | | 2.2, 2.3, 2.5 | 3.2–3<br>4.2–3 |
| 89<br>**Blog-notes** | • Provide extended listening practice recycling the language of the whole unit through a video | | | | 1.2, 1.3, 1.5 | 1.2–3<br>3.2<br>4.2–3 |

| MEDIUM TERM GRID Week-by-week overview (assuming six weeks' work or approximately 10–12.5 hours) | | |
|---|---|---|
| **About Unit 7, *Ma famille*** | | |

In this unit, students learn to talk about their family and other people using *j'ai* and *je n'ai pas de*. They also use *mon*, *ma* and *mes* with family members and *il/elle est* for descriptions with adjectival agreements. They learn to work out meaning using various strategies and ways to remember words and phrases.

New vocabulary includes family members, adjectives to describe physical appearance and personality adjectives. Reading, listening and comprehension skills are developed through a variety of texts, audio and video materials.

| Week | Resources | Objectives |
|---|---|---|
| 1 | 7.1 C'est ma famille | Introducing your family using *c'est*<br>Using *j'ai* and *je n'ai pas de* to say how many brothers and sisters you have<br>Using *mon*, *ma* and *mes*<br>Using visual clues and logic to work out the meaning of words |
| 2 | 7.2 Il est comment? | Saying what someone looks like<br>Using *il/elle est* + adjective<br>Making adjectives agree |
| 3 | 7.3 Mon caractère | Using *je suis* to describe your personality<br>Using *il/elle est* to describe what someone else is like<br>Adjective agreement<br>Ways of remembering words and phrases |
| 4 | **Sound French!** (p58)<br>**À moi** (p82)<br>**Blog-notes** (p89) | Practising pronunciation (pronouncing *r*)<br>Additional reading and writing practice<br>Using the video for reinforcement, extension and follow-up work |
| 5 | 7.4 Vocabulaire<br>Clic-test! | Learning vocabulary<br>Recapping on vocabulary of unit<br>Preparing and carrying out of assessment in all four skills<br>Reviewing progress |
| 6 | **Copymasters (*Feuilles*)**<br>**OxBox** | Reinforcement and extension of the language of the unit using extra resources<br>Reviewing progress via the Checklist on page 58, *Vocabulaire*<br>Going back over aspects of the unit which need reviewing after *Clic-test!* |

# 7.1 C'est ma famille

## *Planner*

> ### Objectives
> - Introduce your family
> - Say how many brothers and sisters you have

> ### Resources
> Students' Book, pages 52–53
> CD 2, tracks 1–2
> Video clip 10, *Clic! 1 Star*
> OxBox *Clic! 1 Star*, *Unité 5, Ma famille; La famille de Théo (multichoice)*
> Copymaster 55, *Clic! 1 Star*

> ### Key language
> *C'est … mes grands-parents, mon grand-père, ma grand-mère, mes parents, ma mère, mon père, ma belle-mère, mon beau-père, mon frère, ma sœur.*
> *J'ai un frère/deux frères.*
> *J'ai une sœur/deux sœurs.*
> *Je n'ai pas de frères et sœurs.*

> ### Grammar
> *j'ai, je n'ai pas de*
> *mon, ma, mes*

> ### Framework reference
> 1.2, 4.6, 5.3, 5.4

> ### Starters
> - In pairs or groups, students try to predict any previously learned language that they might find useful when working on Unit 5, given that the themes are family and other people. For example, colours, numbers (to talk about ages and birthdays), opinions, likes and dislikes. Collect ideas and use this as an opportunity to show that language learned in one context can often be transferred to different contexts.
> - Play Kim's Game with the family vocabulary from this spread. Prepare in advance a few whiteboard screens with the family words. On the first screen note all the family words already met. Then on subsequent screens delete one of the words each time. Allow students one minute to look at the first screen, then display one of the other screens; students work out what is missing.

> ### Plenaries
> - Display some jumbled sentences on the board. Set a time limit for students to put the words into the correct order:
>   *un / J'ai / frère = J'ai un frère.*
>   *Je / pas / n' / frères / de / ai / sœurs / et = Je n'ai pas de frères et sœurs.*
> - Play Word Tennis with the class divided into two teams. One student from team A calls out a word from the spread (*mon*). A student from team B puts the word into a sentence: *C'est mon frère.* A student from team B then calls out a word for team A, and so on.

> ### Assessment opportunities
> - Writing: Students' Book page 53, exercise 7

---

**AT 3.1**

### 1 Lis. C'est qui?

- Ask students to look at the panel which contains family words. Ask them to use strategies they have learned so far to work out what the words mean. Point out the suggestions given in *Top Tips!*

*Answers: mes grandparents* my grandparents; *mon grand-père* my grandfather; *ma grand-mère* my grandmother; *mon beau père* my stepfather; *ma belle-mère* my stepmother; *mon frère* my brother; *ma sœur* my sister

### Top Tips!

- Remind students of strategies to work out new words, such as using picture clues and logic. Ask them what *beau-père* might mean, bearing in mind it is under the sub-heading 'parents'. Students should also use words which look like their English equivalents to help them as well as making sensible guesses.

**AT 1.1**
**AT 2.1**

### 2 Écoute, lis et répète.

- Students can now listen to the family vocabulary and repeat each one, concentrating on accurate pronunciation.
- You could also use the presentation of family members on OxBox, *Ma famille*. This presents the family words from the Students' Book along with some extra family vocabulary, including *cousin, cousine, tante* and *oncle*.

 **CD 2, track 1**   page 52, activité 2

Ma famille …
mes grands-parents
mon grand-père
ma grand-mère
mes parents
mon père
ma mère
mon beau-père
ma belle-mère
mon frère
ma sœur

## Grammaire

- Look at the grammar box with students. It shows the pattern of *mon, ma, mes* and also relates it to the patterns already learned for the words for 'the' and 'a' or 'some'. Explain that *mon* is used for male relatives (it does not matter whether they themselves are male or female); *ma* for female relatives and *mes* for more than one relative. Allow students to listen to the recording from exercise 2 again, noticing which words for 'my' are used for each relative.

### 3 Regarde et présente.

- Students work in pairs. One pretends to be Lisa Simpson and introduces each family member in turn. Their partner points to each person as he/she is mentioned.
- Students can then pretend to be other members of the Simpson family, but you will have to introduce *mon fils/ma fille*.
- As extension, students could do a similar activity pretending to be part of another famous family, such as the Mitchells in 'EastEnders'. This could also be done as a whole class activity.

### 4 Écris.

- Students can use their creativity and artistic flair to invent a character and a family for a new cartoon strip. They can draw and label each family member and also write some sentences to introduce each one.

### Follow-up

- Students could present their cartoon characters from exercise 4 to the rest of the class.
- A display could be made of the new cartoon families and students could vote on which they like the best.

### 5 Choisis et écris deux membres de la famille. Regarde le clip.

- Before watching the video clip, ask students to write down the names of two family members, such as *père, mère*. They then watch the clip and tick their words each time they are mentioned. How many ticks do they have at the end?
- Watch the clip again and pick out some new family words, such as *oncle, tante, cousin* and *cousine*. Explain these words to students so they can use them, if they wish.

 **Video clip 10**     page 53, activité 5

 **CD 2, track 2**

- Aujourd'hui, on parle de la famille … Tu habites avec qui? Tu as des frères et sœurs?

- Salut Yasmina! Aujourd'hui on parle de la famille. Tu habites avec qui?
- J'habite avec mes parents … mon père et ma mère.
- Tu as des frères et sœurs?
- Oui, j'ai un frère et deux sœurs. Voilà une photo …
- Est-ce que tu as des grands-parents?
- Je n'ai pas de grand-père mais j'ai une grand-mère.
- Est-ce que tu as des oncles et des tantes… ou des cousins et des cousines?
- J'ai beaucoup d'oncles et beaucoup de tantes. Et j'ai beaucoup beaucoup beaucoup de cousins et cousines!
- C'est vrai? OK, merci, Yasmina.

- Salut, Manon!
- Salut!
- Tu habites avec qui?
- J'habite avec ma mère et ma grand-mère.
- Et ton père?
- Mes parents sont divorcés, je vois mon père le weekend.
- Tu as des frères et sœurs?
- Non, je n'ai pas de frères et sœurs. Je suis fille unique.
- Tu as donc ta grand-mère … tu n'as pas de grand-père?
- Non, je n'ai pas de grand-père.
- Tu as des oncles et des tantes?
- Oui, j'ai trois oncles et une tante.
- Trois oncles et une tante … Et des cousins et des cousines?
- Oui, j'ai un cousin et une petite cousine.

- Et toi, Thomas … tu habites avec qui?
- J'habite avec ma mère et mon beau-père.
- Tu as des frères et sœurs?
- Oui, j'ai deux frères – un grand et un petit – et j'ai aussi une sœur.
- Une grande sœur?
- Euh, non… une petite sœur.
- Tu as des grands-parents aussi?
- Oui, j'ai des grands-parents … deux grands-mères et deux grands-pères. Ils habitent à Nantes aussi… Mon grand-père est très cool.
- Génial! Et … euh … Tu as des oncles et des tantes?
- Oui, j'ai cinq tantes et cinq oncles. Et beaucoup de cousins … j'ai sept cousins et quatre cousines. C'est sympa!
- Ben oui. Merci, Thomas.

**6 Lis. C'est qui?**

- This reading activity revises *Je m'appelle* and *J'ai un/une ... Je n'ai pas de ...* which was first met in Unit 3 with items. Remind students that *Je n'ai pas de* means 'I don't have'. Give students a few minutes to match the speech bubbles with the pictures.
- As follow-up, do some oral work where students say what brothers and sisters they have, either real or invented.

*Answers:* a 3; b 2; c 5; d 1; e 4

**AT 4.2** **7 Écris.**

- Students write six sentences (of their own choice) about brothers and sisters and draw artwork to match.
- They could also work in pairs, with one student describing orally one of the pictures and his/her partner identifying which one they are describing.

- Students could also write about their own brothers and sisters.

**C55** **Follow-up**

- Additional activities on the theme of family are provided on Copymaster 55. This includes the extended vocabulary *oncle*, *tante*, *cousin* and *cousine*.

*Answers:* 1a 1 vrai; 2 faux; 3 faux; 4 faux; 5 vrai; 6 vrai; 7 faux; 8 vrai

*Answers:* 1b a Romain; b Mathilde; c Ludovic; d Céline; e Françoise; f Robert; g Mathilde; h Clément; i Marie, Céline; j Franck, Vincent; k Marie, Franck, Céline; l Léa, Laura; m Romain

- You could also use the multichoice activity from OxBox, *La famille de Théo*.

## 7.2   Il est comment?

pages 54–55

### *Planner*

> **Objectives**
- Say what someone looks like

> **Resources**
Students' Book, pages 54–55
CD 2, tracks 3–4

> **Key language**
*Il est ... mince, brun, gros, petit, grand, blond, roux.*
*Elle est ... mince, brune, grosse, petite, grande, blonde, rousse.*

> **Grammar**
*il/elle est*
Adjective agreement

> **Framework reference**
4.2, 4.3, 4.5

> **Starters**
- Brainstorm as a class any adjectives students can remember. They have met: *grand, petit, moderne, vieux, joli, moche, super, génial, nul, français, britannique.* Ask which ones could be applied to people. Ask students if they can remember what happens to an adjective when it describes a person (met in Unit 1) and explain that the adjective may change, according to whether it is describing a male or a female.
- Display some magazine photos of celebrities and start describing one of them (using either the first or the third person singular). Students compete to be the first to recognise who you are talking about.

> **Plenaries**
- Students will need access to coloured pencils for this activity. Working in pairs, each student prepares a description of somebody's appearance, which they then read out to a partner. The partner draws a rough sketch. Afterwards, students compare the written description with the drawing: they should be roughly the same!
- Display the photos of celebrities from the Starter activity. Students work in groups to describe one of them. They read out their sentences to the rest of the class who must work out which one they are describing.

> **Assessment opportunities**
- Writing: Students' Book page 55, exercise 6

### Preparation

- This spread introduces *il/elle est* for the first time. Introduce the words before students embark on exercise 1. Present the structures using pictures of celebrities: *Il s'appelle Robert Pattinson. Elle s'appelle Charlotte Church.* Ask students to spot the pattern.

## 1 Écoute, lis et répète.

- Students listen to the descriptions while following the text in their books and repeat, taking care with pronunciation.
- Ask students to deduce what each adjective means from looking at the pictures.
- Ask students if they notice that some words were pronounced and spelled slightly differently when talking about a man and a woman. Look at the differences. Explain that many adjectives simply add *e* for the feminine form (*petite, grande*), but some are irregular (*gros/grosse* and *roux/rousse*).
- Ask students to listen for one word which is the same for both male and female (*mince*) – can they try to explain why? It already ends in *e*.

**CD 2, track 3**                    page 54, activité 1

**1**
Il est grand.
Il est brun.
Il est mince.

**2**
Elle est grande.
Elle est brune.
Elle est mince.

**3**
Il est petit.
Il est roux.
Il est gros.

**4**
Elle est petite.
Elle est blonde.
Elle est grosse.

**AT 3.2**

## 2a Lis et choisis.

- Students choose the correct option for each sentence by looking at the pictures of Harry Potter and Hermione.
- Ask students to work in pairs and read out their answers to each other to practise pronunciation of the feminine and masculine adjectives.

*Answers*: 1 b; 2 b; 3 a; 4 b; 5 a; 6 a

**AT 4.2**

## 2b Écris trois phrases pour Harry et trois pour Hermione.

- Students write three sentences for each character using the sentences from exercise 2a.

**AT 1.1**

## 3 Écoute (1–6). C'est Harry ou Hermione?

- Students listen to individual sentences and note whether each one applies to Harry or Hermione. They can listen out for the use of *il* or *elle* and also any adjectival differences.

*Answers*: 1 Harry; 2 Harry; 3 Hermione; 4 Hermione; 5 Hermione; 6 Harry

**CD 2, track 4**                    page 54, activité 3

**1**  Il est petit.
**2**  Il est brun.
**3**  Elle est rousse.
**4**  Elle est mince.
**5**  Elle est petite.
**6**  Il est mince.

**AT 2.2**

## 4 À deux.

- Students work in pairs to describe people. They each give the names of three famous people to a partner and then describe one of them. Their partner decides which of the three they are describing. Students can use the key language box for support.
- Model an example first with a volunteer to show how this activity works.

**AT 3.2–3**

## 5 Lis les messages et complète les phrases.

- Students read the messages and choose a word from the box to fill each gap.
- Work through a couple of examples first. Ask students to predict what type of word is missing each time, such as *Ma mère est*: what type of word could be missing? If it is an adjective, does it have to be masculine or feminine? Make sure students understand the rest of the messages before they work on the task individually.
- Allow students a few minutes to complete the task, before going over it together. Encourage students to explain their choices.

*Answers*: 1 thin; 2 brown; 3 red; 4 fat; 5 small; 6 sister; 7 tall; 8 blonde

**AT 4.2–3**

## 6 Décris ta famille. Écris 6–10 phrases.

- Students should now use all the language they have met in the last two spreads to describe a few members of their own family. Remind them that the adjectives must be either masculine or feminine.

## Follow-up

- Students could use their sentences from exercise 6 for a pairwork activity. One partner describes a family member and the other one draws him/her.
- Students could also write a description of themselves using *Je suis …*

# 7.3 Mon caractère

## *Planner*

> **Objectives**
> • Describe your personality
> • Describe someone else's personality

> **Resources**
> Students' Book, pages 56–57
> CD 2, tracks 5–6

> **Key language**
> *Je suis … Il/Elle est … bavard(e), drôle, égoïste, gentil(le), généreux/généreuse, intelligent(e), sportif/ sportive, timide*
> *très*

> **Grammar**
> *il/elle est* + adjective agreement

> **Framework reference**
> 1.4, 5.2, 5.6

> **Starters**
> • Ask students to spend two minutes in pairs, without looking at their books, to list as many adjectives as they can from the previous spread.

If possible, they should note both masculine and feminine forms. Recap on what they already know about adjective agreement.
• Display some jumbled sentence sections and give students a time limit to match them up:
*Il est / brun.*
*J'ai / deux / frères.*
*Elle / est gentille / et généreuse.*
*Elle /est / petite.*
*Il / est / petit / et sportif.*

> **Plenaries**
> • Display the personality adjectives in English and French, in jumbled order, on the board. Students race against the clock to match up the pairs.
> • Students choose the odd-one-out in groups of words:
> – *drôle, vert, intelligent* (*vert* because it is a colour and not a personality adjective, or *drôle* because it ends in *e*)
> – *égoïste, gentil, généreuse* (*égoïste* because the other two are good qualities/it could be masculine or feminine; *généreuse* because it is the only one that is definitely feminine.

> **Assessment opportunities**
> • Writing: Students' Book page 57, exercise 8

---

 **AT 3.2**

**1 Lis et explique.**
• Students read Dracula's speech bubbles and work out what he is saying about himself. Pool ideas.

*Answer:* I am Dracula. I am intelligent, sporty and shy!

**AT 3.1**

**2 Lis et relie.**
• Students read the list of personality adjectives and match them to the English words. Remind students to use strategies such as similarity to English words, etc. and only to use the glossary for those they can't work out.

*Answers:* a talkative; b funny; c selfish; d nice; e generous; f intelligent; g sporty; h shy

 **AT 1.1–2**
**AT 2.1–2**

**3 Écoute et répète.**
• Students listen to sentences with *je suis* plus a personality adjective. Both masculine and feminine forms are covered and students should repeat each one. Ask students to explain after each pair (those with different masculine/feminine forms) how they differed.
• Compare the personality adjectives to those met in the previous spread and point out that the same rules apply. Most adjectives add *e* for feminine, some which already end in *e* stay the same and some just act differently, such as *gentil, généreux, sportif*.

 **CD 1, track 5**    page 56, activité 3

**a**
Je suis bavard.
Je suis bavarde.
**b**
Je suis drôle.
**c**
Je suis égoïste.
**d**
Je suis gentil.
Je suis gentille.
**e**
Je suis généreux.
Je suis généreuse.
**f**
Je suis intelligent.
Je suis intelligente.
**g**
Je suis sportif.
Je suis sportive.
**h**
Je suis timide.

AT 4.1

## 4 Écris.

- Students write a list of the adjectives in the order they would like them to apply to themselves. Remind students to choose the correct form of the adjective to show whether they are male or female.

## Top Tips!

- This box offers students a strategy to remember new words and phrases by writing them on two-sided cards and testing themselves at regular intervals. You could give students this as a homework task and see in a subsequent lesson how well they think it works.

AT 1.1

## 5 Joue au Loto.

- Students play Adjective Bingo. They each write four adjectives from the list and then listen and tick them off if they are called. The first person to tick off all their adjectives wins! There are two games provided on the recording, but you could play further games by calling out adjectives of your choice, if liked.

 **CD 2, track 6**    page 57, activité 5

On joue au Loto?

Jeu numéro un. Écoutez bien …
drôle
sportif
timide
égoïste
gentil
bavard
généreux
intelligent

Jeu numéro deux. Écoutez bien …
Je suis timide
Il est gentil
Elle est bavarde
Je suis généreux
Elle est intelligente
Tu es drôle
Je suis sportive
Il est égoïste

AT 2.1

## 6 À deux.

- Students work in pairs and choose three adjectives to describe themselves. How many guesses does their partner need to find them all?

AT 3.2

## 7 Lis et complète.

- Students read Dracula's message and choose the correct words from the web to complete the English sentences. Point out the qualifier *très* means 'very', and encourage students to use this in their own speaking and writing.
- Ask students to read the French sentences out loud in pairs to practise pronunciation.

*Answers*: 1 funny; 2 mother; 3 father; 4 sporty; 5 shy

AT 4.2–3

## 8 Écris.

- Students write a few sentences about their own family, using the key language grid on page 56 as support.
- Ask them to check their partner's work for accurate spelling and for correct use of feminine and masculine adjectives.

# 7.4   Vocabulaire
page 58

## *Planner*

> ### Objectives

- *Vocabulaire*: to provide a theme-based summary of the key language of the unit, which students can use as a reference or as an aid to learning
- To practise pronunciation

> ### Resources
Students' Book, page 58
CD 2, track 7

> ### Framework reference
4.1, 5.5

### Using the vocabulary page

- Encourage students to use the *Vocabulaire* page as a reference point throughout the unit. It can also serve as a useful revision tool before students do the *Clic-test!*
- Vocabulary is listed spread-by-spread and you could either ask students to learn each section for homework after each spread is completed, or set the whole page as a homework task before starting work on the test. Most students learn shorter sections best, so often it is better to give them manageable chunks to learn at a time.
- Encourage students to use different techniques to help them learn the vocabulary:
  - Cover up the English and see what they can remember; write down any words they can't remember and test themselves again on those words.
  - Cover up the French and see if they can remember the words or phrases this way round.
  - Make word cards with English on one side and French on the other. Students can then test themselves to see what they can remember. Put any cards they can't remember on one side and go over those again at the end.
  - Work in pairs to test each other, either using the vocabulary list or the word cards.
  - Record themselves saying the words both in English and French. Saying words and phrases out loud can often help with memorising them.

### Sound French!

- *Aim*: To practise pronunciation
- The point practised here is prounouncing the French *r*.
- Practise the words together and then ask students to spend three minutes finding other words in previous vocabulary lists which use the *r* sound and practise saying them out loud.

 **CD 2, track 7**  page 58, Sound French!

Je suis bavard.
Je suis drôle.
Je suis généreux.
Je suis sportif.

## 7.4  Clic-test!

page 59

### *Planner*

The page is divided into four sections: listening, speaking, reading and writing.

> **Objectives**
- To enable students to recap on the language and structures of the unit

- To provide an opportunity for quick testing of all four skills

> **Resources**
Students' Book, page 59
CD 2, track 8

> **Framework reference**
5.7, 5.8

 **1 Écoute! (1–6)**
- Students listen and match each conversation to a picture.

*Answers*: 1 f; 2 b; 3 d; 4 c; 5 e; 6 a

 **CD 2, track 8**  page 59, activité 1

1  – Tu es grande ou petite, Lucie?
   – Je suis petite.
2  – Tu as des frères et sœurs?
   – Oui, j'ai deux sœurs.
   – Deux sœurs – super!
3  – Ta sœur est blonde ou brune?
   – Elle est blonde.
4  – Je n'ai pas de frères et sœurs. Et toi?
   – Moi non plus, je n'ai pas de frères et sœurs.
5  – Tu as des frères et sœurs?
   – Oui, j'ai une sœur. Elle est brune.
6  – Ils sont comment, tes parents?
   – Ils sont grands et mince. Ma mère est brune et mon père est blond.

 **2 Lis!**
- Students read Claire's message and answer the questions in English.

*Answers*: a fat, tall, brown hair; b sporty, funny, generous

AT 2.1–2 **3 Parle!**
- Students say five things to describe their appearance and personality. Model first with a volunteer, if necessary.

 **4 Écris!**
- Students write a speech bubble for Clément, inventing a family for him, using the example shown. They should write about at least three members of his family.

# À moi

---

## *Planner*

> **Objectives**
> • To provide reinforcement activities for quiet work
> • To provide alternative class and homework material for students who finish other activities quickly

> **Resources**
> Students' Book, page 82

> **Framework reference**
> 2.1, 2.3, 2.5

---

### Problèmes!

 AT 3.2

**1 Read the letters. Find …**

• Students read the letters and answer the questions in English.

*Answers*: a brother, stepfather, mother, sister; b small, slim, tall, fat; c sociable, shy, nice, talkative

AT 3.2–3

**2 Answer the questions in English.**

• Students now answer more detailed questions in English.

*Answers*: a his brother is sociable, he is shy; b he isn't nice; c Chloé; d she's talkative; e small and slim

**3 Write your own problem letter. Copy the letter below and change the highlighted words.**

• Students use the outline to write their own problem letter. Model how to adapt with the class, if necessary.

---

# Blog-notes

---

## *Planner*

> **Objectives**
> • To summarise the main points of the unit in context, in a format that is fun and familiar to students, i.e. a video blog
> • To provide a model enabling students to personalise the language of the unit
> • To provide opportunities for students to ask as well as answer questions

• To provide extended listening practice recycling the language of the whole unit

> **Resources**
> Students' Book, page 89
> CD 2, track 9
> Video clip 11, *Clic! 1 Star*

> **Framework reference**
> 1.2, 1.3, 1.5

---

AT 1.2–3

**1 Watch Yasmina's video diary. Choose a or b to complete each answer.**

• Students watch Yasmina's video diary and choose a or b in answer to each question. Pause the clip after each section to allow students time to answer.

*Answers*: 1 b; 2 b; 3 b; 4 a; 5 a

 **Video clip 11**      page 89, activités 1 et 2

 **CD 2, track 9**

Moteur! Action! Bonjour! Bienvenue sur mon vidéo-blog! Aujourd'hui, c'est un grand jour pour ma famille. C'est le mariage de ma sœur Amina!

a En général, dans la maison, on est six: mon père, ma mère, mon frère et mes deux sœurs. Tu as des frères et sœurs, toi?

b Oh là là! Aujourd'hui, dans la maison, on est 13 personnes! Il y a mon oncle, ma tante, ma cousine. Il y a aussi mes trois cousins et ma grand-mère. En général, ma grand-mère n'habite pas avec nous, elle habite en Algérie. Tu habites avec qui, toi?

c Avec 13 personnes dans la maison, il faut s'organiser le matin! Mes parents, se lèvent à six heures. À six heures trente, mes sœurs et ma cousine se douchent. À sept heures, mon frère et mes cousins se douchent. Moi, je me réveille à sept heures trente. Et toi, en général, tu te lèves à quelle heure?

d Moi, je suis prête en dix minutes! Je m'habille, je me brosse les dents et voilà! Je prends ma douche le soir, je préfère. Et toi, tu fais quoi le matin?

**e** – Yasmina? Yasmina? Tu t'habilles?
Aujourd'hui, pour le mariage de ta sœur, tu
mets ta robe!
Ça, c'est maman …
– Oui maman, je m'habille.
Ah, une robe, je n'aime pas ça. Moi, je suis
grande, mince, sportive! Je suis belle avec
un jean et un tee-shirt! Pas une robe! Et toi,
tu es comment physiquement? Grand, mince,
sportif …?

**f** Oh mes cheveux...! Je déteste mes cheveux
raides! Oh c'est horrible! Je veux des
cheveux frisés. Ma sœur a les cheveux courts
et frisés. Elle porte des lunettes aussi. Et toi?
Tes cheveux sont comment? Tu aimes tes
cheveux? Tu portes des lunettes?
Bon … je m'habille … excusez-moi, hein! Une
minute! …

**g** Hum hum … re-bonjour! Alors, je suis belle!
Regarde, j'ai des beaux yeux marron! Et toi,
de quelle couleur sont tes yeux?

**h** Bon, mais je suis très bavarde, hein, trop
bavarde! C'est mon gros défaut! J'ai un
défaut, mais j'ai beaucoup de qualités … je
suis drôle, gentille, généreuse, travailleuse et
surtout, je suis très très modeste! Et toi, tu as
quelles qualités? Et quels défauts!
– Yasmina! Yasmina! Tu es prête?! On
t'attend, dépêche-toi!
– OK, j'arrive!
Allez, j'y vais! Salut!

**AT 1.2–3**

**2 Watch again. Can you work out ...?**

- Students watch again and choose a or b in answer
to each question.

*Answers*: 1 a; 2 b; 3 b; 4 b

**AT 4.2**

**3 Copy and complete sentences 1–5 in activity 1
with your own details.**

- Students write their own endings to the sentences
from exercise 1.

**AT 4.2–3**

**AT 3.2**

**Follow-up**

- Students use their answers from exercise 3 to help
them write their own blog.
- If the appropriate technology is available, allow
students to record their video blogs and play them
to the class

# 8

# On mange!

| Unité 8: On mange!  Overview grid | | | | | | |
|---|---|---|---|---|---|---|
| **Page reference** | **Contexts and objectives** | **Grammar** | **Language strategies and pronunciation** | **Key language** | **Framework** | **AT level** |
| 60–61<br>**8.1 C'est bon!** | • Name food items<br>• Say what you like eating | • *j'aime/je n'aime pas le, la, les*<br>• *ça* | Words that are similar in English and French<br>Adapting sentences to say different things | *Beurk! Bof! C'est bon! une crêpe, une pizza, une quiche, un steak-frites, un hamburger, un sandwich, des moules, des escargots, des nems J'adore, J'aime bien, Je n'aime pas beaucoup, Je déteste …* | 3.1, 3.2, 5.2, 5.3 | 1.1–2<br>2.1–2<br>3.2–3<br>4.2–3 |
| 62–63<br>**8.2 Je vais au café** | • Say where you go when you eat out<br>• Say what you would like to eat | • *aller (je, tu)*<br>• *au, à la* | | *Je vais … au restaurant, au café, au fast-food, à la pizzeria, à la crêperie, à la cafétéria. Je voudrais (une pizza). On mange (au café).* | 4.3, 4.4, 4.5 | 1.1–3<br>2.1–3<br>3.3<br>4.2–3 |
| 64–65<br>**8.3 S'il vous plait!** | • Name flavours and fillings<br>• Order a snack | • *au, à la, aux*<br>• *je voudrais* | | *une glace à la vanille, à l'orange une pizza à la tomate, aux champignons un sandwich au fromage une crêpe au chocolat Je voudrais … s'il vous plaît.* | 1.4, 4.3, 5.5 | 1.1–3<br>2.1–3<br>3.2–3<br>4.2–3 |
| 66<br>**8.4 Vocabulaire** | • Practise pronunciation | | *ou* sound | | 4.1, 5.5, 5.7 | |
| 67<br>**8.4 Clic-test!** | • Recap on the language and structures of the unit<br>• Provide an opportunity for quick testing of all four skills | | | | 5.8 | 1.2<br>2.2<br>3.2–3<br>4.1–3 |
| 83<br>**À moi** | • Provide reinforcement activities for self-access work | | | | 2.2, 2.3, 2.4 | 2.2–3<br>3.2–3<br>4 2–3 |

| MEDIUM TERM GRID Week-by-week overview (assuming six weeks' work or approximately 10–12.5 hours) |
|---|

**About Unit 8, *On mange!***

In this unit, students discover more about food in France and eating out, using *j'aime* and *je n'aime pas* to express their opinion. They use *aller* to say where they go to eat and they learn to use *au* and *à la* correctly with flavours, fillings and places and to use *je voudrais* to ask for items. They also learn to recognise words that are similar in French and English and how to adapt sentences to say different things. New vocabulary includes food items, opinion phrases, eating places, flavours and fillings and phrases to cope in a café.

Reading, listening and comprehension skills are developed through a variety of texts, audio and video materials.

| Week | Resources | Objectives |
|---|---|---|
| 1 | 8.1 C'est bon! | Naming food items that you would buy in France<br>Saying what you like and don't like eating, *j'aime/je n'aime pas le, la, les*<br>Recognising words that are similar in French and English<br>Adapting sentences to say different things |
| 2 | 8.2 Je vais au café | Using *je vais au/à la* to say where you go when you eat out<br>Using *au* and *à la* correctly with places to eat<br>Saying what you would like to eat with *je voudrais*<br>Using *on* to suggest where to eat |
| 3 | 8.3 S'il vous plait! | Naming flavours and filling in pizzas, ice creams and sandwiches<br>Ordering a snack in a café<br>Using *au, à la* and *aux* correctly for fillings<br>Using *je voudrais* to order something |
| 4 | 8.3 S'il vous plait!<br>Sound French! (p66)<br>À moi (p83)<br>Copymasters, OxBox | Practising pronunciation (pronouncing the *ou* sound)<br>Additional reading and writing practice<br>Using additional resources, such as Copymasters and OxBox activities, to reinforce and extend language met |
| 5 | 8.4 Vocabulaire<br>Clic-test! | Learning vocabulary<br>Recapping on vocabulary of unit<br>Preparing and carrying out of assessment in all four skills<br>Reviewing progress |
| 6 | Copymasters (*Feuilles*)<br>OxBox | Reinforcement and extension of the language of the unit using extra resources<br>Reviewing progress via the Checklist on page 66, *Vocabulaire*<br>Going back over aspects of the unit which need reviewing after *Clic-test!* |

# 8.1 C'est bon!

pages 60–61

## Planner

> ### Objectives
> - Name food items
> - Say what you like eating

> ### Resources
> Students' Book, pages 60–61
> CD 2, tracks 10–11

> ### Key language
> *Beurk! Bof! C'est bon!*
> *une crêpe, une pizza, une quiche, un steak-frites, un hamburger, un sandwich, des moules, des escargots, des nems*
> *J'adore, J'aime bien, Je n'aime pas beaucoup, Je déteste …*

> ### Grammar
> *j'aime, je n'aime pas le, la, les*
> *ça*

> ### Framework reference
> 3.1, 3.2, 5.2, 5.3

> ### Starters
> - Read out the nine food words from the top of page 60. How many items can students work out from how they sound? Explain that French borrows many words from other languages, but also stress that the pronunciation is different.
> - Recap on *j'adore, j'aime bien, je n'aime pas* and *je déteste* (last met in connection with school subjects). Give students two minutes to make as many sentences as they can with these four phrases. Pool ideas.

> ### Plenaries
> - Use this spread as an opportunity to tackle clichés about French food (snails, etc.). Discuss specialities from other countries and cultures. What do people in some countries eat that we in Britain don't? What do we eat that other cultures might not find very appetising? For example, the French aren't particularly keen on Marmite and baked beans!
> - Play Three in a Row, either in pairs or as a whole class, using the grid with the nine photos from the start of page 60.

> ### Assessment opportunities
> - Speaking: Students' Book page 61, exercise 5
> - Writing: Students' Book page 61, exercise 7

---

### 1 Écoute, lis et répète.

- Students listen to the food words and repeat each one, taking care with pronunciation.
- Point out the *Top Tips!* box which focuses on pronunciation of words that are the same in English and French.
- Use the photos as an opportunity to focus on the influence of other countries on French food. Ask students which of the foods shown here are from other countries: *une pizza (un plat italien), des nems (un plat vietnamien), un hamburger (un plat américain)*.
- Can students identify similar influences in Britain? Which dishes are popular in Britain and which countries do they come from?

**CD 2, track 10**      page 60, activité 1

1. Une crêpe!
2. Un steak-frites!
3. Des moules!
4. Une pizza!
5. Un hamburger!
6. Des escargots!
7. Une quiche!
8. Un sandwich!
9. Des nems!

### Top Tips!

- Students find words which are the same in English and French. Do an activity where you read out these words, either with French or English pronunciation. Students only put up their hand if they hear the French version.

### 2 À deux.

- Students work in pairs and look at the photos but cover up the words. They take turns to test their partner on the words, taking care with pronunciation.

### 3 Écris.

- Students write out the nine food items in the order of what they like best. Ask them to check their partner's list for accurate spelling.

### 4 Écoute. (1–9)

- As preparation for this activity, go over the four opinion phrases *j'adore, j'aime bien, je n'aime pas beaucoup* and *je déteste* if you have not already done so in the Starter.
- Students then listen and note the correct symbol for each person speaking.
- As follow-up, play the audio again and ask

students to repeat the answers, but only the ones they agree with, copying the intonation as closely as possible.

*Answers:* 1 ☺; 2 ☹; 3 ♥; 4 😐; 5 ☺; 6 😐; 7 ☹; 8 ☺; 9 ♥

 **CD 2, track 11**          page 61, activité 4

1 – Tu aimes les sandwichs?
  – Oui, c'est bon, j'aime bien ça.
2 – Tu aimes les hamburgers?
  – Beurk! Non, je déteste ça!
3 – Tu aimes les crêpes?
  – Ah oui, j'adore les crêpes!
4 – Les escargots, tu aimes les escargots?
  – Bof, non, je n'aime pas beaucoup ça.
5 – Tu aimes les nems?
  – Oui, c'est bons, les nems, j'aime bien ça.
6 – Tu aimes les pizzas?
  – Non, je n'aime pas beaucoup les pizzas.
7 – Tu aimes les quiches?
  – Non, je déteste les quiches.
8 – Tu aimes le steak-frites?
  – Oui, j'aime bien le steak-frites.
9 – Tu aimes les moules?
  – Ah oui, c'est bon, j'adore ça!

 **5 Parle en classe.**

- Students go round the class asking each other which foods they like and don't like. They each have to find someone who shares at least three of their opinions. Model first with a volunteer.

## Top Tips!

- Encourage students to use *ça* to mean 'it/that' to avoid repeating the name of the food. Practise using it with all four of the opinion phrases.

**AT 3.2–3** **6 Lis et réponds.**

- Students read the passage and answer the questions in English. This passage contains some unknown words, but students should be able to work out the meaning from words which are similar to English ones.
- Read the passage out loud before students start on the activity, if necessary, and encourage students to read out loud in pairs after they have answered the questions.

*Answers:* a Algeria; b couscous; c soup; d Je préfère

**AT 4.2–3** **7 Écris.**

- Students adapt the example to write about a well-known dish from their country, saying whether they like it or not.
- Read out some students' texts as follow-up without saying whose it is. The rest of the class guesses who wrote it.
- Encourage students to adapt sentences they have learned when talking about themselves. Show them how they can adapt a sentence, often by changing just one item (as shown by yellow highlights in this exercise), to say lots of different things: *Je préfère (les pizzas)*. How many different things could they add after *Je préfère* – and not only food items!

# 8.2 Je vais au café

## *Planner*

> ### Objectives
> * Say where you go when you eat out
> * Say what you would like to eat

> ### Resources
> Students' Book, pages 62–63
> CD 2, tracks 12–14
> Video clip 12, *Clic! 1 Star*
> OxBox *Clic! 1 Star, Unité 6, Tu manges où en ville?;*
> *Samedi, 13 heures*

> ### Key language
> *Je vais … au restaurant, au café, au fast-food, à la*
> *pizzeria, à la crêperie, à la cafétéria.*
> *Je voudrais (une pizza).*
> *On mange (au café).*

> ### Grammar
> *aller (je, tu)*
> *au, à la*

> ### Framework reference
> 4.3, 4.4, 4.5

> ### Starters
> * Show students a list of the six places on the
>   whiteboard together with *au* and *à la*. Give them
>   one minute to divide the places into categories,
>   using any reason that is sensible. They can work
>   in pairs or groups. Reasons could include: words

they understand/don't understand; words that are
like English/not like English; words that use
*au/à la*.
* Students draw two columns, headed *au/à la*.
  Display the words for the six places to eat
  (without genders) and set a time limit for students
  to list them in the correct columns. They swap
  with a partner and check each other's lists.

> ### Plenaries
> * Focus on how important it is to learn the gender
>   of nouns in French. Brainstorm words that are
>   affected by gender, such as definite and indefinite
>   articles, adjective agreement and on this spread
>   they have learned *au/à la* to talk about going to
>   places.
> * Write out the lines from a dialogue (similar to
>   the one in exercise 4) in jumbled order on the
>   whiteboard:
>     – *On mange à la crêperie? Je voudrais une*
>       *crêpe.*
>     – *Bof! Je n'aime pas les crêpes. Je préfère les*
>       *hamburgers.*
>     – *Non, merci. Je déteste les hamburgers. Je*
>       *préfère les pizzas.*
>     – *Oui, C'est bon. On mange à la pizzeria*
>     – *OK*
> * Give students a time limit to sort the dialogue into
>   the correct order. Pairs read it aloud.

> ### Assessment opportunities
> * Reading: Students' Book page 63, exercise 4
> * Writing: Students' Book page 63, exercise 6

---

 ### Preparation
* To introduce places for eating out, use the
  flashcard presentation from OxBox, *Tu manges où*
  *en ville?*

 **AT 1.1** ### 1a Écoute. C'est quelle photo? (1–6)
* Students listen to people saying where they go to
  eat out and identify the correct photo.
* Discuss the photos with the class and talk about
  the different types of eating places in France.
  Compare with those in Britain.

*Answers*: 1 photo 2; 2 photo 4; 3 photo 3; 4 photo 1; 5
photo 6; 6 photo 5

 **CD 2, track 12**    page 62, activités 1a et 1b

**1** – Tu vas où?
   – Je vais au café.
**2** – Tu vas où?
   – Je vais à la pizzeria.
**3** – Tu vas où?
   – Je vais au fast-food.
**4** – Tu vas où?
   – Je vais au restaurant.
**5** – Tu vas où?
   – Je vais à la cafétéria.
**6** – Tu vas où?
   – Je vais à la crêperie.

### 1b Réécoute et répète.

- Students listen again and repeat the answers.

- Point out the key language box and, if you have not already done so in the Starter, ask students why they think some places use *à la* and some use *au*. Explain that they both mean 'to the' or 'at the' and that *au* is used with masculine places and *à la* with feminine ones. Practise the sentences with *je vais* orally.

### 2a À deux.

- Students work in pairs and throw a die. They say sentences corresponding to the numbers of the photos. Who is the first to say all six places?

### 2b Écris.

- Students now write sentences about each eating place, starting with the one they like best.

### 3 Regarde le clip.

- Students watch the video clip where people say where they like eating out. They note the places pictured in exercise 1 in the order they hear them mentioned.

*Answers*: 1, 3, 5, 6, 4, 2

 **Video clip 12**    page 62, activité 3

**CD 2, track 13**

Aujourd'hui, on va parler de là où tu manges quand tu vas en ville …

– Tu manges où quand tu vas en ville?
– En ville? Je mange au restaurant avec ma famille. Mes parents aiment bien manger au restaurant.

– Tu manges où quand tu vas en ville?
– En général, avec des copains, on va au fast-food, au Flunch, au MacDo, au Quick. C'est sympa.

– Bonjour! Alors tu aimes manger à la crêperie quand tu vas en ville?
– Oui, j'adore manger à la crêperie quand je vais en ville avec des copines. On adore les crêpes!

– Tu manges où quand tu vas en ville?
– Quand je vais au supermarché avec mes parents, je mange à la cafétéria. C'est pratique.
– Salut! Tu manges où quand tu vas en ville?
– Je vais à la pizzeria. La pizza, c'est mon plat préféré.

– Salut! Tu manges où quand tu vas en ville?
– Des fois, on mange au café. C'est rapide. On prend un sandwich et après on va au cinéma!

### Follow-up

- Play the clip again. Students note down the reasons given for eating at the different places. Ask them to listen for any additional information, e.g. the second boy says he eats at the cafeteria in the supermarket with his parents, and the last boy says he has a sandwich and then goes on to the cinema.

### 4 Lis et réponds.

- Read the scene out loud before giving students a few minutes to answer the questions.
- Students can then read the scene in pairs.
- Recap on the use of *on* to mean 'we' and explain that *je voudrais* means 'I would like'.

*Answers*: a Marie; b doesn't like pizza; c Marie; d pancakes; e eat at the pancake restaurant; f Je voudrais

### 5 Écoute (1–2). Choisis a ou b.

- Students listen to two similar conversations and choose the correct options.

*Answers*: 1 a; 2 b, b

 **CD2, track 14**    page 63, activité 5

**1** – Je voudrais un steak-frites. On va au restaurant?
– Non, je suis végétarien. Je préfère les crêpes.
– Bon, ben, on va à la crêperie!

**2** – On va au fast-food? Je voudrais un hamburger.
– Oh non, merci! Je déteste les hamburgers!
– Alors, une pizza, à la pizzeria? C'est cool.
– Ah non, moi, je préfère un bon steak-frites et une salade au restaurant!

### 6 Adapte et écris la conversation.

- Students adapt the conversation from exercise 4 to create a new dialogue. Words are provided for them and the words they need to change are highlighted in exercise 4.

### 7 À deux.

- In pairs, students perform their dialogues for the rest of the class.

### Follow-up

- Further practice on dialogues can be found on OxBox *Samedi, 13 heures*. This is an interactive sequencing activity.

# 8.3 S'il vous plaît!

## *Planner*

> ### Objectives
> - Name flavours and fillings
> - Order a snack

> ### Resources
> Students' Book, pages 64–65
> CD 2, tracks 15–18
> Copymaster 66, *Clic! 1 Star*

> ### Key language
> *une glace à la vanille, à l'orange*
> *une pizza à la tomate, aux champignons*
> *un sandwich au fromage*
> *une crêpe au chocolat*
> *Je voudrais … s'il vous plaît.*

> ### Grammar
> *au, à la, aux*
> *Je voudrais*

> ### Framework reference
> 1.4, 4.3, 5.5

> ### Starters
> - Play Food Shoot-Out. Two students stand up. Call out a food item or an eating place that has been met in this unit, in English. The pair compete to say the word in French. The first student to answer correctly remains standing; the other one sits down and is replaced by a new challenger.
> - Write the following jumble of words on the board or OHP:
>   *un sandwich / un sandwich / une glace /*

> *une glace / une crêpe / une pizza*
> *au / au / à la / à la / à l' / aux*
> *fromage / tomate / vanille / chocolat / orange / champignons*
> - Give students 30 seconds to match them into appropriate combinations. They must use all the words once only, and each item must be grammatically correct as well as something you'd want to eat!

> ### Plenaries
> - Give students a few new food and drink words in English (e.g. rice, lemon, jam, fish, chicken, soup, potatoes, salad, water). Set a time limit and challenge students to find the French words in a dictionary (together with the gender, if possible). Students compare their answers with a partner and discuss how to pronounce the words. Allow time for feedback, to check answers and pronunciation.
> - Display a café dialogue on the board, OHP or whiteboard, incorporating key language from the spread. Read it with the whole class, then erase one or two words/phrases. Challenge pairs to read the dialogue out loud, filling in the missing words. Erase even more words/phrases, then challenge pairs to read it again. Continue until only a few words/phrases remain. Can any pairs reconstruct the whole dialogue from memory?

> ### Assessment opportunities
> - Writing: Students' Book page 65, exercise 6
> - Speaking: Students' Book page 65, exercise 7

---

AT 1.1
AT 2.1

### 1 Écoute, lis et répète.
- Students listen, read and repeat the names of fillings and flavours. Which are the same or similar in French and English? Discuss as a class.
- Point out the grammar box.

**CD 2, track 15**      page 64, activité 1

1 une glace à la vanille
2 une pizza à la tomate
3 un sandwich au fromage
4 une crêpe au chocolat
5 une pizza aux champignons
6 une glace à l'orange

AT 1.2

### 2 Écoute (1–7). Note les numéros.
- Students listen to people ordering food and note the letter of the snack and the number of the filling or flavouring.

*Answers:* 1 A + 2; 2 B + 3; 3 D + 6; 4 C + 4; 5 D + 1; 6 A + 5; 6 C + 5

**CD 2, track 16**      page 64, activité 2

1 Une pizza à la tomate, s'il vous plaît.
2 Un sandwich au fromage, s'il vous plaît.
3 Une glace à l'orange, s'il vous plaît.
4 Pour moi, une crêpe au chocolat.
5 Pour moi, une glace à la vanille.
6 Je voudrais une pizza aux champignons.
7 Je voudrais une crêpe aux champignons.

**3 Lis et note les numéros.**

- Students read the food orders and note the letter of the snack and the number of the flavour or filling.

*Answers*: a C + 2; b B + 3; c A + 5; d D + 6; e D + 4

## Grammaire

- Look at the grammar box with students and explain that *au, à la, aux, à l'* don't really mean anything in these phrases – they just indicate the type of flavour or filling. Explain which is used for masculine, feminine and plural words and which one for words starting with a vowel. Practise by showing pictures of different items of food and students choose an appropriate flavour or filling.

### Follow-up

- Students take part in a speaking activity. They will need a die. One student chooses item A, B, C or D from page 64 and then throws a die to get a flavour, filling or topping, from pictures 1–6. The student says what it is and their partner says if he/she likes that or not!
  - *[B + 6]: Un sandwich à l'orange! C'est bon?*
  - *Non! Je n'aime pas ça!*

  **4 Écoute, lis et relie.**

- Students listen to the scene at the pancake stall while following the text in their books. They match the French and English expressions. They should be able to match those they know first and work out the rest from deduction and logic.

*Answers*: a 3; b 1; c 4; d 2; e 6; f 5

 **CD 2, track 17**      page 65, activité 4

- Bonjour! Vous désirez?
- Je voudrais une crêpe au fromage, s'il vous plaît.
- C'est tout?
- Oui, merci.
- Voilà, une crêpe au fromage. Bon appétit!
- Merci! Au revoir!

 **5 Écoute et réponds. (1–3)**

- Students listen to three people ordering food and note which person orders the four items pictured.

*Answers*: 1 a; 2 c, d; 3 b

 **CD 2, track 18**      page 65, activité 5

**1**  – Bonjour. Vous désirez?
    – Je voudrais une pizza à la tomate et au fromage, s'il vous plaît.
    – C'est tout?
    – Oui, merci.
    – Merci. Au revoir!

**2**  – Bonjour. Vous désirez?
    – Je voudrais une crêpe aux champignons, s'il vous plaît.
    – C'est tout?
    – Non, je voudrais aussi une glace au chocolat.
    – Voilà. C'est tout?
    – Oui.
    – Merci. Au revoir!

**3**  – Bonjour. Vous désirez?
    – Je voudrais une crêpe, s'il vous plaît.
    – Oui, une crêpe, c'est super bon, hein! Vous désirez une crêpe au chocolat? Ou bien une crêpe au fromage? Aux champignons? Au …
    – Une crêpe au chocolat.
    – Oui, très bien. C'est tout?
    – Oui, merci.
    – Merci à vous. Et bon appétit! Au revoir! Au revoir!

 **6 À deux.**

- Students work in pairs to write a dialogue, changing the highlighted parts of the dialogue in exercise 4.
- Use the whiteboard to show students how to adapt the dialogue, if necessary. Encourage them to have funny combinations, such as *une pizza au chocolat* or *une glace aux champignons*.

  **7 À deux.**

- Students perform their dialogue to the rest of the class.
- Encourage them to assign a mood or personality to the customer and waiter/waitress, such as sad, very grumpy, hard of hearing, over-enthusiastic, very polite or impolite, etc. Explain that it is more polite to use complete sentences (*Je voudrais …, s'il vous plaît*) than to give a short statement of what you want (*Une crêpe, s'il vous plaît*).

 **Follow-up**

- Students can complete exercises 1 and 2 on Copymaster 66 which provide further oral practice of ordering a snack.

## 8.4　Vocabulaire

page 66

---

### *Planner*

➤ **Objectives**
- *Vocabulaire*: to provide a theme-based summary of the key language of the unit, which students can use as a reference or as an aid to learning
- To practise pronunciation

➤ **Resources**
Students' Book, page 66

➤ **Framework reference**
4.1, 5.5, 5.7

---

### Using the vocabulary page

- Encourage students to use the *Vocabulaire* page as a reference point throughout the unit. It can also serve as a useful revision tool before students do the *Clic-test!*
- Vocabulary is listed spread-by-spread and you could either ask students to learn each section for homework after each spread is completed, or set the whole page as a homework task before starting work on the test. Most students learn shorter sections best, so often it is better to give them manageable chunks to learn at a time.
- Encourage students to use different techniques to help them learn the vocabulary:
  - Cover up the English and see what they can remember; write down any words they can't remember and test themselves again on those words.
  - Cover up the French and see if they can remember the words or phrases this way round.
  - Make word cards with English on one side and French on the other. Students can then test themselves to see what they can remember. Put any cards they can't remember on one side and go over those again at the end.
  - Work in pairs to test each other, either using the vocabulary list or the word cards.
  - Record themselves saying the words both in English and French. Saying words and phrases out loud can often help with memorising them.

### Sound French!

- *Aim:* To practise pronunciation
- The point practised here is the *ou* sound.
- Practise the words listed, then ask students to find more examples in previous vocabulary lists and practise saying them out loud.

## 8.4　Clic-test!

page 67

---

### *Planner*

The page is divided into four sections: listening, speaking, reading and writing.

➤ **Objectives**
- To enable students to recap on the language and structures of the unit

- To provide an opportunity for quick testing of all four skills

➤ **Resources**
Students' Book, page 67
CD 2, track 19

➤ **Framework reference**
5.8

---

AT 1.2

**1 Écoute! (1–6)**
- Students listen and match the speakers with the English bubbles.

*Answers*: 1 a; 2 c; 3 e; 4 f; 5 d; 6 b

 **CD 2, track 19**　　　　page 67, activité 1

1 Je vais à la crêperie. C'est super!
2 Je déteste les champignons.
3 J'aime bien les crêpes au fromage.
4 Moi, je n'aime pas beaucoup la glace à la vanille.
5 Je voudrais une pizza. J'adore ça!
6 J'aime les hamburgers mais je préfère le steak-frites.

**2 Lis!**

- Students read the dialogue and answer the questions in English.

*Answers*: a Léo; b quiche; c fast-food place; d hates hamburgers; e Léo; f cheese pancake

**3 Écris!**

- Students copy and complete the café dialogue using the options in the box below. .

*Answers*: 1 Bonjour, je voudrais une crêpe au fromage et à la tomate, s'il vous plaît. 2 Non, je voudrais une crêpe au chocolat, s'il vous plaît. 3 Merci, au revoir.

**AT 2.2** | **4 Parle!**

- Students work in pairs to order the food items selected in the grid.

# À moi

page 83

## *Planner*

> **Objectives**
  - To provide reinforcement activities for quiet work
  - To provide alternative class and homework material for students who finish other activities quickly

> **Resources**
Students' Book, page 83

> **Framework reference**
2.2, 2.3, 2.4

### Arnaud et Juliette au fast-food

**1 Read and answer the questions.**

- Read the text with students first, if you think they need more support to get started.

*Answers*: a hamburger; b pizza; c cheeseburger; d no; e chips

**AT 4.2–3**
**AT 2.2–3**

**2 In groups of three, adapt this conversation and write a new scene. Perform it for the rest of the class.**

- Demonstrate how students might adapt parts of the dialogue to make a new one. Let students practise their conversation in groups and then allow them to do performances for the rest of the class.

### Top Tips!

- Students are encouraged to keep the format of the sentences on the page but just to change specific details.

# 9 Bon appétit!

| Unité 9: Bon appétit! Overview grid | | | | | | |
|---|---|---|---|---|---|---|
| Page reference | Contexts and objectives | Grammar | Language strategies and pronunciation | Key language | Framework | AT level |
| 68–69 **9.1 Les repas** | • Say what you eat at different times of day <br> • Say what you drink | • *du, de la, de l', des* <br> • *le matin, le midi, le soir* | | *Je mange … du pain, du poisson, du fromage, de la soupe, de la viande, de la salade, des céréales, des frites, des légumes.* <br> *Le matin/Le midi/Le soir, je mange/tu manges …* <br> *Je bois … du soda, du chocolat chaud, du café, du lait, du jus de fruit, de l'eau, de la lemonade.* | 1.1, 4.3, 5.4 | 1.1–2 <br> 2.1 <br> 3.1–2 <br> 4.2 |
| 70–71 **9.2 On fait la cuisine** | • Say what food there is and isn't <br> • Follow a simple recipe | • *il y a, il n'y a pas de* <br> • Sequencers: *d'abord, ensuite, pour finir* | | *Il y a … des œufs, du lait, du poivre, du beurre, du pain, du fromage, du jambon, de l'huile.* <br> *Il n'y a pas de …* <br> *d'abord, ensuite, pour finir préparer les ingrédients, mettre du beurre sur le pain, mettre le jambon sur le pain, ajouter du fromage, couvrir avec du pain, mettre 10 minutes dans un four* | 1.5, 2.4, 4.6 | 1.1–3 <br> 2.1–2 <br> 3.2–3 <br> 4.1 |
| 72–73 **9.3 Mange bien!** | • Talk about healthy eating <br> • Say what you are and aren't going to eat | • *je vais +* infinitive | Don't panic when listening | *Je vais … manger des fruits, manger des légumes, boire de l'eau, manger un bon petit déjeuner.* <br> *Je ne vais pas … boire de soda, manger de frites, manger de chocolat, ajouter de sel.* | 1.2, 4.4, 4.5 | 1.2–3 <br> 2.2–3 <br> 3.2–3 <br> 4.2–3 |
| 74 **9.4 Vocabulaire** | • Practise pronunciation | | Last letter of words often not pronounced | | 4.1, 4.2, 5.5 | |
| 75 **9.4 Clic-test!** | • Recap on the language structures of the unit <br> • Provide an opportunity for quick testing of all four skills | | | | 5.8 | 1.2 <br> 2.2 <br> 3.1–2 <br> 4.1–3 |
| 84 **À moi** | • Provide reinforcement activities for self-access work | | | | 2.1, 2.2, 2.5 | 3.2–3 <br> 4.2–3 |
| 90 **Blog-notes** | • Provide extended listening practice recycling the language of the whole unit | | | | 1.2, 1.3, 1.5 | 1.2–3 <br> 2.2–3 <br> 4.2–3 |

| MEDIUM TERM GRID Week-by-week overview (assuming six weeks' work or approximately 10–12.5 hours) |
|---|

**About Unit 9, *Bon appétit!***

In this unit, students learn more about food and drink in France. They learn how to follow a recipe and consider healthy lifestyle. They use *du, de la, de l'* and *des* with food as well as
*il y a* and *il n'y a pas de* and also sequencers. They use *je vais* + infinitive to indicate the future and they cover some strategies for listening.

New vocabulary includes further food items which they eat at different times of day, drinks vocabulary, ingredients and recipe instructions and phrases for a healthy lifestyle.

Reading, listening and comprehension skills are developed through a variety of texts, audio and video materials.

| Week | Resources | Objectives |
|---|---|---|
| 1 | **9.1 Les repas** | Saying what you eat in the morning, at lunch and in the evening<br>Saying what you drink<br>Using *du, de la, de l'* and *des* with food and drink items |
| 2 | **9.2 On fait la cuisine** | Using *il y a* and *il n'y a pas de* to say what food there is and isn't<br>Following a recipe<br>Understanding sequencers |
| 3 | **9.3 Mange bien!** | Talking about healthy eating<br>Talking about what you are and are not going to do to be healthy<br>Using *je vais* and *je ne vais pas* + infinitive to indicate the future<br>Listening strategies |
| 4 | **Sound French!** (p74)<br>**À moi** (p84)<br>**Blog-notes** (p90) | Practising pronunciation (not pronouncing the final letter of words)<br>Additional reading and writing practice<br>Using the video for reinforcement, extension and follow-up work |
| 5 | **9.4 Vocabulaire**<br>**Clic-test!** | Learning vocabulary<br>Recapping on vocabulary of unit<br>Preparing and carrying out of assessment in all four skills<br>Reviewing progress |
| 6 | **Copymasters** (*Feuilles*)<br>**OxBox** | Reinforcement and extension of the language of the unit using extra resources<br>Reviewing progress via the Checklist on page 74, *Vocabulaire*<br>Going back over aspects of the unit which need reviewing after *Clic-test!* |

# 9.1 Les repas

## *Planner*

> **Objectives**
> * Say what you eat at different times of the day
> * Say what you drink

> **Resources**
> Students' Book, pages 68–69
> CD 2, tracks 20–21

> **Key language**
> *Je mange … du pain, du poisson, du fromage, de la soupe, de la viande, de la salade, des céréales, des frites, des légumes.*
> *Le matin/Le midi/Le soir, je mange/tu manges …*
> *Je bois … du soda, du chocolat chaud, du café, du lait, du jus de fruit, de l'eau, de la lemonade.*

> **Grammar**
> *du, de la, de l', des*
> *le matin, le midi, le soir*

> **Framework reference**
> 1.1, 4.3, 5.4

> **Starters**
> * Put the headings for two columns on the whiteboard *midi* and *soir* and explain meanings

if students don't know already. Brainstorm items of food already known, which students may eat at lunchtime or in the evening.
* Play Food Shoot-Out. Two students stand up. Call out a food item from page 68, in English. The pair compete to say the word in French with the correct form of *du, de l', de la, des*. The first student to answer correctly remains standing; the other one sits down and is replaced by a new challenger.

> **Plenaries**
> * Play a game of Word Tennis. Call out a mealtime (*le matin, le soir*, etc.) and a student responds with an appropriate food or drink item in French, including the correct determiner *du, de l', de la, des*. Alternatively, ask students to respond with a full sentence, such as *Je mange des légumes.* Repeat around the class.
> * In pairs, students share their understanding of *du, de l', de la, des*. How do they know when to use each one? They write down some example sentences in French to show correct usage.

> **Assessment opportunities**
> * Writing: Students' Book page 69, exercise 7

---

  **1 Écoute, lis et répète.**
* Students listen and repeat food items spoken with the correct form of *du, de l', de la, des*.

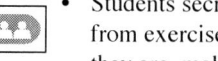 **CD 2, track 20**    page 68, activité 1

Je mange …
du pain
du poisson
du fromage
de la soupe
de la viande
de la salade
des céréales
des frites
des légumes

## Grammaire

* This box explains the three ways of saying 'some' in French with masculine, feminine and plural words; words beginning with vowels are not covered here but you may wish to introduce *de l'*. Explain how we don't always use 'some' in English, e.g. 'I eat bread' but in French you always use a determiner. Practise the words by

calling out a letter of a picture from exercise 1 and students reply with a sentence: h, *Je mange des frites*.

 **2 À deux.**
* Students secretly note down three of the items from exercise 1 and their partner deduces what they are, making as few guesses as possible.

**3 Lis et réponds.**
* Students read the speech bubbles and answer the questions in English.
* Go over the meaning of *le matin, le midi* and *le soir* and explain the use of *ou* and *avec* to make longer sentences.

*Answers*: a in the morning, at lunchtime, in the evening; b cereal or bread; c at lunchtime; d fish or meat with vegetables

 **4 Écris.**
* Students separate out the words to write the complete sentences. They then work out what each means in English.

*Answers*: a *Je mange des frites*. I eat chips. b *Je mange de la viande*. I eat meat. c *Je mange du pain*

*et du fromage.* I eat bread and cheese. d *Tu manges du pain?* Do you eat bread? e *Tu manges des frites ou des légumes?* Do you eat chips or vegetables? f *Le soir, je mange du poisson.* In the evening I eat fish.

 **AT 3.1** | **5 Relie.**

- Students match the names of the drinks to the pictures. They should use strategies to help them, such as using the pictures as clues, looking for words which look like the English and using a process of elimination. Any words they cannot work out, should be looked up in the glossary.
- Do further oral practice of drinks by asking: *Qu'est-ce que tu bois le matin/le midi/le soir?*

*Answers*: a 4; b 7; c 3; d 2; e 5; f 1; g 6

**AT 1.1–2** | **6 Écoute et note.**

- Students listen to the conversation and note three drinks which are mentioned.
- As follow-up, play the audio again and ask students for any other details they can understand.

*Answers*: hot chocolate, water, fizzy drink

 **CD 2, track 21**          page 69, activité 6

- Est-ce que tu manges le matin?
- Oui! Le matin, je mange du pain avec du Nutella. Je bois du chocolat chaud.
- Qu'est-ce que tu manges le midi?
- En général, je mange des frites et je bois de l'eau!
- Tu prends un goûter l'après-midi?
- Oui, de temps en temps: je mange des barres de céréales et je bois du soda.
- Tu manges quoi le soir?
- Ça dépend. J'aime bien manger des pâtes.

**AT 4.2** | **7 Adapte la bulle pour toi.**

- Students write down what they eat and drink at different times of the day. They can adapt the highlighted words.
- Encourage students to use words met in this spread or in Unit 8. Also encourage them to use a dictionary to find words for other items of food they wish to use.

# 9.2    On fait la cuisine

pages 70–71

## *Planner*

> **Objectives**
- Say what food there is and isn't
- Follow a simple recipe

> **Resources**
Students' Book, pages 70–71
CD 2, tracks 22–24
Copymaster 63, *Clic! 1 Star*

> **Key language**
*Il y a … des œufs, du lait, du poivre, du beurre, du pain, du fromage, du jambon, de l'huile.*
*Il n'y a pas de …*
*d'abord, ensuite, pour finir*
*préparer les ingrédients, mettre du beurre sur le pain, mettre le jambon sur le pain, ajouter du fromage, couvrir avec du pain, mettre 10 minutes dans un four*

> **Grammar**
*il y a, il n'y a pas de*
Sequencers: *d'abord, ensuite, pour finir*

**Framework reference**
1.5, 2.4, 4.6

> **Starters**
- Provide a list of food and drink from the previous spread, either on a worksheet or on the

whiteboard, along with the headings *du, de la, des, de l'*. Students see how many they can place in the correct column. Discuss results together as a class.
- In pairs, students play Contradictions. If one student says a positive sentence, their partner has to deny it, and vice versa.
  Student A: *Il y a du pain.*
  Student B: *Il n'y a pas de pain!*
  Student A: *Il y a du beurre.*
  Student B: *Il n'y a pas de beurre.*

> **Plenaries**
- Play Kim's Game. Prepare a few whiteboard screens. The first screen has all the words met in this lesson and subsequent screens each have one word missing. Students work out which word is missing each time. Play as a team game, if preferred.
- Pairs reflect on what they have learned from working on the recipes, e.g. reading strategies, ways to give instructions in French, new vocabulary and how to use sequencers. Ask students to brainstorm other contexts in which they could use the sequencers, such as describing weekend activities, school timetable and daily routine. Allow time for whole class feedback and discussion.

> **Assessment opportunities**
- Speaking: Students' Book page 71, exercise 5
- Reading: Students' Book page 71, exercise 6

**Bon appétit!**

 AT 2.1

**1 Regarde et dis ce qu'il y a.**

- Remind students that *il y a* means 'there is/are'. They met it with places in a town and weather expressions in Unit 6.
- How many sentences can students make with *il y a* and a food item they see in the picture? Encourage students to use the correct words for 'some' each time.

AT 1.1
AT 2.1

**2 Écoute, lis et répète.**

- Students listen to and repeat the ingredients. These are going to be used in a recipe later.

**CD 2, track 22**      page 70, activité 2

- des œufs
- du lait
- du poivre
- du beurre
- du pain
- du fromage
- du jambon
- de l'huile

AT 4.1

**3 Fais ton petit dico.**

- Students make their own picture dictionary to help them remember the food words. They can write them in alphabetical order.
- Ask students to check each other's work when they have finished for accurate spelling and use of accents.
- You could use this opportunity to revise the alphabet. Spell out one of the items and students note which one it is.

AT 1.2

**4 Écoute et note ✓ ou ✗. (1–8)**

- Before listening, remind students of the negative *il n'y a pas de*. Practise this by saying sentences which use *il y a* and *il n'y a pas de* and students give the thumbs-up or thumbs-down sign in response.
- Students listen to identify the items pictured in exercise 2 and note with a tick or a cross whether they are available or not.

*Answers*: 1 a ✓; 2 b ✗; 3 c ✓; 4 d ✓; 5 e ✓; 6 f ✗; 7 g ✓; 8 h ✗

**CD 2, track 23**      page 70, activité 4

1. – Est-ce qu'il y a des œufs?
   – Oui, il y a des œufs.
2. – Il y a du lait?
   – Non, il n'y a pas de lait.
3. – Il y a du poivre?
   – Oui, il y a du poivre.
4. – Est-ce qu'il y a du beurre?
   – Oui, il y a du beurre.
5. – Il y a du pain?
   – Oui, il y a du pain.

6. – Est-ce qu'il y a du fromage râpé?
   – Non, il n'y a pas de fromage râpé.
7. – Il y a du jambon?
   – Oui, il y a du jambon.
8. – Est-ce qu'il y a de l'huile d'olive?
   – Non, il n'y a pas d'huile d'olive.

 AT 2.2

**5 À deux.**

- Students work in pairs and use their answers from exercise 4 to say what ingredients there are or are not. They can use the key language box as support.

AT 3.2–3

**6 Lis et trouve le français.**

- Students read the recipe and find the French equivalents for the English phrases listed. They should be able to identify the answers from phrases they do understand.
- Point out the sequencers which can be used in other contexts.

*Answers*: a 4 tranches de jambon; b préparer les ingrédients; c Mettre du beurre; d Ajouter du fromage râpé; e Couvrir avec du pain; f D'abord; g Ensuite; h Pour finir

AT 1.2–3

**7 Écoute. (1–6)**

- Students listen and note the order of the instructions from the recipe.

*Answers*: 1 D; 2 B; 3 A; 4 E; 5 C; 6 F

**CD 2, track 24**      page 71, activité 7

1. Ajouter du fromage râpé et du poivre.
2. Mettre du beurre sur le pain.
3. D'abord, préparer les ingrédients.
4. Couvrir avec du pain et du fromage râpé.
5. Ensuite, mettre le jambon sur le pain.
6. Pour finir, mettre 10 minutes dans un four à 220°C (thermostat 7–8).

**Follow-up**

- You could show students how to write out other simple recipes, such as fruit salad or an omelette, using similar vocabulary and sequencers.
- Students pretend to be TV chefs and present one of the recipes as if they were on a cookery programme. If possible, record the presentations on video, with students holding up autocue cards for each other.
- Encourage students to use sequencers as a framework for their demonstration.

 C63
- Additional reading and writing activities on ingredients are provided on Copymaster 63, exercises 2 and 3.

*Answers*: **2** a des œufs; b du fromage; c du pain; d de l'huile d'olive; e du jambon; f du beurre; g du sucre; h du lait

*Answers*: **3** a 72; b 100; c 80; d 83; e 68; f 95; g 99; h 76

# 9.3 Mange bien!

## *Planner*

➤ **Objectives**
- Talk about healthy eating
- Say what you are and aren't going to eat

➤ **Resources**
Students' Book, pages 72–73
CD 2, tracks 25–27
Copymaster 67, *Clic! 1 Star*

➤ **Key language**
*Je vais … manger des fruits, manger des légumes, boire de l'eau, manger un bon petit déjeuner.*
*Je ne vais pas … boire de soda, manger de frites, manger de chocolat, ajouter de sel.*

➤ **Grammar**
*je vais* + infinitive

➤ **Framework reference**
1.2, 4.4, 4.5

➤ **Starters**
- Hold a short discussion about healthy eating. Ask students whether their own idea of healthy eating differs from that of their parents/grandparents. Who is the healthiest person in their family?

- Display some anagrams of food and drink items for students to solve and work out whether each word needs *du, de l', de la* or *des*. Write two columns on the board: *C'est bien pour la santé* and *Ce n'est pas bien pour la santé* and ask students to write each food item under the relevant heading and with the correct determiner.

➤ **Plenaries**
- Display the following incomplete sentences:
  *Je vais manger…*
  *Je ne vais pas manger…*
  *Je vais boire …*
  *Je ne vais pas boire …*
- Set a time limit for students, working in pairs, to complete the sentences to make a set of healthy resolutions. Allow time to check answers.
- Display a few single words and phrases from the past few lessons (food and drink). In pairs, students write two sentences containing each word or phrase. Collect in suggestions and write them on the board.

➤ **Assessment opportunities**
- Speaking: Students' Book page 73, exercise 6
- Writing: Students' Book page 73, exercise 8

---

**AT 3.2** **1 Lis et décide.**
- Students read the quiz on their own or you could read it out loud with them. Which of the three sentences correctly describes the quiz? Ask students to explain how they arrived at their choice.

*Answer:* c

**AT 3.2** **2 Relie.**
- Students match the resolutions to the pictures. They may not understand every word in the resolutions but they should be able to do the activity from what they do understand.

*Answers:* 1 c; 2 b; 3 a; 4 f; 5 g; 6 h; 7 d; 8 e

### Grammaire
- The grammar box explains how students can use *je vais* with another verb to talk about what they are going to do. Recap on the negative *Je ne vais pas*, meaning 'I'm not going to'.
- Practise with other items of food and drink.

**AT 1.2** **AT 2.2** **3 Écoute, lis et répète. (Quiz-santé! 1–8)**
- Students listen to and repeat the resolutions.

🎧 **CD 2, track 25**    page 72, activité 3

Je vais manger des fruits.
Je vais manger des légumes.
Je vais boire de l'eau.
Je vais manger un bon petit déjeuner.
Je ne vais pas boire de soda.
Je ne vais pas manger de frites.
Je ne vais pas manger de chocolat.
Je ne vais pas ajouter de sel.

**AT 1.2** **4 Écoute Marie et Max.**
- Students hear Marie and Max answering the questions in the quiz. They note the letters of the pictures from exercise 2 in the order they are mentioned.

*Answers:* Marie a, c, h, f; Max b, d, g, e

**CD 2, track 26**  page 72, activité 4

- Marie ... tu vas boire de l'eau?
- Oui, je vais boire de l'eau.
- Tu vas manger des fruits?
- Oui, je vais manger des fruits.
- Tu vas manger des frites?
- Non, je ne vais pas manger de frites.
- Tu vas manger un bon petit déjeuner?
- Oui, je vais manger un bon petit déjeuner.

- Max, tu vas manger des légumes?
- Oui, je vais manger des légumes.
- Tu vas manger du chocolat?
- Non, je ne vais pas manger de chocolat.
- Tu vas boire du soda?
- Non, je ne vais pas boire de soda.
- Tu vas ajouter du sel?
- Non! Je ne vais pas ajouter de sel.

 **5 Écris.**

- Students write three resolutions they would find hard to keep and three they would find easy.

 **6 Fais des interviews.**

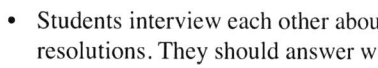

- Students interview each other about their resolutions. They should answer with either a positive or negative sentence, not just *oui* or *non*.
- Make sure students know that *tu vas* is the correct form of the verb they should use in their questions.

 **7 Lis et explique.**

- Students read Toto's resolutions and explain if each one is healthy or not.

*Answers*: It's healthy to eat fish, but it's not healthy to eat hamburgers. It's healthy to drink fruit juice and not to drink fizzy drinks. It's not healthy not to eat salad. It's healthy not to add salt.

 **8 Écris tes bonnes résolutions.**

- Students write a list of what they are and are not going to eat or drink to lead a healthier lifestyle.
- Encourage students to use food and drink vocabulary they have met over the last few weeks, not just the expressions from this spread. Brainstorm food and drink items together, if more support is needed.

 **9 Écoute la chanson.**

- Students listen to the song about what someone is going to buy at the market. They note any food items they recognise.
- You could show students the text of the song and ask them to look up any unfamiliar items of food in a dictionary.

 **CD 2, track 27**  page 73, activité 9

**Au marché**

Aujourd'hui, je fais les courses
Et au marché, je vais acheter ...

... des épinards, une ou deux poires
du camembert et de la bière
et un bout de gruyère
... des champignons, un gros melon
du saucisson et des citrons
et six tranches de jambon
... un ananas et de la glace
des avocats, de la pizza
des crêpes au chocolat.

Aujourd'hui, j'ai fait les courses
mais j'ai oublié d'acheter ...

... des épinards, une ou deux poires
du camembert et de la bière
et un bout de gruyère
... des champignons, un gros melon
du saucisson et des citrons
et six tranches de jambon
... un ananas et de la glace
des avocats, de la pizza
des crêpes au chocolat.

Aïe aïe aïe!

## Top Tips!

- Go over the listening strategies in the box, reassuring students they won't understand every word when they listen to French, but they should just concentrate on what they can understand.
- Before listening, students should try to predict what words they might hear, for example, if it is about what someone is going to buy at the market, what sort of vocabulary might they expect?

**Follow-up**

 **C67**

- Additional reading and writing activities on diet and eating habits are provided on Copymaster 67.

*Answers*: 1 a cereal; b ham sandwich and fruit; c yes, cake/biscuit and a cola; d an omelette and a salad; e he doesn't have a pudding; f quite healthy, but the cake/biscuit and cola for his afternoon snack aren't healthy

*Answers*: 2 a Jean-Christophe mange des céréales le matin. b À midi, il mange un sandwich. c À midi, il mange aussi un fruit. d L'après-midi, il boit un coca. e Le soir, il mange une omelette. f Le soir, il ne mange pas de dessert.

# 9.4 Vocabulaire

## *Planner*

> **Objectives**
> - *Vocabulaire*: to provide a theme-based summary of the key language of the unit, which students can use as a reference or as an aid to learning
> - To practise pronunciation

> **Resources**
> Students' Book, page 74

> **Framework reference**
> 4.1, 4.2, 5.5

### Using the vocabulary page

- Encourage students to use the *Vocabulaire* page as a reference point throughout the unit. It can also serve as a useful revision tool before students do the *Clic-test!*
- Vocabulary is listed spread-by-spread and you could either ask students to learn each section for homework after each spread is completed, or set the whole page as a homework task before starting work on the test. Most students learn shorter sections best, so often it is better to give them manageable chunks to learn at a time.
- Encourage students to use different techniques to help them learn the vocabulary:
  - Cover up the English and see what they can remember; write down any words they can't remember and test themselves again on those words.
  - Cover up the French and see if they can remember the words or phrases this way round.
  - Make word cards with English on one side and French on the other. Students can then test themselves to see what they can remember. Put any cards they can't remember on one side and go over those again at the end.
  - Work in pairs to test each other, either using the vocabulary list or the word cards.
  - Record themselves saying the words both in English and French. Saying words and phrases out loud can often help with memorising them.

### Sound French!

- *Aim:* To practise pronunciation
- The point practised here is not pronouncing the final letters in French words, such as *s* and *d*.
- Model the sentence and ask students to practise reading it out loud. Then ask them to find examples of other similar words in previous vocabulary lists and practise saying them out loud.

# 9.4 Clic-test!

## *Planner*

The page is divided into four sections: listening, speaking, reading and writing.

> **Objectives**
> - To enable students to recap on the language and structures of the unit
> - To provide an opportunity for quick testing of all four skills

> **Resources**
> Students' Book, page 75
> CD 2, track 28

> **Framework reference**
> 5.8

**Bon appétit!**

---

AT 1.2 | **1 Écoute! (1–6)**

• Students listen and match each speaker to a bubble.

*Answers*: 1 f; 2 a; 3 e; 4 b; 5 c; 6 d

 **CD 2, track 28**  page 75, activité 1

– Qu'est-ce que vous faites pour être en forme?

1 Moi, je ne mange pas de viande.
2 Le matin, je mange des céréales.
3 Le soir, je mange du poisson.
4 Je mange des fruits et des légumes tous les jours.
5 Je ne bois pas de soda.
6 Le midi, je bois de l'eau.

AT 3.1–2 | **2 Lis!**

• Students read the menu and explain each item in English.

*Answers*: vegetable soup or tomato salad; grilled fish, chips; cheese; drink: water

AT 2.2 | **3 Parle!**

• Students say what they are going to eat and drink on a picnic.

*Answers*: a Je vais manger du jambon. b Je vais manger du fromage. c Je vais manger de la salade. e Je vais manger du pain. f Je vais manger des fruits. g Je vais boire du jus de fruit.

AT 4.1–3 | **4 Écris!**

• Students complete the sentences about what they eat and drink at different times of the day.

# À moi

## *Planner*

> **Objectives**
• To provide reinforcement activities for quiet work
• To provide alternative class and homework material for students who finish other activities quickly

> **Resources**
Students' Book, page 84

> **Framework reference**
2.1, 2.2, 2.5

### Qu'est-ce que tu manges le matin?

AT 3.2 | **1 Which caption goes with the photo?**

• Students read six captions and identify which one matches the picture.

*Answer*: 2

AT 3.2–3 | **2 Answer in English.**

• This task assesses students' understanding of the detail. They read the captions again and answer the questions in English.

*Answers*: a hot chocolate, milk, fizzy drink, water, coffee; b bread, cereal, egg, chocolate, butter, orange; c 3, it has healthy drink and food choices; d students' own answers

AT 3.2 | **2 Choose one of the captions. Copy it out and draw a picture to match.**

• Students choose one of the breakfast options and copy it out and illustrate it. They could draw arrows to identify each food and drink item.

AT 4.2–3 | **3 Imagine your ideal breakfast. Write what you are going to eat and drink.**

• Students write sentences to describe their ideal breakfast, using the immediate future. There are some prompts given for support, if needed.

# Blog-notes

## *Planner*

➢ **Objectives**
- To summarise the main points of the unit in context, in a format that is fun and familiar to students, i.e. a video blog
- To provide a model enabling students to personalise the language of the unit
- To provide opportunities for students to ask as well as answer questions
- To provide extended listening practice recycling the language of the whole unit

➢ **Resources**
Students' Book, page 90
Video clip 13, *Clic! 1 Star*
CD 2, track 29

➢ **Framework reference**
1.2, 1.3, 1.5

---

**1 Watch Thomas's video diary. Choose a or b to complete each sentence.**

- Students watch Thomas's video diary and choose
- a or b in answer to each question about his eating habits. Pause the clip after each section to allow students time to answer.

*Answers*: 1 a; 2 a; 3 a; 4 b; 5 b

 **Video clip 13**     page 90, activités 1 et 2

**CD 2, track 29**

Salut! Yo, c'est moi! Thomas Garnier. Ça va?
a  Hmmm ... désolé! Je mange mon petit déjeuner! Le matin, au petit déjeuner, je mange une tranche de pain et du Nutella. C'est bon le Nutella! Et toi, qu'est-ce que tu manges le matin?
b  Moi, j'aime bien manger en ville, avec mes copains. En général, on va à la pizzeria près du collège. Et toi, tu manges où quand tu vas en ville?
c  Je vais souvent au restaurant avec mes parents, le dimanche en général. Il y a de très bons restaurants dans la région. Et toi, tu vas quand au restaurant?
d  Moi, j'aime bien manger! Pas toi? Mon plat préféré, c'est le couscous. J'adore ça! C'est de la viande, des légumes et du couscous. Hum! Ton plat préféré, c'est quoi?
e  J'aime bien faire des gâteaux. Ma recette de gâteau préféré, c'est le quatre-quarts. Comme ingrédients, il faut quatre œufs, 250 g de farine, 250 g de sucre, 250 g de beurre et un peu de sel.
f  – Thomas? Je vais faire les courses. Qu'est-ce que tu voudrais manger ce soir?
Ça, c'est ma mère. Qu'est-ce que je voudrais manger ce soir? Euh ... je ne sais pas ... euh, ah oui, je sais!
– Maman! Je voudrais une pizza aux fruits de mer avec de la salade.
– Ah oui! D'accord. Bonne idée! À plus!
– Salut, maman!
Et toi, qu'est-ce que tu voudrais manger ce soir?

g  Je ne mange pas souvent de pizza. La pizza, ce n'est pas "très" bien. Mais bon, je mange bien en général, alors une pizza de temps en temps, ça va! Et toi, tu manges bien en général?
h  Moi, je voudrais être en forme. Alors, j'ai pris deux bonnes résolutions: je vais faire plus de sport et je vais manger moins de Nutella! Et toi, qu'est-ce que tu vas faire pour être plus en forme? Allez, salut!

 **2 Watch again. Can you work out ...?**

- Students watch again and choose a or b in answer to each question.

*Answers*: 1 a; 2 b; 3 a; 4 b

**AT 4.2** **3 Copy and complete sentences 1–5 in activity 1 with your own details.**

- Students write their own endings to the five sentences from exercise 1.

 **Follow-up**

- Students use their answers from exercise 3 to help them write their own blog.
- If the appropriate technology is available, allow students to record their own video blogs and play them to the class.

# Clic!

## Livre du Professeur

### Access 2

Julie Green
Pat Dunn
Danièle Bourdais
Sue Finnie

OXFORD
UNIVERSITY PRESS

# Bienvenue à Paris!

| Unité 1: Bienvenue à Paris  Overview grid | | | | | | |
|---|---|---|---|---|---|---|
| Page reference | Contexts and objectives | Grammar | Language strategies and pronunciation | Key language | Framework | AT level |
| 4–5 **1.1 Bon voyage!** | • Say your name, age and where you live<br>• Welcome a visitor | | To ask a question, make your voice go up | Je m'appelle (Max).<br>J'ai (15) ans.<br>Je suis (français).<br>J'habite à (Paris).<br>Bon voyage! Au revoir!<br>Salut! Bonjour!<br>Ça va? Ça va bien. Et toi?<br>Tu as fait bon voyage?<br>Oui, merci.<br>On y va? OK! | 1.4, 3.1, 3.2 | 1.2–3<br>2.2–3<br>3.2<br>4.2–3 |
| 6–7 **1.2 Mon quartier** | • Say what there is in a town<br>• Say what there isn't in a town | • il y a, il n'y a pas de | Using a dictionary for new words | Il y a … un supermarché, une boulangerie, une poste, un bar-tabac, une gare, un magasin de sport.<br>Il n'y a pas de … | 1.2, 1.3, 1.5, 4.6, 5.2 | 1.1–3<br>2.1–2<br>3.2<br>4.1–2 |
| 8–9 **1.3 Les transports** | • Name different transports<br>• Say how you travel | • en, a + transport | | Je visite Paris (en bus).<br>en métro, en bateau, en taxi, à vélo, à pied<br>Je vais au collège (en voiture). | 4.2, 5.2, 5.6 | 1.1–3<br>2.1–2<br>3.2<br>4.2 |
| 10 **1.4 Vocabulaire** | • Practise pronunciation | | un, une | | 4.1, 5.5 | |
| 11 **1.4 Clic-test!** | • Recap on the language and structures of the unit<br>• Provide an opportunity for quick testing of all four skills | | | | 5.8 | 1.1–2<br>2.2–3<br>3.2<br>4.2 |
| 76 **À moi** | • Provide reinforcement activities for self-access work | | | | 2.1, 2.2, 2.4 | 3.2<br>4.2 |
| 85 **Clic-vidéo** | • Provide extended listening practice recycling the language of the whole unit using a video | | | | 1.2, 1.3 | 1.2–3 |

| MEDIUM TERM GRID Week-by-week overview (assuming six weeks' work or approximately 10–12.5 hours) |
|---|

**About Unit 1, *Bienvenue à Paris!***
In this unit, students discover more about visiting Paris through the eyes of Joe, an English boy who is visiting his penfriend, Max, in Paris. Students learn about using intonation to ask questions. They use *il y a* and *il n'y a pas de* to talk about shops there are and are not in their area and they learn to use *en* and *à* with modes of transport. They use a dictionary to look up new words and they practise the pronunciation of *un* and *une*.
New vocabulary includes asking about a journey, places in a town and modes of transport. Revised language includes greetings vocabulary.
Reading, listening and comprehension skills are developed through a variety of text, audio and video materials.

| Week | Resources | Objectives |
|---|---|---|
| 1 | **1.1 Bon voyage!** | Using general greetings, including talking about a journey<br>Revision of saying name, age, nationality and where you live<br>Familiarisation of places in Paris and travelling to Paris by train<br>Asking a question by making your voice go up at the end |
| 2 | **1.2 Mon quartier** | Using *il y a* and *il n'y a pas de* to say what there is and isn't in a town<br>Using a dictionary to look up words for new places |
| 3 | **1.3 Les transports** | Naming different types of transport using *en* and *à*<br>Saying how you travel around Paris<br>Saying how you travel to school |
| 4 | **Sound French!** (p10)<br>**À moi** (p76)<br>**Clic-vidéo** (p85) | Practising pronunciation (difference between *un* and *une*)<br>Additional reading and writing practice<br>Using the video for reinforcement, extension and follow-up work |
| 5 | **1.4 Vocabulaire**<br>**Clic-test!** | Learning vocabulary<br>Recapping on vocabulary of unit<br>Preparing and carrying out assessment in all four skills<br>Reviewing progress |
| 6 | **Copymasters (*Feuilles*)**<br>**OxBox** | Reinforcement and extension of the language of the unit using extra resources<br>Reviewing progress via the Checklist on page 10, *Vocabulaire*<br>Going back over aspects of the unit which need reviewing after *Clic-test!* |

# 1.1 Bon voyage!

## *Planner*

> **Objectives**
> - Say your name, age and where you live
> - Welcome a visitor

> **Resources**
> Students' Book, pages 4–5
> CD 2, tracks 31–32
> Video clip 1, *Clic! 2 Star*

> **Key language**
> *Je m'appelle (Max). J'ai (15) ans.*
> *Je suis (français). J'habite à (Paris).*
> *Bon voyage! Au revoir! Salut! Bonjour!*
> *Ça va? Ça va bien. Et toi?*
> *Tu as fait bon voyage? Oui, merci.*
> *On y va? OK!*

> **Framework reference**
> 1.4, 3.1, 3.2

> **Starters**
> - Look at the map and visuals on the spread. Ask if any students have visited France and share experiences. Has anyone travelled by Eurostar? What was it like? Has anyone visited Paris? Show pictures of Paris, if you have any, or from the internet.

> - Look at the photos of Max and Joe and explain that they are characters who will appear throughout the Students' Book on video clips. Brainstorm anything students could say about themselves if they met somebody new, using language they know (they can invent details): *J'aime le sport. J'ai deux frères. Mon anniversaire, c'est le deux mai. J'habite dans une grande ville.*

> **Plenaries**
> - Allow students to watch the video clip again, so they can make up their own quiz, in English, with a partner. Questions can be based on the dialogues or the visual content: Which station do we see at the beginning? What time is shown on the big station clock?
> - Ask students to work with a partner to build up a short dialogue, imagining one of them is a French person arriving to visit their English penfriend. If necessary, display jumbled phrases on the board: *Tu as fait bon voyage? Ça va?*

> **Assessment opportunities**
> - Writing and Speaking: Students' Book page 5, exercise 6

## Preparation

- This spread introduces students to two of the recurring characters who appear in the video clips. Joe is an English boy visiting Paris to stay with his penfriend, Max. Nina, one of Max's friends, will be introduced later on.

 **1 Lis et explique.**

- Students look at the pictures and captions and explain what they understand, in English. The phrases are all ones they met in Book 1.
- When going over the answers with the class, discuss different ways of travelling from Britain to France.

*Answers*: a Joe is an English boy. He is 15 and lives in London. b Max is a French boy. He is 16 and lives in Paris. c He is going to Paris to stay with Max. d Eurostar

 **2 Présente-toi.**

- Students adapt Max's message to write about themselves. They state their name, age, nationality and where they live. Do some oral practice around the class, if necessary, to revise these phrases.
- Remind girls they will need to make their nationality adjective agree. Go over any nationalities that your class will need.

AT1 1.2–3 **3 Regarde le clip. Choisis a ou b.**

- Before playing the video clip, ask students to try predicting the answers to the five multichoice questions.
- Students watch the clip and check how many of their predictions were correct.

*Answers*: 1 b; 2 b; 3 b; 4 b; 5 a

**Video clip 1** page 4, activité 3 et page 5, activitié 5

 **CD 2, track 31**

Joe: *Hi. I'm Joe. I've got my ticket and my passport. I'm off to Paris on the Eurostar. I'm going to visit my French pen pal, Max. Je m'appelle Joe. J'ai mon billet et mon passeport. Je vais à Paris. Je vais prendre l'Eurostar pour visiter mon correspondant français, Max.*

Eurostar person: Bonjour. Votre ticket, s'il vous plaît. Merci.
Joe : Merci. Au revoir.
Eurostar person: Bon voyage.
Joe : Salut!

Joe : Max?
Max : Joe?
Joe : Oui.
Max : Oui. Ça va?
Joe : Oui, ça va bien, et toi?
Max : Bien. Tu as fait bon voyage?
Joe : Oui, oui. Bon voyage.
Max : Très bien ! Bienvenue alors.
Joe : Merci.
Max : Allez. On y va!
Joe : OK!
Max: C'est Paris!
Joe : Et en plus, il pleut, comme en Angleterre!

 **4 Relie.**

- Students match the French speech bubbles to the English phrases.

*Answers*: 1 c; 2 a; 3 d; 4 b; 5 e

 **5 Regarde encore le clip. C'est dans quel ordre?**

- Students watch the clip again and note the order they hear the five speech bubbles spoken.

*Answers*: a, c, e, b, d

 **6 À deux.**

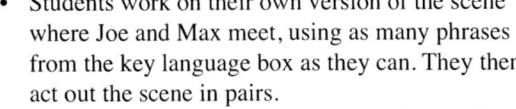

- Students work on their own version of the scene where Joe and Max meet, using as many phrases from the key language box as they can. They then act out the scene in pairs.
- Choose the best scene and ask the pair to perform it for the rest of the class.

## Top Tips!

- Recap on intonation when asking a question. Give students some statements to turn into questions simply by making their voice go up at the end.

**AT 1.2** **7 Paris, tu connais? Écoute. (1–6)**

- This activity familiarises students with a few places in Paris. They look at the map of Paris and point to each sight as they hear it mentioned.
- Point out that red numbers on the map are for *arrondissements* (districts). Revise numbers, if appropriate, by giving a number and students name a sight in that district.
- Bring in pictures of any places in Paris to discuss and share any experiences you have or anyone in the class has of Paris.
- For homework, ask students to do some research on one sight in Paris. Pool ideas next lesson.

*Answers*: 1 la Tour Eiffel; 2 l'Arc de Triomphe; c la Gare du Nord; 4 le Sacré-Cœur; 5 Notre-Dame; 6 le Centre Pompidou

**CD 2, track 32**       page 5, activité 7

1 – Oh ... c'est la Tour Eiffel!
  – Ah oui, la Tour Eiffel.
2 – Regarde, c'est l'Arc de Triomphe.
  – L'Arc de Triomphe, OK!
3 – Ici, c'est la Gare du Nord?
  – Oui, c'est la Gare du Nord.
4 – Le Sacré-Cœur ... tu vois?
  – Le Sacré-Cœur! Super!
5 – Ah ... Notre-Dame!
  – Oui, c'est la cathédrale de Notre-Dame.
6 – Et ça, c'est le Centre Pompidou.
  – Oui, c'est le Centre Pompidou.

# 1.2   Mon quartier

## *Planner*

➤ **Objectives**
- Say what there is in a town
- Say what there isn't in a town

➤ **Resources**
Students' Book, pages 6–7
CD 2, tracks 33–34
Video clip 2, *Clic! 2 Star*
OxBox, *Clic! 2 Star, Unité 1, Dans mon quartier, il y a; La Rue Monorgeuil*
Copymaster 10, *Clic! 2 Star*

➤ **Key language**
*Il y a un supermarché, une boulangerie, une poste, un bar-tabac, une gare, un magasin de sport.*
*Il n'y a pas de …*

➤ **Grammar**
*il y a, il n'y a pas de*

➤ **Framework reference**
1.2, 1.3, 1.5, 4.6, 5.2

➤ **Starters**
- Talk about the six photos on page 6. How many clues can students spot which tell them this is France? Ask them to predict which places will feature in the video clip (they can check their predictions after viewing the clip).
- Working in pairs, students memorise the six places photographed. Partner A begins by closing the book and trying to name them in order, including the correct gender: *La photo numéro un, il y a un supermarché. Numéro deux, il y a une boulangerie.* Partner B checks carefully against the Students' Book and awards a point for each place in the correct order with the correct gender. The pair swap roles to see who wins the most points.

➤ **Plenaries**
- In pairs or small groups, students play a memory game to practise places in town.
  Student A: *Dans ma rue, il y a une poste.*
  Student B: *Dans ma rue, il y a une poste et une boulangerie.*
  Student C: *Dans ma rue, il y a une poste, une boulangerie et …*
  Once students have practised *il y a un/une* sufficiently, ask them to swap to *il n'y a pas de.*
  Student A: *Dans ma rue, il n'y a pas de poste.*
  Student B: *Dans ma rue, il n'y a pas de poste et il n'y a pas de boulangerie.*
- Students take part in a paired challenge on gender and places in town. Ask them to draw two columns headed *un* and *une*. With the Students' Book closed, they take turns to write places in town into the correct gender column, each adding one place at a time. Students continue for a set time or until neither partner can add anything further. They then open the Students' Book, check their work and award points for correct spellings and placement in the correct columns. The partner with the most points is the winner.

➤ **Assessment opportunities**
Listening: Students' Book page 6, exercise 2
Speaking: Students' Book page 7, exercise 7

---

AT 1.1
AT 2.1

**1 Écoute, lis et répète.**
- Students listen to and repeat the places in a town, taking care with accurate pronunciation.
- Look at the photos and discuss them as a class, if you have not already done so in the Starter.
- Recap on the meaning of *il y a* with students (first met in Book 1) and also point out the negative *il n'y a pas de.*

**CD 2, track 33**          page 6, activité 1

1  Il y a un supermarché.
2  Il y a une boulangerie.
3  Il y a une poste.
4  Il y a un bar-tabac.
5  Il y a une gare.
6  Il y a un magasin de sport.

AT 1.2.3

**2 Regarde le clip. Il y a quoi?**
- Play the video clip. Max is showing Joe around his local area of Paris. Students note which of the places from the photos are mentioned in the video. (Note that students only need to watch part of this video clip. See transcript below for required section.)
- Watch the video again and see if students can spot any additional places that are pictured or mentioned.

*Answers*: 2, 3, 5, 4

**Video clip 2**   page 6, activité 2

 **CD 2, track 34**

Max: Voilà, Joe. C'est mon quartier. Là, c'est le marchand de fruits et légumes. Et là-bas, c'est la boulangerie. Elle est géniale! Les croissants y sont super bons! Ici, il y a beaucoup de magasins. Juste là, il y a une pharmacie ... et derrière, un petit supermarché. Là-bas, à gauche, il y a une pizzeria.

Joe: Et est-ce qu'il y a une poste ici?
Max: Non, il n'y a pas de poste ici ... Regarde, là, c'est le fromager, c'est super bon.
Joe: Et le bus?
Max: L'arrêt de bus? Il est juste ici.
Joe: Et est-ce qu'il y a un métro par ici?
Max: Oui, bien sûr, juste en face.

Max: Bonjour, Madame Jantier.
Mme: Ah, bonjour, Max. Tu vas bien?
Max: Très bien. Et vous? Comment allez-vous?
Mme: Ça va bien, oui.
Max: Je vous présente Joe, mon correspondant anglais.
Mme: Bonjour, Joe.
Joe: Bonjour, madame.
Mme: Euh ... bienvenue à Paris.
Joe: Merci beaucoup.
All: Au revoir.

Max: Donc, le bar-tabac. Tu vas acheter les tickets de bus. Tu sais comment faire? Alors, tu commences: Bonjour, monsieur/madame.
Joe: Bonjour, monsieur/madame. Je veux des...
Max: Non, non, non. Je voudrais.
Joe: Ah oui. Je voudrais des tickets de bus. C'est combien, s'il te plaît?
Max: Non. S'il vous plaît. C'est une personne adulte, tu ne la connais pas. S'il vous plaît.
Joe: Ah oui. Je voudrais des tickets de bus, s'il vous plaît.
Max: Bon. Très bien. On y va.
Joe: OK.

**Follow-up**

- Play the clip again and ask students to look out for any additional shops or places from the photos that don't appear
- Discuss similarities and differences between British and French streets.

 **3 À deux.**

- Students take turns to throw a die, match the number to one of the six photos and say whether the place is or isn't in their neighbourhood.
- Ask students to use the key language box as support and point out that after the negative *il n'y a pas* they should use *de* instead of *un/une*.

**AT 4.1** **4 Fais ton petit dico.**

- Students make a picture dictionary to help them remember the names of places in a town. They write the words in alphabetical order and draw pictures or symbols to go with each.
- Students also use a dictionary to look up three new places to add to their list. Look up a few words together as a class to demonstrate how to find new words.

**C10** • Copymaster 10 provides further practice of using a dictionary.

*Answers*: 1
Places in town: 1 église; 2 musée; 3 patinoire; 4 boutique
Drinks: 1 limonade; 2 lait; 3 vin; 4 eau
Countries: 1 Inde; 2 Australie; 3 Nouvelle-Zélande; 4 Canada
Vegetables: 1 haricot; 2 chou-fleur; 3 oignon; 4 carotte
Fruits: 1 pêche; 2 raisin; 3 cerise; 4 mûre
Sports: 1 natation; 2 patinage; 3 escalade; 4 voile
Clothing: 1 écharpe; 2 ceinture; 3 haut; 4 botte

*Answers*: 2

| noun or verb? | French word |
| --- | --- |
| verb | j'arrose (arroser) |
| noun | l'eau |
| verb | regarder |
| noun | une montre |

 **5 Lis la bulle. Réponds "oui" ou "non" aux questions.**

- Students read the speech bubble where Alicia describes what there is and isn't in her area. Students answer *oui* or *non* depending on whether there is the place pictured or not.

*Answers*: a oui; b oui; c non; d oui; e non; f oui

 **6 Écris.**

- Students write about three places which their area has and three which it doesn't.

 **7 À deux.**

 • Students work in pairs. One student questions the other one to find out which places he/she listed in exercise 6. Students should only answer using *oui* or *non*. Who finds out in the fewest questions?

**Follow-up**

- As extension, students could work in pairs to prepare a PowerPoint presentation about the area around the school: *Dans le quartier de l'école, il y a ... Dans le quartier de l'école, il n'y a pas de ...*
- Show students the video clip from exercise 2 again and ask them to see how much they can now understand.
- Further activities on places in a town can be found on OxBox, *Dans mon quartier, il y a* (matching activity) and *La Rue Monorgeuil* (sequencing activity). These two activities contain a couple of new places not met on this spread.

# 1.3 Les transports

## *Planner*

> **Objectives**
> • Name different transports
> • Say how you travel

> **Resources**
> Students' Book, pages 8–9
> CD 2, tracks 35–37
> OxBox, *Clic! 2 Star, Unité 1, On va au collège; Tu y vas comment?*
> Copymaster 6, *Clic! 2 Star*

> **Key language**
> *Je visite Paris (en bus).*
> *en métro, en bateau, en taxi, à vélo, à pied*
> *Je vais au collège (en voiture).*

> **Grammar**
> *en, à* + transport

> **Framework reference**
> 4.2, 5.2, 5.6

> **Starters**
> • Before opening the Students' Book, ask students to suggest, in English, six different ways to travel around Paris, such as by bus, metro, on foot, etc. They can then open their books on page 8 and check against the photos. How many means of transport did they guess correctly?

> • To begin a lesson, once the means of transport have been introduced, display the six transport phrases on the board with the vowels missing: *_n b_t_ _ _.* Students race against the clock to fill in the missing letters. To increase the challenge, omit the dotted lines that indicate the number of missing letters: *en bateau* would be *n bt; à pied* would be *pd.*

> **Plenaries**
> • Students play a dice game in pairs to practise talking about means of travel. Numbers 1–6 on the die correspond to photos a–f on page 8: 1 = *en bus*, 2 = *en métro*, etc. Students take turns to throw the die and say a sentence containing the appropriate means of transport.
> Student A: *cinq – Je vais au collège à vélo. / Je visite Paris à vélo.*

> • Students do a word chain around the class or in groups, building sentences on the theme of transport. Each student adds a couple of words to what the previous person has said. Whoever finishes a sentence must start off a new one.
> Student A: *Je vais ...*
> Student B: *au collège en ...*
> Student C: *bus. Je visite ...*
> Student D: *Paris en ...*
> Student E: *métro. Je vais ...*

> **Assessment opportunities**
> • Speaking: Students' Book page 9, exercise 6

---

 **1 Écoute, lis et répète.**
• Students listen to and repeat the different forms of  transport.
• Discuss the photos which show transport around Paris, if you have not already done so in the Starter. How does the transport differ to what students have where they live?

 **CD 2, track 35**   page 8, activité 1

Je visite Paris ...
en bus
en métro
en bateau
en taxi
à vélo
à pied

**AT 2.2** **2 À deux: jeu de mémoire.**
• Students play a memory game. They start with a sentence including a form of transport and take turns to add a different transport each time. How many can they remember in the correct order?

**AT 1.2** **3 Écoute (1–6). Note les transports.**
• Students listen to how people get around Paris and note for each speaker which transport method they mention.

*Answers*: 1 b; 2 a; 3 c; 4 e; 5 d; 6 f

**CD 2, track 36**　　　　　page 8, activité 3

1 – On peut visiter Paris comment?
　 – On peut visiter Paris en métro! C'est super!
2 – On peut visiter Paris comment?
　 – En bus! Visiter Paris en bus, c'est sympa.
3 – On peut visiter Paris comment?
　 – On peut visiter le centre de Paris en bateau,
　　 c'est génial! C'est le batobus.
4 – On peut visiter Paris comment?
　 – On peut visiter Paris à vélo! Les vélos à
　　 Paris, ça s'appelle les vélib'!
5 – On peut visiter Paris comment?
　 – On peut visiter Paris en taxi.
6 – On peut visiter Paris comment?
　 – On peut visiter Paris à pied! Marcher à pied,
　　 c'est écolo!

**AT 4.2** **4 Écris une phrase pour chaque touriste.**

- Students write a sentence for each picture to describe how the tourists get around Paris.
- Ask students to check each other's sentences for accuracy of spelling.
- These pictures could be used for some additional speaking practice. One partner says a sentence out loud and another student says which picture it refers to.

*Answers:* Je visite Paris ... a à pied et en métro; b à pied et en taxi; c en bus et en bateau; d en métro et en bus; e à vélo et en bateau; f en taxi et à vélo

**AT 3.2** **5 Lis les bulles et complète les phrases.**

- Students read the five speech bubbles about how people get to school and answer the questions in English. Remind students that *au collège* means 'to school' and point out the new form of transport mentioned, *en voiture* (by car).
- Ask students to read the speech bubbles out loud in pairs and to correct each other on pronunciation.

*Answers:* a Samira; b Babacar; c Léa; d metro; e bike

**AT 2.2** **6 Sondage: tu vas comment au collège? Écolo ou pas?**

- Students carry out a class survey to find out how everyone travels to school. How environmentally friendly is the class?
- Discuss how best to show the results of the survey, for example in a graph, diagram, pie chart, etc.

**AT 1.3** **7 Écoute la chanson.**

- Students listen to the song and note any means of transport mentioned in it.
- You may wish to show students the words for the song and ask them to sing along, if appropriate.

 **CD 2, track 37**　　　　　page 9, activité 7

**Ça roule en roller!**

*Refrain 1:*
Ce matin, c'est l'enfer:
Pas de bus, pas de train,
Pas de tram, pas d'métro.
Aïe aïe aïe, comment faire
Pour aller au boulot?

En voiture? Pas question.
Ça pollue la nature.
À vélo? Pas question.
Il n'fait pas assez beau!

*Refrain 1*

Et à pied? Non, non, non!
Ça, ça use les souliers!
En roller? Mais bien sûr!
Le roller, c'est super! Écolo, rigolo
Et presto au boulot!

*Refrain 2:*
Ce matin, c'est super:
Pas de bus, pas de train,
Pas de tram, pas d'métro.
Pour aller au boulot
Le roller, c'est le bonheur!

**Follow-up**

- Further activities on transport are provided on OxBox, *On va au collège* (matching activity) and *Tu y vas comment?* (sequencing activity).

 **C6**
- Further speaking practice on transport is provided on Copymaster 6.

## 1.4 Vocabulaire

### *Planner*

> **Resources**
Students' Book, page 10

> **Objectives**
- *Vocabulaire:* to provide a theme-based summary

of the key language of the unit, which students can use as a reference or as an aid to learning
- To practise pronunciation

> **Framework reference**
4.1, 5.5

### Using the vocabulary page

- Encourage students to use the *Vocabulaire* page as a reference point throughout the unit. It can also serve as a useful revision tool before students do the *Clic-test!*
- Vocabulary is listed spread-by-spread and you could either ask students to learn each section for homework after each spread is completed, or set the whole page as a homework task before starting work on the test. Most students learn shorter sections best, so often it is better to give them manageable chunks to learn at a time.
- Encourage students to use different techniques to help them learn the vocabulary:
  - Cover up the English and see what they can remember; write down any words they can't remember and test themselves again on those words.
  - Cover up the French and see if they can remember the words or phrases this way round.
  - Make word cards with English on one side and French on the other. Students can then test

themselves to see what they can remember. Put any cards they can't remember on one side and go over those again at the end.
  - Work in pairs to test each other, either using the vocabulary list or the word cards.
- Record themselves saying the words both in English and French. Saying words and phrases out loud can often help with memorising them.

### Sound French!

- *Aim:* To practise pronunciation
- The point practised here is the difference in pronunciation between *un* and *une*. Demonstrate how each one is pronounced: *un* sounds more like *euh-n* and students could practise the sound by pinching their nose and making the sound at the back of their throat. To pronouce *une*, students should put their tongue behind their bottom teeth, push their lips forward to make a tiny circle and let out the *oo* sound.
- Practise with the words listed, before giving students a couple of minutes in pairs to practise with other familiar words.

## 1.4 Clic-test!

### *Planner*

The page is divided into four sections: listening, speaking, reading and writing.

> **Objectives**
- To enable students to recap on the language and structures of the unit

- To provide an opportunity for quick testing of all four skills

> **Resources**
Students' Book, page 11
CD 2, track 38

> **Framework reference**
5.8

 **1 Écoute! (1–6)**
- Students listen and match the six speakers with the correct form of transport.

*Answers:* 1 e; 2 f; 3 b; 4 a; 5 d; 6 c

 **CD 2, track 38**      page 11, activité 1

**1** – Comment est-ce que tu visites Paris?
  – Je visite Paris en métro.

2 – Comment est-ce que tu visites Paris?
– Moi, je visite Paris en bus.

3 – Comment est-ce que tu visites Paris?
– Moi, je visite Paris à vélo.

4 – Comment est-ce que tu visites Paris?
– Normalement, je visite Paris à pied.

5 – Comment est-ce que tu visites Paris?
– Je visite Paris en taxi.

6 – Comment est-ce que tu visites Paris?
– Je visite Paris en bateau.
– En bateau?!
– Oui, en bateau-mouche sur la Seine!

 **2 Lis!**

- Students read the six sentences and say whether they refer to picture A or picture B.

*Answers*: 1 A; 2 A; 3 B; 4 A; 5 B; 6 A

AT 2.2–3 **3 Parle!**

- Students carry out a guided conversation in pairs, converting the English parts into French with their own details.

AT 4.2 **4 Écris!**

- Students copy out the sentence beginnings and write their own endings.

# À moi

page 76

## *Planner*

> **Objectives**
- To provide reinforcement activities for quiet work
- To provide alternative class and homework material for students who finish other activities quickly

> **Resources**
Students' Book, page 76

> **Framework reference**
2.1, 2.2, 2.4

### Mr Bean en France

 **1 Find a caption for each photo. Be careful! You only need four of the six captions.**

- This page reinforces the different types of transport. Students match the four photos of Mr Bean in France to the correct captions.

*Answers*: 1 d; 2 a; 3 c; 4 e

AT 3.2 **2 Copy out the two left-over captions. Draw a picture to illustrate each one.**

- Encourage students to use the glossary if they need to look up any of the words for this task.

AT 4.2 **3 Imagine that Mr Bean uses the following means of transport. Write a caption for each picture.**

- Students use the vocabulary support to write new captions, using the different means of transport.

# Clic-vidéo

## *Planner*

> **Objectives**
  - To provide extended listening practice recycling the language of the whole unit

> **Resources**
Students' Book, page 85
Video clip 2, *Clic! 2 Star*
CD 2, track 39

> **Framework reference**
1.2, 1.3

---

 **1 Which of the following places are in Max's area? Watch the video clip to find out.**

- Students watch the video clip and note the letters of the places listed they see.

*Answers*: a, c, e, b

 **Video clip 2**     page 85, activités 1, 2 et 3

 **CD 2, track 39**

Max:   Voilà, Joe. C'est mon quartier. Là, c'est le marchand de fruits et légumes. Et là-bas, c'est la boulangerie. Elle est géniale! Les croissants y sont super bons! Ici, il y a beaucoup de magasins. Juste là, il y a une pharmacie ... et derrière, un petit supermarché. Là-bas, à gauche, il y a une pizzeria.
Joe:    Et est-ce qu'il y a une poste ici?
Max:   Non, il n'y a pas de poste ici ... Regarde, là, c'est le fromager, c'est super bon.
Joe:    Et le bus?
Max:   L'arrêt de bus? Il est juste ici.
Joe:    Et est-ce qu'il y a un métro par ici?
Max:   Oui, bien sûr, juste en face.

Max:   Bonjour, Madame Jantier.
Mme:  Ah, bonjour, Max. Tu vas bien?
Max:   Très bien. Et vous? Comment allez-vous?
Mme:  Ça va bien, oui.
Max:   Je vous présente Joe, mon correspondant anglais.
Mme:  Bonjour, Joe.
Joe:    Bonjour, madame.
Mme:  Euh ... bienvenue à Paris.
Joe:    Merci beaucoup.
All:     Au revoir.

Max:   Donc, le bar-tabac. Tu vas acheter les tickets de bus. Tu sais comment faire? Alors, tu commences: Bonjour, monsieur/ madame.
Joe:    Bonjour, monsieur/madame. Je veux des...
Max:   Non, non, non. Je voudrais.
Joe:    Ah oui. Je voudrais des tickets de bus. C'est combien, s'il te plaît?

Max:   Non. S'il vous plaît. C'est une personne adulte, tu ne la connais pas. S'il vous plaît.
Joe:    Ah oui. Je voudrais des tickets de bus, s'il vous plaît.
Max:   Bon. Très bien. On y va.
Joe:    OK.

Joe:    Bonjour, monsieur.
Man:   Bonjour.
Joe:    Je voudrais des tickets de bus, s'il vous plaît. C'est combien?
Man:   C'est dix euros dix le paquet.
Joe:    Tenez.
Man:   Merci.
Joe:    Merci. Au revoir.

Max:   Eh, Nina!
Max/Nina: Ça va?
Nina:   Ça va, et toi?
Max:   Je te présente Joe, mon correspondant anglais.
Joe/Nina: Salut!
Max:   On va se balader?
Nina:   Ben oui. Pourquoi pas?

**Point langue**
Ici, il y a beaucoup de magasins.
Juste là, il y a une pharmacie.
Et derrière, un petit supermarché.
Là-bas, à gauche, il y a une pizzeria.
Non, il n'y a pas de poste ici.

 **2 How observant are you? Watch again and find:**

- Students watch the clip again and answer the more detailed questions.

*Answers*: a le Palais du fruit; b green; c pharmacie; d la Perla (pizza et pasta); e Paul

 **3 Listen carefully. Choose a or b.**

- Students watch the clip again and choose a or b in answer to each question.

*Answers*: 1 b; 2 b; 3 b; 4 a

# 2

# Le weekend dernier

| Unité 2: Le weekend dernier  Overview grid | | | | | | |
|---|---|---|---|---|---|---|
| **Page reference** | **Contexts and objectives** | **Grammar** | **Language strategies and pronunciation** | **Key language** | **Framework** | **AT level** |
| 12–13 **2.1 Qu'est-ce que tu as fait?** | • Say what you did earlier today | • Perfect tense with *avoir* + *-er* verbs (*je, tu*) | Saying different things using the same verbs | *J'ai trouvé des souvenirs. J'ai regardé un film. J'ai visité un musée. J'ai acheté un T-shirt. J'ai joué sur l'ordinateur. J'ai mangé un hamburger. Tu as* + same verbs | 4.4, 4.5, 5.3, 5.6 | 1.2–4 2.2 3.2–3 4.2–3 |
| 14–15 **2.2 J'ai joué au foot!** | • Say what you did last weekend | • Negative in perfect tense • More perfect tense verbs: irregulars | Using connectives *et, mais, après* | *J'ai écouté mon iPod. J'ai aidé à la maison. J'ai vu mes copains. J'ai lu mon magazine. J'ai fait mes devoirs. J'ai joué au foot. Je n'ai pas … et, mais, après* | 1.5, 2.5, 4.6, 5.1 | 1.2–3 2.2–3 3.2–3 4.2–4 |
| 16–17 **2.3 C'est mon idole!** | • Say who you are a fan of • Say what he or she has done | • Using *il, elle* + perfect tense | Giving yourself time to think in speaking activities with *alors, euh* | *Il a fait des films. Elle a fait des CD. Il a joué dans des films. Elle a joué dans l'équipe de France. Il a gagné des matchs. Elle a gagné un prix.* | 1.4, 2.4, 4.3, 5.2 | 1.3 2.3–4 3.3–4 4.3–4 |
| 18 **2.4 Vocabulaire** | • Practise pronunciation | | Pronouncing present and past: *je trouve, j'ai trouvé* | | 4.1, 5.5 | |
| 19 **2.4 Clic-test!** | • Recap on the language structures of the unit • Provide an opportunity for quick testing of all four skills | | | | 5.8 | 1.2 2.2–3 3.2–3 4.2–3 |
| 77 **À moi** | • Provide reinforcement activities for self-access work | | | | 2.2, 2.3, 2.5 | 3.2–3 4.2–3 |
| 86 **Clic-vidéo** | • Provide extended listening practice recycling the language of the whole unit using the video | | | | 1.2, 1.3 | 1.2–4 3.2 |

## MEDIUM TERM GRID Week-by-week overview (assuming six weeks' work or approximately 10–12.5 hours)

**About Unit 2, _Le weekend dernier_**

In this unit, students learn how to say what they have and someone else has done in the past, and learn more about Paris. Students learn to use the perfect tense with _avoir_ in the
_je, tu, il_ and _elle_ forms, using both regular and irregular verbs and using sentences in the negative. They learn how to adapt sentences by using the same verbs to say different things. They also learn how to use connectives _et, mais_ and _après_ and how to give themselves time to think in speaking by using _alors, euh_, etc.

New vocabulary includes activities in the past with a variety of verbs, activities done earlier today and last weekend and what someone famous has done.

Reading, listening and comprehension skills are developed through a variety of text, audio and video materials.

| Week | Resources | Objectives |
|---|---|---|
| 1 | 2.1 Qu'est-ce que tu as fait? | Using the perfect tense of regular -er verbs to say what you did earlier today<br>Using _Tu as …?_ to ask questions in the perfect tense (_trouver, regarder, visiter, acheter, jouer, manger_)<br>Saying sentences using the same verbs but changing the endings |
| 2 | 2.2 J'ai joué au foot! | Saying what you did last weekend using -er verbs, including irregulars (_écouter, aider, voir, lire, faire, jouer_)<br>Using the negative of the perfect tense to say what you did not do<br>Using connectives _et, mais_ and _après_ to make longer sentences |
| 3 | 2.3 C'est mon idole! | Saying who your idol is<br>Using the perfect tense _il/elle_ form to say what your idol has done in the past<br>Gaining time to think while speaking by using _alors, euh_, etc. |
| 4 | Sound French! (p18)<br>À moi (p77)<br>Clic-vidéo (p86) | Practising pronunciation (difference between past and present verbs: _je trouve_ and _j'ai trouvé_)<br>Additional reading and writing practice<br>Using the video for reinforcement, extension and follow-up work |
| 5 | 2.4 Vocabulaire<br>Clic-test! | Learning vocabulary<br>Recapping on vocabulary of unit<br>Preparing and carrying out of assessment in all four skills<br>Reviewing progress |
| 6 | Copymasters (_Feuilles_)<br>OxBox | Reinforcement and extension of the language of the unit using extra resources<br>Reviewing progress via the Checklist on page 18, _Vocabulaire_<br>Going back over aspects of the unit which need reviewing after _Clic-test!_ |

## 2.1  Qu'est-ce que tu as fait?

### *Planner*

➤ **Objectives**
- Say what you did earlier today

➤ **Resources**
Students' Book, pages 12–13
CD 2, tracks 40–42
Video clip 3, *Clic! 2 Star*

➤ **Key language**
*J'ai trouvé des souvenirs. J'ai regardé un film. J'ai visité un musée. J'ai acheté un T-shirt. J'ai joué sur l'ordinateur. J'ai mangé un hamburger.*
*Tu as* + same verbs

➤ **Grammar**
Perfect tense with *avoir* and *-er* verbs (*je, tu*)

➤ **Framework reference**
- 4.4, 4.5, 5.3, 5.6

➤ **Starters**
- Draw attention to the spread objective: Say what you did earlier today. Display the six pictures from page 12 and write their English equivalents on the board. Challenge students to match them up. Can they spot the pattern in the French sentences ( *j'ai* + final *é* )?

- In pairs, students try to make as many sentences as they can using the six perfect tense verbs from page 12: *J'ai visité … le musée, ma grand-mère, mon copain/ma copine, Paris. J'ai acheté … un T-shirt, un CD, un sandwich, un vélo.* Pairs provide feedback to the class to see which pair has the most correct sentences.

➤ **Plenaries**
- Display a grid of nine squares, numbered 1–9, with a word in each square relating to the six perfect tense phrases met on this spread: *un film, une pizza, un jean,* etc. Divide the class into two teams for a game of Noughts and Crosses. Teams take turns to choose a square and build a sentence in the perfect tense using the word or phrase in the square: *J'ai mangé une pizza.*
- In pairs, students note down what they have learned about the perfect tense. Elicit feedback and build up a mind map to summarise students' knowledge so far – keep a copy of this, so you can add to it as you work through Unit 2.

➤ **Assessment opportunities**
- Reading: Students' Book page 13, exercise 6
- Writing: Students' Book page 13, exercise 7

---

AT 1.2
AT 2.2

**1 Écoute, lis et répète.**
- Students listen, while following the perfect tense captions in their books, and repeat each one.
- If you have not already done so in the Starter, write up the six phrases and ask students what pattern they notice. Explain that all the sentences refer to actions which happened in the past.

 **CD 2, track 40**      page 12, activité 1

a  J'ai trouvé des souvenirs.
b  J'ai regardé un film.
c  J'ai visité un musée.
d  J'ai acheté un T-shirt.
e  J'ai joué sur l'ordinateur.
f  J'ai mangé un hamburger.

AT 1.2  **2 Écoute. Note l'ordre des activités a-f.**
- Students listen to the same six phrases and note the order in which they hear them,

*Answers*: 1 c; 2 f; 3 a; 4 d; 5 b; 6 e

 **CD 2, track 41**      page 12, activité 2

Ce matin, j'ai visité un musée. Super!
Ce midi, j'ai mangé un hamburger.
Après, j'ai trouvé des souvenirs.
Cet après-midi, j'ai acheté un T-shirt.
Après, j'ai regardé un film. Génial!
Ce soir, j'ai joué sur l'ordinateur. Et voilà.

AT 3.2  **3 Compléte.**
- Students complete the English sentences with words from the box to translate the French sentences from exercise 1.
- To provide further oral practice, call out the English sentences in a random order and ask students to say the equivalent French sentences.

*Answers*: a I found souvenirs. b I watched a film. c I visited a museum. d I bought a T-shirt. e I played on the computer. f I ate a hamburger.

AT 1.3–4  **4 Regarde et note.**
- Students watch a section at the end of the video clip (before the *Point langue*) and note which of

**121**

the French verbs they hear Joe use.
- Play the clip again and see if students can understand any further details. Discuss the places in Paris that Joe visited.

*Answers:* 3, 4

 **Video clip 3**   page 12, activité 4

 **CD 2, track 42**

Nina: Salut, Max!
Joe: Max!
Max: Eh, salut! Vous allez bien?
Joe: Oui, ça va.
Nina: Ça va, et toi?
Max: Oui, très bien. Tu as fait quoi aujourd'hui alors?
Joe: J'ai visité le Musée Grévin. J'ai vu des célébrités.
Nina: Oui. Moi, j'ai beaucoup aimé Céline Dion. Elle est très belle. Elle a les cheveux longs. Elle a les cheveux blonds et elle est très mince.
Joe: Oui. Et moi, j'ai vu Fabien Barthez.
Max: Cool! Et tu as acheté des souvenirs?
Joe: Oui, j'ai acheté un cahier.
Max: Eh! Alors tu as passé une bonne journée?
Joe: Oui, c'était super!
Max: À ton séjour à Paris!

## Grammaire

- Look at the grammar box with students. It explains how to say what they did in the past. For regular *-er* verbs, show how to use *j'ai* + past participle which ends in *é*. Also point out that the

*tu* form is *tu as*. Students will need to use this to ask questions.
- Look at the key language box together and ask students to work in pairs and practise saying as many past tense sentences as they can in one minute.

 AT 2.2 **5 À deux.**

- Students work in pairs. One partner chooses three activities from the key language box. The other student asks questions to work out which ones they are. How many questions does it take to find all three activities?

AT 3.3 **6 Lis. Note l'ordre.**

- Students read an account in the past tense. They note the pictures in the order Anya mentions them.
- For more support, read the passage out loud with the class first and encourage students to practise reading it with a partner, taking care with the pronunciation of *é*.

*Answers:* a, d, e, b, c

## Top Tips!

- Point out to students that they can use the same verbs to say many different things. Look at each of the six verbs from this spread in turn and gather together other possible endings for each one.

AT 4.2–3 **7 Écris.**

- Students write four true and four false sentences about what they did yesterday, using some of the expressions listed or ones you gathered together earlier. Their partner has to work out which sentences are true and which are false.

# 2.2 J'ai joué au foot!                   pages 14–15

---

## *Planner*

> **Objectives**
- Say what you did last weekend

> **Resources**
Students' Book, pages 14–15
CD 2, track 43
Copymaster 17, 19, 20, *Clic! 2 Star*

> **Key language**
*J'ai écouté mon iPod. J'ai aidé à la maison. J'ai vu mes copains. J'ai lu mon magazine. J'ai fait mes devoirs. J'ai joué au foot. Je n'ai pas …*
*et, mais, après*

> **Grammar**
Negative in perfect tense
More perfect tense verbs: irregulars

> **Framework reference**
1.5, 2.5, 4.6, 5.1

> **Starters**
- Play a memory game as a class, using the perfect tense phrases.
  Student A: *Le weekend dernier, j'ai regardé un film.*
  Student B: *Le weekend dernier, j'ai regardé un film et j'ai acheté un T-shirt.*
  Student A: *Le weekend dernier, j'ai regardé un film, j'ai acheté un T-shirt et …*
- Display ten perfect tense sentences split in half on the board. Students have one minute to match as many as they can:
  *J'ai écouté / J'ai fait / J'ai vu / J'ai acheté / J'ai lu / J'ai aidé / J'ai joué / J'ai mangé / J'ai visité / J'ai trouvé*
  *mon iPod / mes devoirs / mes copains / un T-shirt / à la maison / au foot / une pizza / un musée / des souvenirs*

> **Plenaries**
> - Students work in pairs or groups for two to three minutes and make up further questions in the *tu* form to add to the quiz on page 14. They can either use the verbs from this spread with different nouns or use verbs from the previous spread. Pool ideas to see who has the most suggestions.

- Students give a mini-presentation about what they did last weekend. Confident volunteers could present to the whole class and others could present to each other in small groups of three or four.

> **Assessment opportunities**
> - Writing: Students' Book page 15, exercise 5

## Grammaire

- Look at the grammar box with students before doing the activities. Explain that to form a negative in the past tense (i.e. to say 'I did not'), they should use *je n'ai pas* rather than *j'ai*. Ask students to look at the quiz and spot sentences which are in the negative.

 **1 Lis et relie.**

- Students read the quiz and match each one to its correct English phrase.

*Answers*: 1 F; 2 B; 3 E; 4 A; 5 D; 5 C

AT 1.2–3 **2 Écoute et note.**

- Students listen to Max and Nina to find out what they did or didn't do.

*Answers*: Max 1 ✓; 2 ✗; 3 ✗; 4 ✗; 5 ✗; 6 ✓
Nina 1 ✗; 2 ✓; 3 ✗; 4 ✓; 5 ✓; 6 ✗
Neither of them did their homework.

🎧 **CD 2, track 43**　　　　　page 14, activité 2

- – Qu'est-ce que tu as fait le weekend dernier? Tu as écouté ton iPod?
- – Oui, j'ai écouté mon iPod.
- – Tu as aidé à la maison?
- – Non, je n'ai pas aidé à la maison.
- – Tu as fait tes devoirs?
- – Non, je n'ai pas fait mes devoirs!
- – Tu as joué au foot?
- – Je n'ai pas joué au foot.
- – Tu as vu tes copains?
- – Non, je n'ai pas vu mes copains.
- – Tu as lu ton magazine?
- – Oui, j'ai lu mon magazine de sport. Super!
- – Qu'est-ce que tu as fait le weekend dernier? Tu as écouté ton iPod?
- – Non, je n'ai pas écouté mon iPod.
- – Tu as aidé à la maison?
- – Eh oui! J'ai aidé à la maison.
- – Tu as fait tes devoirs?
- – Non, je n'ai pas fait mes devoirs.
- – Tu as joué au foot?
- – Oui, j'ai joué au foot.
- – Tu as vu tes copains?
- – J'ai vu mes copains.
- – Tu as lu ton magazine?
- – Je n'ai pas lu mon magazine.

 AT 4.2 **3a Écris tés reponses.**

- Students write out their own responses to each quiz question.

 AT 2.2–3 **3b À deux.**

- Students ask each other the quiz questions and reply with full sentences.

## Grammaire

- On the previous spread, only regular -er verbs were introduced in the perfect tense. Explain that not all verbs are regular and that some verbs form the past tense in other ways, but most still use *j'ai*. Look at the irregular verbs *vu*, *fait* and *lu* and ensure students understand what they mean. Can they think of other things they could say using these verbs?

 AT 3.3 **4 Lis et complète.**

- Students read an account in the past tense and complete the gaps with the correct verbs from the box. For further practice in accurate writing, students could copy out the whole account.
- Explain the use of connectives, *et*, *mais* and *après*, which are used to join phrases together and make longer sentences.

*Answers*: 1 joué; 2 écouté; 3 lu; 4 vu; 5 joué; 6 aidé; 7 fait

AT 4.3–4 **5 Écris.**

- Students use verbs from this spread and the previous one to write six sentences about what they did last weekend. Encourage students to use the connectives *et*, *mais* and *après*.
- Model on the board how students might adapt sentences, if more support is needed.

**Follow-up**

 C17 - Further work on the perfect tense can be found on Copymaster 17, exercise 1.

*Answers*: J'ai visité Paris. Tu as mangé un hamburger. J'ai acheté un DVD. Tu as regardé la télé. J'ai écouté la radio.

 C19 - Copymaster 19 provides a Battleships-style game which practises questions as well as positive and negative statements in the perfect tense.

C20 - Copymaster 20, exercise 1, provides further reading and writing practice of the perfect tense.

*Answers*: a samedi dernier; b c'était une journée; excellente; c l'une des attractions; d j'ai mangé; e du poulet; f j'ai bu; g j'ai acheté

# 2.3 C'est mon idole!

## *Planner*

> ### Objectives
> - Say who you are a fan of
> - Say what he or she has done

> ### Resources
> Students' Book, pages 16–17
> CD 2, track 44
> OxBox *Clic! 2 Star, Unité 2, Jenifer;* Perfect tense with *avoir*

> ### Key language
> *Il a fait des films. Elle a fait des CD.*
> *Il a joué dans des films. Elle a joué dans l'équipe de France. Il a gagné des matchs. Elle a gagné un prix.*

> ### Grammar
> Using *il, elle* + perfect tense

> ### Framework reference
> 1.4, 2.4, 4.3, 5.2

> ### Starters
> - Before beginning work on the spread, ask students to find on page 16 three examples of *-er* verbs in the past tense and one irregular verb. What else is different about the past tense in these captions? They use *il/elle* a instead of *j'ai*.
> - Play a game to practise first and third person of the perfect tense. Prepare some cards with a subject pronoun, a past participle or a noun on each one. Hold up a subject pronoun card together with one of the others and challenge students to say a simple sentence using the two words you hold up: *il* + *musée* or *je* + *acheté* or *elle* + *au foot*.

> ### Plenaries
> - Divide the class into teams. Call out words or phrases from the spread and team members collaborate to put each word or phrase into a sentence.
>   Teacher: *l'équipe de France*
>   Student: *Il a joué dans l'équipe de France.*
>   Teacher: *un prix*
>   Student: *Jenifer a gagné un prix.*
>   Students work from memory without referring to the Students' Book, if possible. Teams feed back their sentences. Award points for correct sentences.
> - In pairs, students tell each other as much as they can remember about the people featured on the spread, taking turns to supply a detail each.
>   Student A: *Yoann Gourcuff est footballeur.*
>   Student B: *Il a gagné des matchs.*
>   Student A: *Il a joué dans l'équipe de France.*

> ### Assessment opportunities
> - Speaking: Students' Book page 17, exercise 3
> - Writing: Students' Book page 17, exercise 4

## Preparation

- In this spread the perfect tense with *il/elle* is introduced. Remind students what *il/elle* mean and explain that instead of using *j'ai*, if you are talking about what 'he' or 'she' did in the past, use *il a* or *elle a* instead.

AT 1.3 **1 Écoute et lis. Réponds.**

AT 3.3

- Students listen to the interviews while following the text in their books. They identify the four people and then find the French equivalents to some English phrases.
- Encourage students to read the interviews out loud in pairs to practise correct pronunciation.

*Answers:* a Nicolas; b Yoann Gourcuff; c Jenifer; d Gaspard Ulliel; e Elle a gagné un jeu télévisé. f Il a joué dans l'équipe de France. g Elle a joué dans le film. h Il a gagné un prix.

 **CD 2, track 44**  page 16, activité 1

- C'est qui, ton idole?
- Alors, mon idole, c'est Jenifer. C'est une chanteuse.
- Qu'est-ce qu'elle a fait?
- Euh … Elle a gagné un jeu télévisé, la *Star Academy*. Elle a fait beaucoup de CD.

- C'est qui, ton idole?
- Mon idole, euh … c'est Yoann Gourcuff. C'est un footballeur.
- Qu'est-ce qu'il a fait?
- Alors, il a joué dans l'équipe de France. Il a gagné des matchs!

- C'est qui, ton idole?
- Mon idole, c'est Gaspard Ulliel. C'est un acteur.
- Qu'est-ce qu'il a fait?
- Il a joué dans beaucoup de films français. Euh … Il a gagné un prix aux Césars.

– C'est qui, ton idole?
– Alors, mon idole, c'est Marion Cotillard. C'est une actrice.
– Qu'est-ce qu'elle a fait?
– Elle a joué dans le film Taxi. Euh … Elle a gagné un prix aux Oscars.

### 2 Relis. C'est qui?

* Students read the interviews again and say whom each of the French sentences refers to. Remind students to look out for any negative sentences as well as key words.

*Answers*: a Gaspard Ulliel; b Marion Cotillard; c Jenifer; d Yoann Gourcuff; e Jenifer; f Gaspard Ulliel

### Follow-up

* Students could carry out the interactive activity from OxBox, *Jenifer*. This has further information on **Jenifer**, who won Star Academy in 2002 – a famous French reality television series.
* Students could also research more information on the interviewees by using the internet and finding out three things they have each done. Pool ideas at the end.

### 3 À deux.

* Students work in pairs. One of them chooses to be one of the four teenagers from the interviews and answers questions from the other, using the example given as support.
* Model first with a volunteer, if necessary.

## Top Tips!

* Students are encouraged to use words, such as *alors* and *euh*, to give themselves time to think when speaking. Explain to them that it is always best to sound French, and making French hesitation sounds is always more convincing than making English ones!

### 4 Écris.

* Students write about their favourite celebrity and what he or she has done. They can use a dictionary to find key words they may need for their texts and they could download a picture from the internet to accompany it.
* Model how to do a text first on the board. You could then make a display with students' work.

### Follow-up

* Carry out some extension work on the perfect tense, using the PowerPoint presentation from OxBox, Perfect tense with *avoir*.
* Show students the mind map on the perfect tense that you began on spread 2.1 Plenary. Ask them, in pairs, to consider what they have learned about the perfect tense on this spread. Elicit feedback from the class and add students' suggestions to the mind map.

# 2.4  Vocabulaire

page 18

## *Planner*

> **Resources**
Students' Book, page 18

> **Objectives**
* *Vocabulaire:* to provide a theme-based summary of the key language of the unit, which students can use as a reference or as an aid to learning
* To practise pronunciation

> **Framework reference**
4.1, 5.5

### Using the vocabulary page

* Encourage students to use the *Vocabulaire* page as a reference point throughout the unit. It can also serve as a useful revision tool before students do the *Clic-test*!
* Vocabulary is listed spread-by-spread and you could either ask students to learn each section for homework after each spread is completed, or set the whole page as a homework task before starting work on the test. Most students learn shorter sections best, so often it is better to give them manageable chunks to learn at a time.

* Encourage students to use different techniques to help them learn the vocabulary:
  – Cover up the English and see what they can remember; write down any words they can't remember and test themselves again on those words.
  – Cover up the French and see if they can remember the words or phrases this way round.
  – Make word cards with English on one side and French on the other. Students can then test themselves to see what they can remember.

Put any cards they can't remember on one side and go over those again at the end.
 – Work in pairs to test each other, either using the vocabulary list or the word cards.
• Record themselves saying the words both in English and French. Saying words and phrases out loud can often help with memorising them.

## Sound French!

• *Aim:* To practise pronunciation
• The point practised here is making a clear difference in pronunciation between the present and the perfect tense.
• Practise, using the example, then do some oral discrimination activities. Read out some simple phrases in either the present or the past and students note which tense you are using.

# 2.4  Clic-test!

page 19

---

## *Planner*

The page is divided into four sections: listening, speaking, reading and writing.

➢ **Objectives**
• To enable students to recap on the language and structures of the unit

• To provide an opportunity for quick testing of all four skills

➢ **Resources**
Students' Book, page 19
CD 2, track 45

➢ **Framework reference**
5.8

---

**AT 1.2** **1 Écoute!**
• Students listen and list the pictures in the correct order.

*Answers:* 1 c; 2 f; 3 d; 4 b; 5 a; 6 e

 **CD 2, track 45**      page 19, activité 1

1  – Qu'est-ce que tu as fait le weekend dernier?
   – J'ai joué au football.
   – C'est bien.
2  – Qu'est-ce que tu as fait après?
   – Après, j'ai mangé un hamburger.
   – Un hamburger? Bof!
3  – Et après? Qu'est-ce que tu as fait?
   – J'ai regardé la télé.
   – D'accord.
4  – Qu'est-ce que tu as fait après?
   – J'ai acheté un T-shirt.
   – OK, encore un T-shirt!
5  – Et ensuite, qu'est-ce que tu as fait?
   – J'ai lu mon magazine.
   – D'accord.
6  – Qu'est-ce que tu as fait après?
   – J'ai joué sur mon ordinateur.
   – Super! Merci.

**AT 3.2–3** **2 Lis!**
• Students read the passage about Natacha's idol and complete the summary in English.

*Answers:* 1 actor, singer; 2 French films; 3 Les Choristes; 4 CDs

**AT 4.2–3** **3 Écris!**
• Students write a sentence about each picture in the past tense, using the grid as support. Some students may be able to write a short paragraph using connectives.

*Answers:* 1 J'ai écouté mon iPod. 2 J'ai lu mon magazine. 3 J'ai joué au foot. 4 J'ai aidé à la maison. 5 J'ai fait mes devoirs. 6 J'ai regardé un film.

**AT 2.2–3** **4 Parle!**
• Students refer to the pictures to say what they did or didn't do last weekend. Prompts are provided for support with forming the perfect tense structures.

*Answers:* a J'ai vu mes copains. b Je n'ai pas regardé la télé. c J'ai mangé un hamburger. d J'ai acheté un T-shirt. e Je n'ai pas joué sur mon ordinateur. f Je n'ai pas visité un musée.

# À moi

---

## *Planner*

> **Objectives**
> - To provide reinforcement activities for quiet work
> - To provide alternative class and homework material for students who finish other activities quickly

> **Resources**
> Students' Book, page 77
> CD 2, track 46

> **Framework reference**
> 2.1, 2.3, 2.5

---

### C'est la vie!

**1 Read and match each picture to a verse of the song.**

 • You may wish to play the song at the beginning to set the scene before letting students work on the activities by themselves.

*Answers*: a verse 2; b verse 3; c verse 1; d verse 4

 **CD 2, track 46**          page 77, activité 1

**C'est la vie!**

J'ai mangé un gâteau énorme
Maintenant, je n'suis pas en forme.

Mais j'ai ri
Et j'ai dit:
C'est la vie

J'ai acheté un p'tit chaton
Maintenant, c'est un très gros lion.

Mais j'ai ri …

À la montagne, j'ai fait du ski
Maintenant, je suis dans mon lit.

Mais j'ai ri …

Hier soir, j'ai vu un film d'horreur
Maintenant, j'ai encore très peur.

Mais j'ai ri …

**AT 3.2** **2 Find these verbs in French in the song.**

• Students find the verbs in the perfect tense.

*Answers*: j'ai mangé; j'ai acheté; j'ai fait; j'ai vu

**AT 4.2–3** **3 In pairs, use the rhyming words below to write two more verses for the song. Change the highlighted words in the example.**

• Students find rhyming words in the box, or use their own ideas, and write additional verses for the song. The basic structure is provided for them to follow.

**4 Listen to the song. Sing along if you can.**

• If you have not already played the song to the class, play it now and encourage students to sing along!
• Students could also perform their own verses from exercise 3 for the rest of the class to enjoy.

# Clic-vidéo

---

## *Planner*

> ### Objectives
> • To provide extended listening practice recycling the language of the whole unit

> ### Resources
> Students' Book, page 86
> Video clip 3, *Clic! 2 Star*
> CD 2, track 47

> ### Framework reference
> 1.2, 1.3

---

### Preparation

• Before you watch the video clip, explain that the *Musée Grévin* is a waxworks museum in Paris. It contains models of famous people, past and present, as well as scenes from history. You could encourage students to visit the museum's website, www.grevin.com.

 **AT 1.2–4**

**1 In pairs, predict the answers to questions 1–4 before watching the video. Then watch the clip and check your answers. Which is true, a or b?**

• Students watch the clip and choose a or b in answer to each question. Pause the clip after each section to allow students enough time to answer.

*Answers*: 1 a; 2 b; 3 a; 4 b

 **Video clip 3**     page 86, activités 1, 2 et 3

 **CD 2, track 47**

Nina: Voilà, c'est le Musée Grévin.
Joe: Le Musée Grévin, c'est quoi exactement?
Nina: Le Musée Grévin, c'est un musée de cire. Il y a des personnages historiques, des stars de cinéma, des sportifs. Il y a des personnages en cire. On y va?
Joe: Allez, on y va!

Joe: C'est qui cet homme là-bas, avec les cheveux blancs et courts et la petite moustache?
Nina: Oui, c'est le général de Gaulle.
Joe: De Gaulle?
Nina: Oui. Pendant la Deuxième Guerre mondiale, c'est lui qui a aidé à la libération de la France. Ensuite, il a été président de la République. C'est un très grand homme, très autoritaire.
Joe: Oui, il est très grand. Il a un grand nez et de grandes oreilles.

Nina: Et lui aussi, il est grand, non?
Joe: Qui, lui?
Nina: Oui, le type qui n'a pas de cheveux.
Joe: Oui, attends. Comment s'appelle-t-il?
Nina: C'est Fabien Barthez.
Joe: Ah oui.

Nina: Le joueur de foot, enfin le gardien de but. Il est très célèbre aussi. Il est beau, non?
Joe: Bof! Pas trop. Il est fort en goal.
Nina: Oui, il est très bon et en plus, tout le monde l'embrasse sur la tête.
Joe: Alors, Jean, ça va?
Nina: Comment allez-vous?
Joe: Le café, il est bon?

Nina: Salut, Max!
Joe: Max!
Max: Eh, salut! Vous allez bien?
Joe: Oui, ça va.
Nina: Ça va, et toi?
Max: Oui, très bien. Tu as fait quoi aujourd'hui alors?
Joe: J'ai visité le Musée Grévin. J'ai vu des célébrités.
Nina: Oui. Moi, j'ai beaucoup aimé Céline Dion. Elle est très belle. Elle a les cheveux longs. Elle a les cheveux blonds et elle est très mince.
Joe: Oui. Et moi, j'ai vu Fabien Barthez.
Max: Cool! Et tu as acheté des souvenirs?
Joe: Oui, j'ai acheté un cahier.
Max: Eh! Alors tu as passé une bonne journée?
Joe: Oui, c'était super!
Max: À ton séjour à Paris!

### Point langue
Il est très grand.
Il a un grand nez et de grandes oreilles.
Elle est très belle. Elle a les cheveux longs. Elle a les cheveux blonds et elle est très mince.
J'ai visité le Musée Grévin. J'ai vu des célébrités.

 **AT 3.2**

**2 From what you saw on the clip, decide which sentences Joe could say about his trip to the Musée Grévin:**

• Students select the sentences that they think Joe could have said.

*Answers*: a, c, d, f, g

 **AT 1.2–4**

**3 Watch the end again and listen carefully. You will hear Joe say four of sentences a–h above. Which ones?**

• Students watch the final section again and see which of the sentences Joe says.

*Answers*: a, c, d, g

# 3 Vacances et voyages

| Unité 3: Vacances et voyages  Overview grid | | | | | | |
|---|---|---|---|---|---|---|
| Page reference | Contexts and objectives | Grammar | Language strategies and pronunciation | Key language | Framework | AT level |
| 20–21 **3.1 Les pays** | • Say which country you went to<br>• Say what it was like | • *je suis allé(e)*<br>• *en* + countries<br>• *c'était* | Giving an opinion in the past: *c'était* + adjective | *Je suis allé(e) en France, Espagne, Irlande, Grande-Bretagne, Belgique, Allemagne, Suisse, Italie.*<br>*C'était amusant, ennuyeux, intéressant, nul, cool, sensationnel, génial.* | 3.1, 4.5, 5.4, 5.6 | 1.2<br>2.2<br>3.1–3<br>4.2 |
| 22–23 **3.2 À Paris** | • Say where you went in Paris | • Other verbs which take *être*<br>• Agreement of the past participle | Asking questions: *où, quand* | *Je suis allé(e) à Notre-Dame, au Sacré-Cœur, à la Tour Eiffel, à l'Arc de Triomphe.*<br>*Je suis arrivé(e) à (neuf heures).*<br>*Je suis parti(e) à (six heures).*<br>*Je suis monté(e) à la Tour Eiffel.*<br>*Je suis rentré(e) à (quatre heures).*<br>Days of the week (revised) | 1.1, 1.2, 4.4 | 1.3–4<br>2.2–4<br>3.2–3 |
| 24–25 **3.3 En vacances** | • Talk about a past holiday | Verbs in the past with *avoir* and *être* | | *Je suis/Tu es allé(e) en (Espagne).*<br>*Je suis parti(e) en juin.*<br>*J'ai fait du sport, du ski, du surf, du shopping.*<br>*J'ai visité (le musée).*<br>*C'était …* | 2.1, 2.5, 4.5, 5.1 | 1.3<br>2.2<br>3.3<br>4.2 |
| 26 **3.4 Vocabulaire** | • Practise pronunciation | | Nasal sounds: *an* and *en* | | 4.1, 5.5 | |
| 27 **3.4 Clic-test!** | • Recap on the language structures of the unit<br>• Provide an opportunity for quick testing of all four skills | | | | 5.7, 5.8 | 1.2<br>2.2–4<br>3.3<br>4.2–4 |
| 78 **À moi** | • Provide reinforcement activities for self-access work | | | | 2.1, 2.2, 2.4 | 3.3–4<br>4.3–4 |
| 87 **Clic-vidéo** | • Provide extended listening practice recycling the language of the whole unit using the video | | | | 1.2, 1.3 | 1.3–4 |

| MEDIUM TERM GRID Week-by-week overview (assuming six weeks' work or approximately 10–12.5 hours) |
|---|

**About Unit 3, *Vacances et voyages***

In this unit, students learn how to talk about holidays and they find out more about Paris. They learn to use the perfect tense with *être* in the *je* and *tu* forms, including the agreement of the past participle. They learn to give an opinion in the past using *c'était* + adjective and they ask questions using *où* and *quand*. Students also mix *avoir* and *être* verbs in the past.

New vocabulary includes activities in the past with *être* verbs (*aller, arriver, partir, monter, rentrer*), countries in Europe and places in Paris. Revised language includes days of the week and avoir verbs.

Reading, listening and comprehension skills are developed through a variety of text, audio and video materials.

| Week | Resources | Objectives |
|---|---|---|
| 1 | 3.1 Les pays | Using *en* + country to say where you went on holiday<br>Using *c'était* + adjective to say what it was like<br>Making the past participle agree: *je suis allé* and *je suis allée* |
| 2 | 3.2 À Paris | *Saying where you went in Paris*<br>Naming places in Paris<br>Using different *être* verbs in the perfect tense (*aller, arriver, partir, monter, rentrer*)<br>Asking questions with *où* and *quand*<br>Revising days of the week and times |
| 3 | 3.3 En vacances | Consolidating work on the perfect tense<br>Using *avoir* and *être* verbs met so far to talk about a past holiday |
| 4 | **Sound French!** (p26)<br>**À moi** (p78)<br>**Clic-vidéo** (p87) | Practising pronunciation (nasal sounds *an* and *en*)<br>Additional reading and writing practice<br>Using the video for reinforcement, extension and follow-up work |
| 5 | **3.4 Vocabulaire**<br>**Clic-test!** | Learning vocabulary<br>Recapping on vocabulary of unit<br>Preparing and carrying out of assessment in all four skills<br>Reviewing progress |
| 6 | **Copymasters (*Feuilles*)**<br>**OxBox** | Reinforcement and extension of the language of the unit using extra resources<br>Reviewing progress via the Checklist on page 26, *Vocabulaire*<br>Going back over aspects of the unit which need reviewing after *Clic-test!* |

# 3.1 Les pays

## *Planner*

> **Objectives**
> - Say which country you went to
> - Say what it was like

> **Resources**
> Students' Book, pages 20–21
> CD 2, tracks 48–49
> OxBox *Clic! 2 Star*, Unité 3, *Vive l'Europe; Selon Nicolas et Natacha*

> **Key language**
> *Je suis allé(e) en France, Espagne, Irlande, Grande Bretagne, Belgique, Allemagne, Suisse, Italie.*
> *C'était amusant, ennuyeux, intéressant, nul, cool, sensationnel, génial.*

> **Grammar**
> *je suis allé/allée*
> *en* + countries
> *C'était*

> **Framework reference**
> - 3.1, 4.5, 5.4, 5.6

> **Starters**
> - Brainstorm and make a list of any European countries students can name (in English). Prepare a list of countries from page 20 in French on the board. How many of these countries can students recognise? How many can they match up with their English equivalents?

- In pairs, students think of additional places outside Europe where people may go on holiday. Provide dictionaries for students to look up spellings and whether the countries are masculine or feminine. How many can they find and note correctly in three minutes? Pool ideas and make a list on the board for later reference.

> **Plenaries**
> - Divide some of the country names into halves and mix them on the board. Students race to write a complete list of the six countries, taking care with their spellings.

| Esp | ande |
|---|---|
| Alle | Bretagne |
| Grande- | sse |
| Irl | agne |
| Sui | magne |
| Bel | gique |

- Give students three minutes to work in pairs. Challenge them to write correctly as many adjectives as they can to describe a holiday (with their books closed!). They receive one point for each adjective and a further point for spelling it correctly. They swap lists with other pairs to mark.

> **Assessment opportunities**
> - Reading: Students' Book page 21, exercise 6
> - Writing: Students' Book page 21, exercise 7

## Preparation

- This spread introduces the perfect tense with *je + être + allé(e)*. You may like to refer to the grammar box at the beginning of the spread and explain that some verbs of movement form the past tense with *je suis* instead of *j'ai* (as met in Unit 2). Write up on the board: *Je suis allé* and *Je suis allée*. Ask students to think about why there are two different forms and establish that *je suis allée* is used for females. Remind students of adjectives agreeing and adding *e* for the female form, which they have met before.

 **1 Écoute, lis et répète.**

- Students listen to the sentences and repeat each one with accurate pronunciation. Point out that *en* is used to say 'to' with a feminine country. All the countries listed are feminine.
- Look at the map and discuss the countries listed. Have students visited any of them? Discuss any experiences of these countries.

- Play the audio again and students point to the country mentioned each time on the map.

 **CD 2, track 48**     page 20, activité 1

- Je suis allé en France.
- Je suis allée en Espagne.
- Je suis allé en Irlande.
- Je suis allée en Grande-Bretagne.
- Je suis allé en Belgique.
- Je suis allée en Allemagne.
- Je suis allé en Suisse.
- Je suis allée en Italie.

 **2 À deux.**

- Students use the key language box and work in pairs to say they have been to one of the countries on the map. Their partner points to the country mentioned each time.

**3 Écoute et choisis. (1–6)**

- Students listen and choose the country each person mentions from the options provided.

*Answers*: 1 b; 2 b; 3 a; 4 b; 5 a; 6 a

**CD 2, track 49**                    page 20, activité 3

**1** – Tu es allée où?
   – Je suis allée en Italie.
**2** – Tu es allé où?
   – Je suis allé en Grande-Bretagne.
**3** – Tu es allée où?
   – Je suis allée en Allemagne.
**4** – Tu es allé où?
   – Je suis allé en Irlande.
**5** – Tu es allée où?
   – Je suis allée en Belgique.
**6** – Tu es allé où?
   – Moi? Je suis allé en France!

**AT 4.2** **4 Écris.**

- Students write sentences to show which countries the people pictured have been to. Remind them to use *allée* for the females. Also remind them to use *et* to link the two countries in their sentences.

*Answers*: a Je suis allé en France et en Belgique. b b Je suis allé en Espagne et en Italie. c Je suis allée en Irlande et en Grande-Bretagne. d Je suis allée en France et en Suisse. e Je suis allé en Allemagne et en Belgique. f Je suis allée en Grande-Bretagne et en Espagne.

**Follow-up**

- Students can do the matching activity from OxBox, *Vive l'Europe*. This covers the countries from this spread, as well as some additional European countries.
- To revise colours, do some further work on the flags of the countries mentioned.
- If students show an interest in the countries, they could carry out some research to find out interesting facts about a few of them, such as capital city, area, population, tourist attractions, geographical features, etc.

## Preparation

- The rest of the spread concentrates on giving opinions in the past tense with *c'était*.
- First, gather a list of adjectives on the board which students know. Explain that opinions can easily be given in the past by using *c'était* + any of the adjectives they have come up with.

**AT 3.1** **5 Trouve les paires.**

- Students match the English and French adjectives.
- Encourage them to work out as many as they can by using prior knowledge and cognates and only to use the glossary as a final resort.

*Answers*: *ennuyeux* boring; *amusant* fun; *cool* cool; *génial* great; *intéressant* interesting; *nul* rubbish; *sensationnel* amazing

**Follow-up**

- Students can do the matching activity from OxBox, *Selon Nicolas et Natacha*. This contains the adjectives from this spread, as well as some additional ones.

**AT 3.2–3** **6 Lis et réponds en anglais.**

- Students read the short texts and answer the questions in English.
- Read the texts out loud with the class, if more support is necessary. Encourage students to read the texts out loud in pairs once they have answered the questions.

*Answers*: a Morgane Italy; Victor Switzerland; Amy Great Britain; b Amy: fun; Morgane: interesting; Victor: boring; c Morgane: Rome; Victor: with dad; Amy: in December

**AT 4.2** **7 Écris.**

- Students write sentences about three countries they have visited and give their opinion. They can invent details.

**Follow-up**

- Students could play Speaking Snap. They use the three countries and opinions they chose in exercise 7 and circulate in the class saying where they have been and what it was like. If they discover somebody with the same country and opinion, it's a Snap. Who is the first to get a Snap?

# 3.2 À Paris

## *Planner*

> ### Objectives
> * Say where you went in Paris

> ### Resources
> Students' Book, pages 22–23
> CD 2, track 50
> Video clip 4, *Clic! 2 Star*
> OxBox *Clic! 2 Star, Unité 3, Je suis allé à Paris*
> Copymaster 29, 39, *Clic! 2 Star*

> ### Key language
> *Je suis allé(e) à Notre-Dame, au Sacré-Cœur, à la Tour Eiffel, à l'Arc de Triomphe.*
> *Je suis arrivé(e) à (neuf heures).*
> *Je suis parti(e) à (six heures).*
> *Je suis monté(e) à la Tour Eiffel.*
> *Je suis rentré(e) à (quatre heures).*
> Days of the week (revised)

> ### Grammar
> Other verbs which take *être*
> Agreement of the past participle

> ### Framework reference
> 1.1, 1.2, 4.4

> ### Starters
> * As a class, discuss any personal experiences or knowledge of Paris. Have students visited the city or any of the attractions pictured on page 22? Which ones would they like to visit? Look at the photos and see which, if any, students can recognise. Give some basic information on the places pictured by way of an introduction to Paris.
> * Recap on days of the week. Can students remember them? Can they remember how to spell them? Once they have recited the days, recap on

the alphabet by asking students to write out as many days as they can and then challenge others in the class to spell them out.

* **Écris des phrases**
Ask students to separate the words and write out the sentences. Then give the English. Exemple: JesuisalléenFrance. → Je suis allé en France. = I went to France.
  a JesuisalléenFrance.
  b JesuismotéeàlaTourEiffel.
  c Jesuispartidimanche.
  d Jesuisarrivéàsixheures.
  e Jesuispartieàdeuxheures.
  f Jesuisrentréeàtroisheures.

> ### Plenaries
> * Ask students to work in pairs and discuss what they know about the perfect tense from their recent work. Ask them to prepare two or three sentences in the perfect tense by way of example. Pool ideas and establish that most verbs use *j'ai* + verb which sometimes end in *é* but some are irregular. A few verbs of movement, such as *aller*, are preceded by *je suis*.
> * Play Speed Duel to practise the perfect tense with *être*. Two students stand up. Call out an infinitive and the students compete to put it into the *je* form of the perfect tense.
>   Teacher: *arriver*
>   Student: *Je suis arrivé!*
>   The first student to answer remains standing. The opponent sits down and is replaced by another challenger. Continue in the same way. Depending on the ability of your class and what you want to focus on, you could stick to verbs with *être* or you could use a mixture of *avoir* and *être* verbs.

> ### Assessment opportunities
> * Speaking: Students' Book page 23, exercise 5

---

**1a Regarde le clip. Tu vois quels monuments?**
* Play the video clip. Max and Joe have just returned from a sightseeing trip around Paris and are telling Nina about their day.
* Students watch and identify which of the places shown in the photos are shown on the video. This relies on the visual content of the clip rather than an understanding of the script.
* Once students have identified the places, play the clip again and challenge students to listen for extra details by providing them with a list of adjectives and opinions to spot.

*Answers*: 1 b; 2 d; 3 c; 4 a

 **Video clip 4**   page 22, activités 1a et 1b

 **CD 2, track 50**

Max: Salut, Nina! Nina: Salut!
Max: Ça va? Nina: Ça va?
Joe: Ça va, et toi?
Nina: Oui, oui, ça va. Alors, Joe, tu es allé où?
Joe: J'ai visité Paris. C'était super beau, mais c'était fatigant.
Nina: Mais, vous êtes allés où alors?
Max: Nous sommes allés à Notre-Dame.
Joe: Oui, c'était très beau et très intéressant. Et tu as lu le livre *The Hunchback of Notre-Dame?*

Nina: *The Hunchback* ... Ah, le bossu. *Notre-Dame de Paris* de Victor Hugo.

Max: Et puis, on est allés voir l'Arc de Triomphe.

Joe: Oui, c'était super impressionnant.

Max: C'était très drôle. On s'est bien amusés avec des Japonaises.

Joe: Oui, attends, j'ai des photos. Regarde.

Nina: Fais voir ...

Joe: Wouah! C'est super!

Max: C'est magnifique!

Nina: Ah – trop marrant là!

Nina: Et vous êtes allés à la Tour Eiffel?

Joe: Oui, c'était génial!

Nina: Et vous êtes montés au premier étage?

Max: Non, il y avait trop de monde.

Joe: Non, je ne suis pas monté au premier étage. Mais regarde, j'ai pris des photos.

Max: Et puis, on est allés à Sacré-Cœur.

Joe: Ah oui. Là, il y avait plein de touristes. Je suis monté jusqu'en haut, c'était fatigant

Max: Oui, mais on n'est pas entrés dans l'église. On a regardé le panorama et on a vu tout Paris.

Joe: Ah oui, c'était très, très beau.

Nina: Et vous voulez encore visiter Paris?

Max: Oui, mais pas à pied.

Nina: Parfait. On va prendre la péniche alors.

Joe: Euh ... c'est quoi un* péniche?

Nina: Une péniche, c'est un bateau.

Joe: Ah super!

Joe: J'adore Paris!

**Point langue**
Vous êtes allés où?
Nous sommes allés à Notre-Dame.
Je ne suis pas monté ...
C'était très drôle.

*Remind students that Joe is English and sometimes makes mistakes when speaking French. Here, he says "un péniche" when it should be "une".*

 **1b Regarde encore. Lis les questions.**
  **Oui ou non?**

• Students watch the clip again and answer the questions.

*Answers*: a yes; b yes; c no; d yes; e yes

**Follow-up**

 • Students could carry out the multichoice activity from OxBox, *Je suis allé à Paris*. This uses parts of the video clip to identify places in Paris.

 • Copymaster 39 (*Clic-vidéo*) can be used at this point.

*Answers*: **1** <u>Paris</u>: beau, fatigant; <u>Notre-Dame</u>: beau, intéressant; <u>l'Arc de Triomphe</u>: impressionnant, drôle; la <u>Tour Eiffel</u>: génial; <u>le Sacré-Cœur</u>: fatigant, beau
*Answers*: **2** a 2; b 3; c 4; d 1
*Answers*: **3** a ii; b ii; c ii; d ii

 **2 À deux.**

 • Students work in pairs. One partner secretly writes down one of the places in Paris and the other asks questions to find out which place he/she has chosen. Which partner can guess the location in the fewest number of questions?

AT 3.2 **3 Trouve les paires.**

• Students match the English verbs in the perfect tense with the French ones provided in the grammar box. Allow students a minute or two to match the pairs on their own, before going over other verbs which take *être* in the past.

*Answers*: a je suis monté; b je suis arrivé; c je suis rentré; d je suis parti

## Grammaire

• Explain that a few other verbs of movement, like *aller* which was met in the previous spread, use *je suis* in the perfect tense instead of *j'ai*. Give examples of sentences using these other verbs before gathering other possible sentence endings.

• Explain that all these past participles need to add an extra *e* if you are talking about a female.

## Preparation

• Do a quick revision of days of the week at this point, if you have not already done so in the Starter.

• Point out the feminine agreement on the past participle, if you have not done so already.

AT 3.3 **4 Lis les bulles.**

• Students read two texts which contain the verbs from exercise 3. They note details in English for each person.

*Answers*: Lucas: a Saturday; b 9 o'clock; c Eiffel Tower; d 6 o'clock. Chloé: a Sunday; b 10 o'clock; c Notre-Dame; d 4 o'clock.

AT 2.3–4 **5 À deux.**

 • Students ask and answer questions as if they were Lucas or Chloé from exercise 4. This also provides practice and a recap of the question words *où* and *quand*.

• Ask some students to perform their interview for the rest of the class.

**Follow-up**

C29 • Further work on perfect tense sentences and adjectives is provided on Copymaster 29.
*Answers:* **1** see right.
**2** *she went* – elle est allée; *I went (f.)* – je suis allée; *you left (m.)* – tu es parti; *I went up (f.)* – je suis montée; *I left (m.)* – je suis parti; *he went* – il est allé

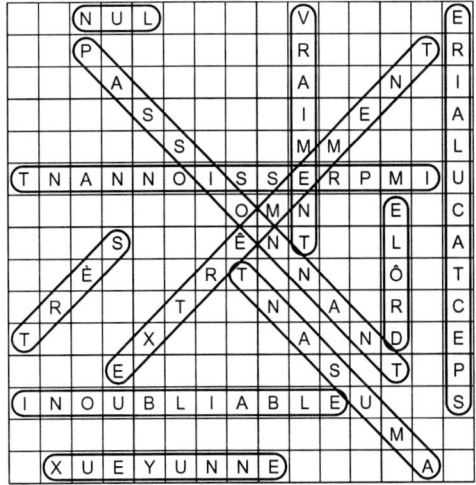

# 3.3   En vacances

page 24–25

## Planner

> **Objectives**
  • Talk about a past holiday

> **Resources**
  Students' Book, pages 24–25
  CD 2, tracks 51–52
  OxBox *Clic! 2 Star, Unité 3, Qu'est-ce que tu as fait en vacances?*
  Copymaster 31, 32
  CD 3, tracks 60–61 *Clic! 2 Star*

> **Key language**
  *Je suis/Tu es allé(e) en (Espagne).*
  *Je suis parti(e) en juin.*
  *J'ai fait du sport, du ski, du surf, du shopping.*
  *J'ai visité (le musée).*
  *C'était …*

> **Grammar**
  Verbs in the past with *avoir* and *être*

> **Framework reference**
  2.1, 2.5, 4.5, 5.1

> **Starters**
  • Display jumbled vocabulary on the board for four categories, such as months, means of transport, countries and adjectives. Challenge students, in pairs, to sort the jumbled vocabulary into the categories.
    *en: mai, juillet, août, mars*
    *en: train, bus, hélicoptère, métro*
    *en: France, Espagne, Italie, Allemagne*
    *amusant, ennuyeux, cool, génial*
    Ask students to add two more words to each category, if they can, then go through the answers as a whole class.

• Display four columns of words and phrases on the board and challenge students to build seven sentences by choosing a word or phrase from each column. Point out that there are various possibilities, but students can only use each word/phrase once.

| Je<br>J' | suis<br>ai | allé<br>fait<br>allé<br>mangé<br>allée<br>joué<br>fait | en France.<br>au foot.<br>à la plage.<br>du shopping.<br>des crêpes.<br>au cinéma.<br>du vélo. |
|---|---|---|---|

> **Plenaries**
  • Display some groups of words on the themes of the unit and ask students to choose an odd-one-out in each group, giving a reason for their choice. Point out there may be more than one possible odd-one-out in each group.
    – *Allemagne, Espagne, Europe* (*Europe* because it is the only continent.)
    – *je suis restée, resté, je suis allé, j'ai mangé* (*j'ai mangé* because it doesn't use *être* in the perfect tense.)
    – *Grande-Bretagne, France, Sénégal* (*Sénégal* because it is the only country in Africa.)
  • Split the class up into small groups and ask each group to produce a short text about a real or imaginary holiday. Ask them to include: where they went, when, two activities they did, somewhere they visited and their opinion. Offer a point for each of these elements successfully mentioned. Students could use the blog from exercise 4 as a model. Provide key language on the board as support, if necessary.

> **Assessment opportunities**
  • Writing: Students' Book page 25, exercise 6
  • Speaking: Students' Book page 25, exercise 7

## Introduction

- This spread consolidates work done in this unit on the perfect tense and includes verbs which take *avoir* and those which take *être*.

| Alex | Irlande | mère, père, 2 sœurs | très ennuyeux |
|------|---------|---------------------|---------------|
| Sophie | Italie | mère, tante, cousine | inoubliable |

AT 1.3 **1 Regarde les dessins et écoute Léa. Choisis titre a ou titre b.**

- Students listen to Léa's account of her holiday and follow the story in their books. They then choose the best title for her story.

*Answer:* a

 **CD 3, track 60** Feuille 31, *Clic! 2 Star*, activité 1

- Clarice, tu es allée à l'étranger?
- Oui, je suis allée en Suisse avec un groupe scolaire.
- Tu as aimé la Suisse?
- Oui, énormément, c'était spectaculaire – les montagnes étaient très impressionnantes.

- Alex, tu es allé en vacances cet été?
- Oui, je suis allé en Irlande avec ma mère, mon père et mes deux sœurs.
- Et tu as aimé le pays?
- Non, pas du tout. Je l'ai trouvé très ennuyeux. Je n'aime pas faire des randonnées.

- Et Sophie, tu es déjà allée à l'étranger?
- Oui, je suis allée en Italie, à Venise.
- Comment tu as trouvé la ville?
- C'était inoubliable. Je l'ai beaucoup aimée.
- Et tu étais avec qui?
- J'étais avec ma mère, ma tante et ma cousine.

 **CD 2, track 51**          page 24, activité 1

1. Je m'appelle Léa et je suis allée à la montagne.
2. Je suis partie en février.
3. J'ai fait du ski tous les jours.
4. J'ai acheté un cadeau pour mon frère.
5. Je suis tombée – aïe!
6. Je suis rentrée en hélicoptère: c'était nul!

AT 3.3 **2 Trouve une légende pour chaque dessin.**

- Students match the captions with the pictures depicting Léa's holiday account.

*Answers:* 1 c; 2 a; 3 f; 4 e; 5 b; 6 d

### Follow-up

- For more writing practice, ask students to write Léa's story in the correct order.
- To go over the correct order, play the audio again from exercise 1 for students to check their answers.
- To ensure comprehension of the verbs used, do further oral practice by calling out a verb in English, such as 'I left' and students look at the captions and say the French equivalent.

AT 2.2 **3 À deux.**

- Students do some speaking practice of the phrases in the story. They take it in turns to start reading out loud one of the sentences for a partner to complete.

## Grammaire

- Summarise work on the perfect tense by gathering in a list of all verbs students have met which take *j'ai* and those which take *je suis*. Establish also that verbs which take *je suis* add an extra *e* when describing something a female has done.

### Follow-up

C31 - Students could work on Copymaster 31 which provides listening activities on the perfect tense.

*Answers:* **1**

| nom | pays | avec | opinion |
|-----|------|------|---------|
| Clarice | Suisse | un groupe scolaire | spectaculaire, impressionnant |

*Answers:* **2**

| where? | Disneyland Paris |
|--------|------------------|
| with? | mother, father, brother |
| when? | 6 April |
| transport? | Eurostar/train |
| what time? | she left home at 10 a.m. she arrived at around 1 p.m. |
| how many nights? | 2 |
| favourite show? | car show |
| opinion? | great |

 **CD 3, track 61** Feuille 31, *Clic! 2 Star*, activité 2

- Astrid, où es-tu allée pendant les vacances?
- Je suis allée à Disneyland Paris avec ma mère, mon père et mon frère.
- Tu es partie quand?
- Je suis partie le six avril.
- Comment tu y es allée?
- J'ai pris l'Eurostar qui va directement de Londres au parc qui est à côté de Paris. Je suis partie à dix heures du matin et on est arrivés au parc vers une heure.
- Tu es restée combien de jours?
- J'ai dormi deux nuits à l'hôtel, donc on a passé trois journées complètes au parc.
- Tu as vu des spectacles?
- Oui, beaucoup, mon spectacle préféré s'appelle "Moteurs … Action!", un spectacle avec des voitures.
- C'était bien?
- Oui, c'était génial. Je voudrais y retourner un jour.

• Students could work on Copymaster 32 which provides speaking activities on the perfect tense.

 • If you wish to do some work on the third person form of the perfect tense, you could use the activity from OxBox, *Qu'est-ce que tu as fait en vacances?*

 **4 Recopie et complète.**

• Students look at Ludo's blog and match the sentence beginnings with the correct endings. They then write out the complete blog.

• Go over the starts of the sentences, one at a time, with the class. For example, what might they expect to come after the verb *je suis allé*? Collect ideas and then see which ending fits best. Do the same for the other sentence beginnings.

*Answers*: Je suis allé en Espagne. Je suis parti en juillet. J'ai fait du surf. J'ai visité le musée de la Mer. C'était amusant.

**5 Écoute. Choisis a ou b.**

• Students listen to Charlotte answering questions about her hozliday and choose a or b for each question.

*Answers*: 1 a; 2 b; 3 b; 4 a

 **CD 2, track 52**   page 25, activité 5

– Charlotte, pendant les vacances, tu es allée où?
– Je suis allée à Paris.
– Tu es partie quand?
– Je suis partie en juin.
– Qu'est-ce que tu as fait?
– J'ai fait du shopping.
– C'était comment?
– C'était un peu ennuyeux.

 **6 Adapte le blog pour Martin.**

• Students adapt Ludo's blog from exercise 4 , putting in Martin's details instead. Model on the board how to adapt the blog with other details and show students how to add different endings to the sentence beginnings. Students can use the key language box as support.

*Answers*: Je suis allé en Irlande. Je suis parti en août. J'ai fait du sport. J'ai visité le musée. C'était génial.

 **7 Interviews: les vacances de rêve.**

 • Students work in pairs to interview each other about their ideal holiday, using the four questions provided in Activity 5. They can use the key language box to help with their answers.

• Model an interview with a volunteer first.

**Follow-up**

• For further oral practice, students could do a similar interview pretending to be Ludo or Martin from this spread.

• For writing practice, students could write up their interviews.

# 3.4   Vocabulaire                              page 26

## *Planner*

➤ **Resources**
Students' Book, page 26

➤ **Objectives**
• *Vocabulaire:* to provide a theme-based summary of the key language of the unit, which students can use as a reference or as an aid to learning
• To practise pronunciation

➤ **Framework reference**
4.1, 5.5

### Using the vocabulary page

• Encourage students to use the *Vocabulaire* page as a reference point throughout the unit. It can also serve as a useful revision tool before students do the *Clic-test!*

• Vocabulary is listed spread-by-spread and you could either ask students to learn each section for homework after each spread is completed, or set the whole page as a homework task before starting work on the test. Most students learn shorter sections best, so often it is better to give them manageable chunks to learn at a time.

• Encourage students to use different techniques to help them learn the vocabulary:
   – Cover up the English and see what they can remember; write down any words they can't remember and test themselves again on those words.
   – Cover up the French and see if they can remember the words or phrases this way round.

– Make word cards with English on one side
and French on the other. Students can then test
themselves to see what they can remember.
Put any cards they can't remember on one side
and go over those again at the end.
– Work in pairs to test each other, either using
the vocabulary list or the word cards.
• Record themselves saying the words both in
English and French. Saying words and phrases out
loud can often help with memorising them.

## Sound French!

• *Aim:* To practise pronunciation
• The points practised here are nasal sounds *an*
and *en*.
• Practise the words listed, asking students to repeat
each one.
• Ask students to find more examples of nasal
sounds in the vocabulary list and practise saying
them out loud.

# 3.4 Clic-test! page 27

---

## *Planner*

The page is divided into four sections: listening,
speaking, reading and writing.

➢ **Objectives**
• To enable students to recap on the language and
structures of the unit

• To provide an opportunity for quick testing of all
four skills

➢ **Resources**
Students' Book, page 27
CD 2, track 53

➢ **Framework reference**
5.7, 5.8

---

AT 1.2 **1 Écoute! (1–6)**

• Students listen and choose picture a or b to match
Lucie's answers about her holiday.

*Answers:* 1 a; 2 a; 3 b; 4 b; 5 b; 6 a

 **CD 2, track 53** page 27, activité 1

**1** – Salut, Lucie! Tu es allée où en vacances?
– Je suis allée en Angleterre, à Londres.
**2** – Tu es partie quand?
– Je suis partie en avril.
**3** – Tu es arrivée quand?
– Je suis arrivée à quatre heures.
**4** – Qu'est-ce que tu as fait là-bas?
– J'ai fait du shopping.
**5** – Qu'est-ce que tu as acheté?
– J'ai acheté un cadeau.
**6** – C'était comment?
– C'était super!

AT 3.3 **2 Lis!**

• Students read the dialogue and answer the
questions in English.

*Answers:* a Ireland and Spain; b no; c France and
Belgium; d Switzerland; e great

AT 2.2–4 **3 Parle!**

• Students describe a day trip to Paris using the
prompts given.

AT 4.2–4 **4 Écris!**

• Students copy the sentence beginnings and add
suitable endings to describe Norbert's holiday.

# À moi

---

### *Planner*

> **Objectives**
> * To provide reinforcement activities for quiet work
> * To provide alternative class and homework material for students who finish other activities quickly

> **Resources**
> Students' Book, page 78

> **Framework reference**
> 2.1, 2.2, 2.4

---

### Une excursion intéressante

 **1 Read the interview, then answer questions a–e in English.**

* Students read Natacha's interview about her holiday and answer the questions in English.

*Answers*: a on Saturday; b 11 o'clock; c watched the shows; d went home; e amazing/sensational

 **2 From the interview questions, pick out the French words for:**

* This task asks students to pick out the correct question words from the interview.

*Answers*: a où; b quand; c Qu'est-ce que

 **3 Think of a day trip you have been on. Copy out the interview questions and write your own answers.**

* Students write their own interview about a day trip they have been on, either real of imaginary, which they can then act out with a partner.
* Ask some pairs to perform their interviews for the rest of the class.

---

# Clic-vidéo

---

### *Planner*

> **Objectives**
> * To provide extended listening practice recycling the language of the whole unit

> **Resources**
> Students' Book, page 87
> Video clip 4, *Clic! 2 Star*
> CD 2, track 54

> **Framework reference**
> 1.2, 1.3

---

 **1 Watch the video clip. Which place do you think Joe finds most tiring and difficult to get to?**

* Students watch the video clip and choose one of the places.

*Answer*: d Sacré-Cœur

 **Video clip 4**      page 87, activités 1–4

 **CD 2, track 54**

*See tapescript from 3.2, pages 133–134*

 **2 Watch again. Match the statements below to the four places, according to what is said in the clip.**

* Students watch the clip again and match the statements to the four places mentioned.

*Answers*: a l'Arc de Triomphe; b Sacré-Cœur; c Notre-Dame; d la Tour Eiffel

 **3 Can you remember who said the following: Joe, Max or Nina? Watch again to check.**

* Students watch the clip again to listen to the detail of who said what.

*Answers*: a Joe; b Nina; c Joe; d Joe; e Max; f Nina

 **4 Which of these adjectives do you hear in the clip?**

* Students note which adjectives they hear on a further viewing.

*Answers*: beau, fatigant, intéressant, super, génial

# Planète mode!

| Unité 4: Planète mode! Overview grid | | | | | | |
|---|---|---|---|---|---|---|
| Page reference | Contexts and objectives | Grammar | Language strategies and pronunciation | Key language | Framework | AT level |
| 28–29 **4.1 Une robe jaune, j'adore!** | • Name clothes and colours<br>• Say which clothes you like or dislike | • Agreement of colours with clothes, masculine/ feminine | | *une robe, un pantalon, un T-shirt, un sweat à capuche, une chemise, une veste, un blouson, une jupe, des baskets*<br>*noir(e), vert(e), bleu(e), gris(e), blanc/blanche, rouge, jaune, rose*<br>*Je n'aime pas. J'aime bien. Ça va. J'adore! C'est très cool! Bof, c'est pas terrible. Je déteste! C'est moche!* | 1.1, 1.3, 4.3 | 1.1–2<br>2.1–3<br>3.2<br>4.1–2 |
| 30–31 **4.2 C'est quoi, ton style préféré?** | • Say what your favourite look is<br>• Say what you normally wear | • Agreement of plural adjectives | English words sometimes mean different things | *C'est quoi, ton style préféré?*<br>*Mon style préféré, c'est le style (rappeur, surfeur, gothique).*<br>*En générale, je mets des chaussures (noires), un jean (noir), une casquette (bleue), un short (baggy).* | 2.1, 4.2, 5.2 | 1.2<br>2.1–2<br>3.2–3<br>4.2–3 |
| 32–33 **4.3 Je peux essayer?** | • Shop for clothes | • *je voudrais,*<br>• *je peux* | | *Bonjour! Je peux vous aider?*<br>*Je voudrais (une robe).*<br>*Je peux essayer?*<br>*Bien sûr. Les cabines sont là.*<br>*Ça va?*<br>*Oui, ça va, je prends./Non, c'est trop (petit, grand, cher).* | 1.4, 3.1, 5.8 | 1.2–4<br>2.2–4<br>3.2<br>4.3–4 |
| 34 **4.4 Vocabulaire** | • Practise pronunciation | | Pronouncing the *ch* sound | | 4.1, 5.5 | |
| 35 **4.4 Clic-test!** | • Recap on the language structures of the unit<br>• Provide an opportunity for quick testing of all four skills | | | | 5.7, 5.8 | 1.2<br>2.2–3<br>3.2<br>4.2–3 |
| 79 **À moi** | • Provide reinforcement activities for self access work | | | | 2.1, 2.3, 3.1 | 3.3<br>4.2 |
| 88 **Clic-vidéo** | • Provide extended listening practice recycling the language of the whole unit using the video | | | | 1.2, 3.1, 3.2 | 1.3–4<br>2.2 |

140

| MEDIUM TERM GRID Week-by-week overview (assuming six weeks' work or approximately 10–12.5 hours) |
|---|

**About Unit 4, *Planète mode!***

In this unit, students learn to talk about fashion, clothes and shopping. They learn about the agreement of adjectives when describing clothes and they use *je voudrais* and *je peux* when shopping. They also learn that similar looking English words can mean different things in French.

New vocabulary includes items of clothing, opinions, fashion styles and shopping phrases. Revised language includes colours and some opinions.

Reading, listening and comprehension skills are developed through a variety of text, audio and video materials.

| Week | Resources | Objectives |
|---|---|---|
| 1 | **4.1 Une robe jaune, j'adore!** | Naming clothes and colours<br>Saying which clothes you like and dislike<br>Expressing specific opinions about items of clothing<br>Using agreement of adjectives to describe clothes (masculine and feminine singular) |
| 2 | **4.2 C'est quoi, ton style préféré?** | Saying what your favourite look is<br>Saying what you normally wear<br>Using adjective agreements (plural)<br>Learning that similar looking English words can mean different things in French |
| 3 | **4.3 Je peux essayer?** | Shopping for clothes<br>Saying which item of clothing you would like<br>Asking if you can try something on<br>Saying whether an item of clothing fits you or not<br>Using *je voudrais* and *je peux* when shopping for clothes |
| 4 | **Sound French!** (p34)<br>**À moi** (p79)<br>**Clic-vidéo** (p88) | Practising pronunciation (*ch* sound)<br>Additional reading and writing practice<br>Using the video for reinforcement, extension and follow-up work |
| 5 | **4.4 Vocabulaire**<br>**Clic-test!** | Learning vocabulary<br>Recapping on vocabulary of unit<br>Preparing and carrying out of assessment in all four skills<br>Reviewing progress |
| 6 | **Copymasters (*Feuilles*)**<br>**OxBox** | Reinforcement and extension of the language of the unit using extra resources<br>Reviewing progress via the Checklist on page 34, *Vocabulaire*<br>Going back over aspects of the unit which need reviewing after *Clic-test!* |

# 4.1 Une robe jaune, j'adore!

## *Planner*

> ### Objectives
> - Name clothes and colours
> - Say which clothes you like and dislike

> ### Resources
> Students' Book, pages 28–29
> CD 3, tracks 1–3
> OxBox *Clic! 2 Star, Unité 4, J'aime ou Je n'aime pas; C'est quelle couleur?; Gender Matters*
> Copymaster 42, 45, 49, *Clic! 2 Star*

> ### Key language
> *une robe, un pantalon, un T-shirt, un sweat à capuche, une chemise, une veste, un blouson, une jupe, des baskets*
> *noir(e), vert(e), bleu(e), gris(e), blanc/blanche, rouge, jaune, rose*
> *Je n'aime pas. J'aime bien. Ça va. J'adore! C'est très cool! Bof, c'est pas terrible. Je déteste! C'est moche!*

> ### Grammar
> Agreement of colours with clothes, masculine/feminine

> ### Framework reference
> 1.1, 1.3, 4.3

> ### Starters
> - Recap on colours in French. How many colours can students remember from Book 1? Write a list of colours as they are mentioned, then delete them and play a game of Hangman with the words.
> - Use the grid of clothes on page 28 for a *Loto* game. Students list four numbers between one and nine, corresponding to the numbered squares in the grid. Call out an item of clothing from the grid, such as *une chemise*. Students tick off the corresponding number (2), if they have it on their list. The winner is the first person to tick everything off their list. Keep a note of what you call and ask the winner to read back their list. A confident student could take over as the *Loto* caller.

> ### Plenaries
> - Working in pairs, students estimate how many of the nine items of clothing from the key language they think they will be able to list from memory, including correct gender. Explain that they will score a point for each item they recall but will lose points if they fail to meet their estimated figure. Tell them also that they cannot attempt more than the number of items they estimate. For example, a student estimates nine items, but can only manage eight, so he/she wins eight points but loses a point because of failing to meet the original estimate, giving a total of seven points. Another student estimates seven items but finds after naming seven items that he/she can actually remember eight; he/she must stop at seven because this was the original estimate. This means that the game is a gamble: students need to take risks in order to win points, but if they take too big a risk they could end up losing.
> - After working on the opinion phrases, suggest a few other topics for discussion, such as music, food, film titles, sports and holiday destinations. As a class, exchange opinions on some of the topics.
>   Student A: *Le nouveau film de …, c'est pas terrible.*
>   Student B: *Bof, c'est terrible.*
>   Student C: *Mais non! Moi, j'adore!*
>   Encourage students to speak as convincingly as possible, using appropriate intonation, facial expressions, gestures, etc.

> ### Assessment opportunities
> - Listening: Students' Book page 29, exercise 6
> - Writing: Students' Book page 29, exercise 7

---

AT 1.1

AT 2.1

**1 Écoute, lis et répète.**

- Students listen, while looking at the pictures and captions in their books, and repeat each one, taking care with accurate pronunciation.
- Ask students to look carefully at the words for the items of clothing. How many of them are like the English words? One or two could be confusing, such as *une veste* meaning 'a jacket', not a vest and *un blouson* also meaning 'a jacket', not a blouse.

 **CD 3, track 1**    page 28, activité 1

1 un sweat à capuche
2 une chemise
3 un T-shirt
4 une veste
5 un blouson
6 un pantalon
7 une jupe
8 une robe
9 des baskets

## Preparation

- Make sure that students are familiar with the colours, if you have not already done so in the Starter.
- Point out that colour words act like adjectives, so they have to agree with the item they are describing. Some colours need to add e on the end for feminine items. However, those already ending in e don't change (*rouge, rose*). There are also some irregular adjectives, such as *blanc/blanche*. Point out the difference in pronunciation the additional e makes in some cases, such as *vert(e)* and *gris(e)*.

 - Further practice of colours is provided on OxBox, *C'est quelle couleur?* A few extra colours are also included.

 **2 Écoute et lis (1–9). C'est quelle photo? Note la couleur.**

- Students hear the clothes mentioned, this time with colours. They note the number of the item from the photos in exercise 1 as well as the colour in French.
- Point out that, unlike in English, colour words come after the item they are describing in French.

*Answers*: 1 picture 8 jaune; 2 picture 6 vert; 3 picture 9 bleu; 4 picture 3 rose; 5 picture 1 gris; 6 picture 2 bleue; 7 picture 4 blanche; 8 picture 5 rouge; 9 picture 7 rouge et noire

🎧 **CD 3, track 2**      page 28, activité 2

1. une robe jaune
2. un pantalon vert
3. les baskets bleues
4. un T-shirt rose
5. un sweat à capuche gris
6. une chemise bleue
7. une veste blanche
8. un blouson rouge
9. une jupe rouge et noire

 **3 À deux.**

 - Students work in pairs. One covers up an item of clothing from the grid and the other student says what it is, including the colour.

 **4 Dessine et écris la couleur.**

- Students choose four or five items of clothing from the grid to draw. They change the colour and write a new label for each picture. Remind students to make the colour adjective agree with the item each time. Point out that if they are describing *les baskets*, they will need to make the adjective feminine and add an *s* as it is a plural word.

## Preparation

- Recap on opinion phrases students already know. Make a note of suggestions on the board. The next part of the spread concentrates on opinion phrases, some of which will already be familiar to students from other topics.

 **5a Relie chaque photo et deux bulles.**

- Students match each of the speech bubbles to one of the three images depicting opinions. If students need more support, read out the texts and students can use voice intonation as an additional clue.
- Go over precisely what each phrase means and encourage students to repeat them all with correct intonation and expressions.

*Answers*: 1 b, d; 2 a, f; 3 c, e

**5b Écoute et vérifie. (1–3)**

- Students listen to the audio to check their answers, using intonation to help understanding of positive, negative and indifferent opinions.

**Follow-up**

- Further practice of clothes and opinions (including a couple of extra opinions) is provided on OxBox *J'aime ou Je n'aime pas*.

🎧 **CD 3, track 3**      page 29, activités 5b et 6

1. – Un blouson rouge. J'adore! C'est très cool!
   – Un sweat à capuche gris, j'aime bien.
2. – Une jupe rouge et noire? Je n'aime pas!
   – Une veste blanche ... Je déteste! C'est moche!
3. – Une chemise bleue? Euh ... Ça va ...
   – Un pantalon vert? Bof, c'est pas terrible.

**6 Réécoute. C'est quels vêtements?**

- Students listen again to the audio and note which items of clothing are mentioned each time from the grid of clothes in exercise 1.

*Answers*: 1 pictures 5, 1; 2 pictures 7, 4; 3 pictures 2, 6

**7 Écris.**

- Students write sentences for each item from the grid of clothes in exercise 1. They write the item, its colour and also their opinion of it.

**Follow-up**

 - Further activities on clothes, colours and opinions are provided on Copymaster 42.

**4** Planète mode!

*Answers*: **1** a blue jeans; b white and pink socks; c red skirt; d grey and black scarf; e purple baseball cap; f green shorts; g brown jacket; h white and blue trainers; i orange dress; j grey shoes

Answers: **2** <u>positive</u>: il est trop beau, la classe, j'adore, c'est cool, elle est trop belle, c'est pas mal; <u>negative</u>: je déteste, c'est moche, c'est nul, c'est l'horreur, c'est pas terrible, c'est pas mal

- Copymaster 45 has a Battleships-style game where students can practise asking questions and giving positive or negative responses.

- If you wish to do further work on feminine and masculine adjectives and gender in general, this is covered on an OxBox PowerPoint, Gender Matters.

**C49**
- For further work on gender, students could work from Copymaster 49.

*Answers*:

|  | masculine | feminine | plural (m. and f.) |
|---|---|---|---|
| **determiners:** |  |  |  |
| a | un | une | – |
| some |  |  | des |
| the | le | la | les |
| my | mon | ma | mes |
| this/these | ce | cette | ces |
| **pronouns** (it/them) | le | la | les |
| **adjectives** (e.g. black) | noir | noire | noirs, noires |
| **nouns with masc/fem forms** | musicien | musicienne | musiciens, musiciennes |
|  | acteur | actrice | acteurs, actrices |
|  | vendeur | vendeuse | vendeurs, vendeuses |
|  | boucher | bouchère | bouchers, bouchères |
|  | client | cliente | clients, clientes |
|  | facteur | factrice | facteurs, factrices |
|  | électricien | électricienne | électriciens, électriciennes |
|  | boulanger | boulangère | boulangers, boulangères |
|  | conducteur | conductrice | conducteurs, conductrices |

# 4.2 C'est quoi, ton style préféré?

pages 30–31

## *Planner*

> ### Objectives
> - Say what your favourite look is
> - Say what you normally wear

> ### Resources
> Students' Book, pages 30–31
> CD 3, tracks 4–5
> OxBox *Clic! 2 Star, Unité 4, C'est quoi, ton style?*

> ### Key language
> *C'est quoi, ton style préféré?*
> *Mon style préféré, c'est le style (rappeur, surfeur, gothique).*
> *En générale, je mets des chaussures (noires), un jean (noir), une casquette (bleue), un short (baggy).*

> ### Grammar
> Agreement of plural adjectives

> ### Framework reference
> 2.1, 4.2, 5.2

> ### Starters
> - Ask students to choose a teenager pictured on page 30 and to write down as many words and phrases as they can to describe him/her. Encourage students to refer to clothes, colours and physical appearance, and to invent details of personality, likes and dislikes, etc. Pool ideas.

- Speed Duel. Two students stand up. Call out one of the three styles from page 30 and students compete to name an accessory associated with the style. Teacher: *le style rappeur*
  Student: *un pantalon baggy*
  The first student to give a correct answer, remains standing, while the opponent sits down and is replaced by another challenger. Continue around the class.

> ### Plenaries
> - Working in pairs, students close their books and try to remember as much as they can about each teenager's style from page 30. Encourage students to give full sentences, but if this is too difficult, ask them to list words. Students take turns to give a detail each. The aim is to be the last person to speak, so when neither partner can add anything further, the winner is the person who had the final word.
> - Ask students to choose a celebrity, such as a sportsperson, singer, musician, television personality or actor. They should imagine they are this person and write a magazine article about their favourite style: *Mon style préféré, c'est …* *En général, je mets …* Ask students to read their descriptions to the rest of the class to see if they can identify the celebrity being described.

> ### Assessment opportunities
> - Writing: Students' Book page 31, exercise 5

**1a Écoute, lis et répète.**

- Students listen to three people saying what their favourite style is and repeat both the question and answer, copying intonation as well as pronunciation.
- If you have not already done so in the Starter, look at the photos together and discuss the styles of surfer, rapper and goth. Ask students what they know about the clothes people following these groups would wear.

**CD 3, track 4**  page 30, activité 1a

1 – C'est quoi, ton style préféré?
  – Mon style préféré, c'est le style rappeur.
2 – C'est quoi, ton style préféré?
  – Mon style préféré, c'est le style surfeur.
3 – C'est quoi, ton style préféré?
  – Mon style préféré, c'est le style gothique.

 **1b Relie.**

- Students listen again and match each speech bubble to the correct picture.

*Answers*: A 3; B 1; C 2

## Top Tips!

- This box points out that sometimes clothes words are the same or similar in English and French. However, some clothes words do not mean the same: *robe* means 'dress' not 'robe' and *baskets* have nothing to do with 'basket' in English!

 **2 Parle.**

- Students choose their favourite style and go round the class asking others what their favourite style is. They have to find three people with the same style choice as themselves.

 **3a Lis. Trouve le français.**

- Students read the speech bubbles and find the French phrases for the English ones listed. Even if students do not understand every word, they should be able to work out the phrases from the words they do understand.

*Answers*: 1 Tu mets quoi ...? 2 En général, je mets une robe; 3 et des chaussures noires; 4 Je mets aussi une casquette; 5 je mets un jogging; 6 ben ... en général

**3b Relis. Qui parle?**

- Students read the speech bubbles again and match them to a picture from page 30.
- Point out that *je mets* means 'I wear', as students will use this phrase in subsequent activities.

*Answers*: a C; b A; c B

 **4 Écoute et regarde les photos. Qui parle? (1–3)**

- Students listen and say which of the three pictures each person speaking is referring to.

*Answers*: 1 b; 2 a; 3 c

 **CD 3, track 5**  page 31, activité 4

1 – En général, je mets un jean bleu, un T-shirt rouge et une veste bleue.
2 – En général, je mets un pantalon baggy bleu, un sweat à capuche bleu et des baskets blanches.
3 – En général, je mets une veste noire, un T-shirt noir et un pantalon noir.

 **5 Écris des bulles.**

- Students write a speech bubble for each of the people pictured in exercise 4, starting with *Je mets ...*

## Grammaire

- Point out what happens to adjectives of colour when they describe plural items: if they are masculine; they add *s* and if they are feminine plural, they add es (*baskets, chaussures*).

**Follow-up**

- As extension, you could do further work on the different styles, using two interactive activities on OxBox, *C'est quoi, ton style? (1) (2)*.
- Students choose someone from the class as a model and invent a new look for him/her. They could work on this individually or in pairs. Ideally, allow students to produce 'before and after' photos, by taking a digital photo of their model, and then (if suitable software is available) manipulating the digital image to show the new look. Perhaps this could be done as a cross-curricular project with art or ICT. Alternatively, students could draw or find pictures of the proposed new clothing, hairstyle, accessories, etc. and build up a collage of the new look.

## 4.3 Je peux essayer?

---

# *Planner*

> **Objectives**
- Shop for clothes

> **Resources**

Students' Book, pages 32–33
CD 3, tracks 6–8
Video clip 5, *Clic! 2 Star*
OxBox *Clic! 2 Star, Unité 4, Le shopping; Faire les magasins*
Copymaster 43, 44, 52, *Clic! 2 Star*
CD 3, tracks 62–63

> **Key language**

*Bonjour! Je peux vous aider?*
*Je voudrais (une robe).*
*Je peux essayer?*
*Bien sûr. Les cabines sont là.*
*Ça va?*
*Oui, ça va, je prends/Non, c'est trop (petit, grand, cher).*

> **Grammar**

*je voudrais*
*je peux*

> **Framework reference**

1.4, 3.1, 5.8

> **Starters**
- To prepare for work on the *Mini-guide du shopping*, ask students to work in pairs to gather, in English, any key phrases they would expect to hear when shopping for clothes. Tell them to list the language in two columns: things they as the shopper might say (No, thanks, I'm just looking. Can I try this on, please?) and things the shop assistant might say (Can I help you? What size

are you?). After looking at the *Mini-guide* in their books, students find out how many phrases they guessed correctly.
- Display two columns of key language from the *Mini-guide*, with the French in one column and the English translations in the other, but in the wrong order. Challenge students to match the English to the French within a time limit.

> **Plenaries**
- Display a shopping dialogue on the board, like the one below, but place the lines out of sequence. Challenge students to sort the lines into the correct sequence. Point out that the dialogue is in two halves (before and after trying on clothes) and the first line of each part is in the correct position.
  - *Bonjour! Je peux vous aider?*
  - *Oui, je voudrais une veste bleue.*
  - *Voilà – une veste bleue.*
  - *Je peux essayer?*
  - *Oui, bien sur, les cabines sont là, à droite …*
  *(Plus tard)*
  - *Ça va?*
  - *Oui, ça me va. C'est combien?*
  - *C'est 20 euros.*
  - *Oui, je prends. Merci, madame.*
- Display the correct version of the dialogue from the above Plenary and read it through with the class a few times. Delete one or two words or phrases and challenge pairs of students to read it out loud, filling in the missing words from memory. Delete even more words and phrases and challenge pairs to read it again. Continue until only a skeleton of the original text remains. Can any pairs reconstruct the whole dialogue from memory?

> **Assessment opportunities**
- Writing: Students' Book page 33, exercise 5a
- Speaking: Students' Book page 33, exercise 5b

---

## Preparation
- Look together at the photos on page 32 and ask students to say as much as they can about them, such as the items of clothing and colours, etc. Look at the speech bubbles along with the photos, if you have not already done so in the Starter, and elicit what the phrases mean. If necessary, give students the English phrases to match up.

| AT 1.2 |
| AT 2.2 |
| AT 3.2 |

**1 Écoute, lis et répète. Qui parle?**
- Students listen to nine extracts from the shopping guide and repeat each one. They then identify whether it is the customer or the shop assistant speaking each time.

*Answers:* 1 shop assistant; 2 customer; 3 customer; 4 shop assistant; 5 shop assistant; 6 customer; 7 customer; 8 customer; 9 customer

**CD 3, track 6**  page 32, activité 1

1 Bonjour! Je peux vous aider?
2 Je voudrais un T-shirt.
3 Je peux essayer?
4 Bien sûr. Les cabines sont là.
5 Ça va?
6 Oui, ça va, je prends.
7 Non, c'est trop petit.
8 Non, c'est trop grand.
9 Non, c'est trop cher.

**2 Écoute et note. (1–4)**

- Students listen to four shopping dialogues and answer the questions in English for each one.

*Answers*: 1 pink dress; no, too small; 2 jeans; no, too big; 3 skirt and jacket; yes; 4 trainers; no, too expensive

**CD 3, track 7**                     page 32, activité 2

1 – Bonjour! Je peux vous aider?
  – Je voudrais une robe rose. Je peux essayer?
  – Bien sûr. Les cabines sont là.
  – Ça va?
  – Non, c'est trop petit.

2 – Bonjour! Je peux vous aider?
  – Je voudrais un jean. Je peux essayer?
  – Bien sûr. Les cabines sont là.
  – Ça va?
  – Non, c'est trop grand.

3 – Bonjour! Je peux vous aider?
  – Je voudrais une jupe et une veste. Je peux essayer?
  – Bien sûr. Les cabines sont là.
  – Ça va?
  – Oui, ça va, je prends.

4 – Bonjour! Je peux vous aider?
  – Je voudrais des baskets. Je peux essayer?
  – Oui, bien sûr.
  – Ça va?
  – Non, c'est trop cher.

 **3a À deux.**

- Students adapt the dialogue from the shopping guide to purchase the items pictured.

 **3b Écris une conversation.**

- Students write one of their shopping dialogues, taking care with accurate spellings. Ask students to check their partner's work for spelling and use of accents.

 **4 Regarde le clip. Réponds.**

- Play the video clip which shows Nina, Joe and Max shopping for clothes in Paris.
- Students answer the questions in English.

*Answers*: a cap, 10 euros; b Joe; c T-shirt, no, it's a bit big; d it's great

 **Video clip 5**          page 33, activité 4

**CD 3, track 8**

Nina: Ah, trop cool, cette casquette! J'adore mettre des casquettes pour sortir. En plus, elle est pas chère, dix euros, ça va. Et toi, Joe, tu aimes mettre quoi pour sortir?

Joe: Moi, mon* tenue préférée, c'est un T-shirt, un jean et des baskets.
Max: Oui, c'est pas très original, mais c'est ce qu'il y a de mieux.
Max: J'adore cette boutique, il y a plein de trucs super ici.
Nina: Oui, moi, j'achète mes jeans et mes T-shirts ici. J'aime bien ce sweat à capuche. Et toi, Joe?
Joe: Moi, j'aime bien ce sweat au* capuche.
Max: Moi, je déteste les capuches. Mais j'adore les jeans.
Joe: Oui, les jeans, c'est cool.
Nina: Pas mal, la jupe noire à pois.
Max/Joe: Bof!
Nina: Ouais … Ah non, je préfère ce T-shirt à rayures … Bonjour.
Shop assistant: Bonjour. Je peux vous renseigner?
Nina: Oui, je voudrais essayer ce T-shirt, s'il vous plaît.
Shop assistant: Oui, les cabines d'essayage sont au fond du magasin.
Nina: Merci.

Joe: Je peux essayer ce sweat à carreaux? Je ne connais pas la taille française.
Shop assistant: Je pense que ça ira. Tu peux y aller.
Joe: OK, merci.

Nina: Qu'est-ce que tu en penses?
Max: Ça va.
Nina: C'est un peu grand quand même.
Joe: Qu'est-ce que vous en pensez? C'est cool, non?
Max: Oui, c'est cool. Bon, à moi. Je vais essayer ça.

Max: Qu'est-ce que vous en pensez?
Nina: La classe!
Joe: La classe?
Nina: Ben oui. Ça lui va bien.
Joe: Ah oui. La classe!

Nina: Je n'ai pas acheté le T-shirt à rayures.
Joe: J'ai acheté une* sweat à carreaux et à capuche.
Max: J'ai acheté un T-shirt bleu.

**Point langue**
Pas mal, la jupe noire à pois.
C'est un peu grand …
Je n'ai pas acheté le T-shirt à rayures.
J'ai acheté un T-shirt bleu.

*\* Remind students that Joe is English and sometimes makes mistakes when speaking French. Here, he says "mon tenue préférée" when it should be "ma", "ce sweat au capuche" instead of "à capuche", and at the end of the clip "une sweat" instead of "un".*

### Follow-up

 C52

- Further activities on the video clip are provided on page 88, *Clic-vidéo* of the Students' Book and also on Copymaster 52.

*Answers:* **1** a Nina; b Joe; c Max; d Nina, Max; e Joe; f Nina; g Nina, Joe; h Joe; i Max
Answers: **2** ma tenue préférée – *my favourite outfit*; je peux vous renseigner? – *can I help you?*; les cabines d'essayage – *the fitting rooms*; ça lui va bien – *it suits/ fits him*; je n'ai pas acheté – *I haven't bought/didn't buy*
Answers: **3** a 4; b 6; c 5; d 1; e 2; f 3

- An interactive activity on parts of the video clip is also available on OxBox, *Le shopping*.
- Play the video again and talk about the types of shop that appear, the clothing styles, colours, patterns, etc. Compare with students' local shops and their clothing styles. Elicit the meanings of *à rayures* and *à carreaux*, and *à pois*.

 AT 4.3–4 **5a Invente une scène et écris.**

- Students imagine a scene in a clothes shop. They adapt the dialogue in the example to produce their own scene. Encourage students to add humour to their dialogues.

 AT 2.3–4 **5b À deux.**

- Students act out their scene from exercise 5. Choose a few students to perform for the rest of the class. The class evaluates each performance.

### Follow-up

 C43

- Further reading activities on shopping can be found on Copymaster 43.

*Answers:* **1** a 3; b 8; c 6; d 10; e 9; f 2; g 1; h 7; i 4; j 5; k 14; l 16; m 12; n 15; o 11; p 13
Answers: **2** a red and blue; b yellow and orange; c purple; d black; e brown; f pink and red

 C44

- For further listening activities on shopping, see Copymaster 44.

*Answers:* 1 1 e; 2 d; 3 b; 4 c; 5 f; 6 a

---

 **CD 3, track 62** Feuille 44, *Clic! 2 Star*, activité 1

**1** – C'est quoi, ton style préféré?
– Euh, j'aime mettre un jean, un sweat, un T-shirt et des baskets. Je mets ça tous les weekends.

**2** – Paul, qu'est-ce que tu mets le weekend?
– D'habitude, je mets un pantalon, une chemise et un blouson. C'est confortable.

**3** – Et Claire, tu mets quoi pendant les vacances?
– Ah, j'aime les vacances! Je mets un short, un T-shirt, des lunettes de soleil et des sandales.

**4** – Sophie, qu'est-ce que tu portes au mariage de ta cousine?
– Ah, c'est moche! Je dois porter une jupe, une chemise, une veste et des chaussures roses.

**5** – Et Simon, tu portes quoi quand tu vas à un mariage?
– Je mets un pantalon, une chemise, une veste et des chaussures. Je déteste ça!

**6** – Et Caroline, qu'est-ce que tu portes pour faire du sport?
– Je mets un short, un T-shirt, un sweat à capuche, des chaussettes et des baskets. Je voudrais porter une marque de sport mais on ne peut pas au lycée!

*Answers:* 2 1 a; 2 c; 3 d; 4 b, c

---

 **CD 3, track 63** Feuille 44, *Clic! 2 Star*, activité 2

**1** – Je peux vous aider, mademoiselle?
– Oui, je voudrais essayer ce pantalon.
– D'accord, les cabines sont là-bas …
– Ça va?
– Non, il est beaucoup trop grand.

**2** – Vous avez essayé le blouson, monsieur?
– Oui, et il me va bien. C'est combien?
– C'est 45 euros.
– Oh, c'est trop cher. Je ne le prends pas!

**3** – Regarde! J'ai trouvé cette robe – elle est superbe!
– Ah, oui, je l'adore!
– Mais où sont les cabines?

**4** – Vous avez essayé la veste, monsieur?
– Oui, mais elle est trop petite.
– Vous voulez essayer une veste plus grande.
– Euh, non merci … elle est aussi très chère

---

- Students can carry out the multichoice activity from OxBox, *Faire les magasins*.

# 4.4 Vocabulaire

## Planner

> **Resources**
Students' Book, page 34

> **Objectives**
• *Vocabulaire*: to provide a theme-based summary of the key language of the unit, which students can use as a reference or as an aid to learning
• To practise pronunciation

> **Framework reference**
4.1, 5.5

### Using the vocabulary page

• Encourage students to use the *Vocabulaire* page as a reference point throughout the unit. It can also serve as a useful revision tool before students do the *Clic-test!*
• Vocabulary is listed spread-by-spread and you could either ask students to learn each section for homework after each spread is completed, or set the whole page as a homework task before starting work on the test. Most students learn shorter sections best, so often it is better to give them manageable chunks to learn at a time.
• Encourage students to use different techniques to help them learn the vocabulary:
  – Cover up the English and see what they can remember; write down any words they can't remember and test themselves again on those words.
  – Cover up the French and see if they can remember the words or phrases this way round.

– Make word cards with English on one side and French on the other. Students can then test themselves to see what they can remember. Put any cards they can't remember on one side and go over those again at the end.
  – Work in pairs to test each other, either using the vocabulary list or the word cards.
• Record themselves saying the words both in English and French. Saying words and phrases out loud can often help with memorising them.

### Sound French!

• *Aim:* To practise pronunciation
• The point practised here is the *ch* sound.
• Ask students to repeat the phrases on the page several times.
• Ask students to find more examples of the *ch* sound in the vocabulary list and practise saying the words out loud.

# 4.4 Clic-test!

## Planner

The page is divided into four sections: listening, speaking, reading and writing.

> **Objectives**
• To enable students to recap on the language and structures of the unit

• To provide an opportunity for quick testing of all four skills

> **Resources**
Students' Book, page 35
CD 3, track 9

> **Framework reference**
5.7, 5.8

**AT 1.2** **1 Écoute! (1–5)**
• Students listen and match each item of clothing to its correct colour.

*Answers*: 1 c; 2 f; 3 b; 4 a; 5 d

 **CD 3, track 9**     page 35, activité 1

1 Je mets un pantalon bleu.
2 J'adore le sweat à capuche rouge.
3 Je voudrais un short noir et blanc, s'il vous plaît.
4 Le blouson jaune est trop grand et trop cher.
5 Je n'aime pas les baskets vertes. C'est moche.

**AT 3.2** **2 Lis!**
• Students match each speech bubble to one of the pictures of four teenagers.

*Answers*: a 3; b 1; c 4; d 2; e 4

**AT 4.2–3** **3 Écris!**
• Students write a speech bubble for each person, describing what they are wearing.

*Answers*: a Je mets un pantalon noir, un T-shirt blanc et des chaussures noires. b Je mets une casquette bleue, un T-shirt noir, une veste rouge, un pantalon/jeans bleu et les baskets blanches.

## 4 Planète mode!

**4 Parle!**

AT 2.2–3

• Students complete the conversation in a clothes shop with a partner.

*Answers:* a Bonjour! b Je voudrais une chemise verte et jaune. c Je peux essayer? d Non, c'est trop petit et cher.

# À moi

## *Planner*

➤ **Objectives**
• To provide reinforcement activities for quiet work
• To provide alternative class and homework material for students who finish other activities quickly

➤ **Resources**
Students' Book, page 79

➤ **Framework reference**
2.1, 2.3, 3.1

### La Tecktonik

AT 3.3 **1 Read about this look. Which paragraph (A–D) …**

• Students read for gist before looking out for key words to help them answer the questions about a new look.

*Answers:* 1 A; 2 C; 3 B; 4 D

AT 3.3 **2 Read again. Choose a or b in each sentence.**

• Students now look at more of the detail in the text to choose the correct multichoice answers.

*Answers:* 1 b; 2 a; 3 b; 4 b; 5 a

AT 4.2 **3 Write your opinion about the Tecktonik look.**

• Students use the example given, plus any other opinion phrases they know, to write what they think about the *Tecktonik* look.

# Clic-vidéo

## *Planner*

➤ **Objectives**
• To provide extended listening practice recycling the language of the whole unit

➤ **Resources**
Students' Book, page 88
Video clip 5, *Clic! 2 Star*
CD 3, track 10

➤ **Framework reference**
1.2, 3.1, 3.2

AT 1.3–4 **1 Watch the video clip. Which of the following do you see Nina, Max and Joe try on. Choose a or b?**

• Students watch the video and choose a or b for each answer.

*Answers:* 1 a; 2 b; 3 b; 4 a; 5 b

 **Video clip 5**      page 88, activités 1, 2 et 3

 **CD 3, track 10**

*See tapescript from 4.3, page 147*

 **2 Watch again. Who says the following? Max, Nina or Joe?**

• Students watch the clip again and identify which teenager says each phrase.

*Answers:* a Joe; b Max; c Nina; d Nina; e Joe; f Max

AT 1.3–4 **3a Which of these opinion words do you hear?**

• Students now listen for the opinion words listed.

*Answers:* C'est cool! Bof! Ça va. La classe! J'adore! Je déteste!

AT 1.3–4 / AT 2.2 **3b Use the opinions in 3a to say what you think of the clothes in the clip.**

• Students give their opinion of the clothes shown in the video clip. Play the clip again and pause it when each item is shown to elicit various opinions.

# 5 En forme

| Unité 5: En forme  Overview grid | | | | | | |
|---|---|---|---|---|---|---|
| **Page reference** | **Contexts and objectives** | **Grammar** | **Language strategies and pronunciation** | **Key language** | **Framework** | **AT level** |
| 36–37<br>**5.1 Le sport, j'adore!** | • Say which sports you like and don't like<br>• Say which sports you play and don't play | • Negative: *je ne joue pas*<br>• *je joue au* + sports | | *J'aime/Je n'aime pas le tennis, le football, le ping-pong, le hockey, le basket, le rugby.*<br>*Je joue au (football).*<br>*Je ne joue pas au (tennis).* | 1.1, 5.5, 5.6 | 1.1–2<br>2.1–2<br>3.1–3<br>4.2 |
| 38–39<br>**5.2 Fais du sport!** | • Talk about more sports you do<br>• Say how often you do sport | • *du, de la, de l'* + sports | Frequency expressions | *Je fais du ski, du jogging, du skateboard, du vélo, de la natation, de l'équitation.*<br>*tous les jours, de temps en temps*<br>*une, deux, trois fois par semaine* | 1.2, 2.4, 4.4, 5.1 | 1.2–4<br>2.2<br>3.3<br>4.2–3 |
| 40–41<br>**5.3 Futur champion?** | • Talk about daily routine<br>• Talk about healthy lifestyle | • Reflexive verbs: *je, tu* | | *Je me réveille à (huit heures).*<br>*À midi, je mange un sandwich/des chips.*<br>*Je joue (au basket).*<br>*Je fais (de la natation).*<br>*Je m'entraîne (une fois par semaine).*<br>*Je fume. Je ne fume pas.*<br>*Je me couche à (dix) heures.* | 1.4, 4.5, 5.4 | 1.2–3<br>2.2–3<br>3.2–3<br>4.2–3 |
| 42<br>**5.4 Vocabulaire** | • Practise pronunciation | | *tion* sound | | 4.1, 5.5 | |
| 43<br>**5.4 Clic-test!** | • Recap on the language structures of the unit<br>• Provide an opportunity for quick testing of all four skills | | | | 5.7, 5.8 | 1.1–2<br>2.2<br>3.2<br>4.2–3 |
| 80<br>**À moi** | • Provide reinforcement activities for self-access work | | | | 2.1, 2.2, 2.4 | 3.2–3<br>4.2 |
| 89<br>**Clic-vidéo** | • Provide extended listening practice recycling the language of the whole unit using the video | | | | 1.2, 1.3 | 1.3–4 |

| MEDIUM TERM GRID Week-by-week overview (assuming six weeks' work or approximately 10–12.5 hours) | | |
|---|---|---|

**About Unit 5, *En forme***

In this unit, students learn to talk about sports, daily routine and a healthy lifestyle. They use *je joue au* + sport and the negative *je ne joue pas au* + sport. They use the verb *faire* with *du, de la* and *de l'*, some reflexive verbs in the *je/tu* forms and frequency expressions.

New vocabulary includes types of sports used with *jouer* and *faire*, frequency expressions and phrases and verbs to do with a healthy lifestyle. Revised language includes *j'aime* and
*je n'aime pas* to give opinions.

Reading, listening and comprehension skills are developed through a variety of text, audio and video materials.

| Week | Resources | Objectives |
|---|---|---|
| 1 | **5.1 Le sport, j'adore!** | Naming sports<br>Using *j'aime* and *je n'aime pas* to say which sports you like and don't like<br>Using *je joue au* and *je ne joue pas au* to say which sports you play and don't play |
| 2 | **5.2 Fais du sport!** | Using *faire* + *du, de la, de l'* to talk about other sports you do<br>Saying how often you do sport<br>Using frequency expressions |
| 3 | **5.3 Futur champion?** | Using reflexive verbs in the *je* and *tu* forms to talk about daily routine (*se réveiller, s'entraîner*)<br>Talking about healthy lifestyle |
| 4 | **Sound French!** (p42)<br>**À moi** (p80)<br>**Clic-vidéo** (p89) | Practising pronunciation (*tion* sound)<br>Additional reading and writing practice<br>Using the video for reinforcement, extension and follow-up work |
| 5 | **5.4 Vocabulaire**<br>**Clic-test!** | Learning vocabulary<br>Recapping on vocabulary of unit<br>Preparing and carrying out of assessment in all four skills<br>Reviewing progress |
| 6 | **Copymasters (*Feuilles*)**<br>**OxBox** | Reinforcement and extension of the language of the unit using extra resources<br>Reviewing progress via the Checklist on page 42, *Vocabulaire*<br>Going back over aspects of the unit which need reviewing after *Clic-test!* |

# 5.1 Le sport, j'adore!

## *Planner*

> ### Objectives
> - Say which sports you like and don't like
> - Say which sports you play and don't play

> ### Resources
> Students' Book, pages 36–37
> CD 3, tracks 11–12

> ### Key language
> *J'aime/Je n'aime pas le tennis, le football, le ping-pong, le hockey, le basket, le rugby.*
> *Je joue au (football).*
> *Je ne joue pas au (tennis).*

> ### Grammar
> Negative: *je ne joue pas*
> *je joue au* + sports

> ### Framework reference
> 1.1, 5.5, 5.6

> ### Starters
> - Display the photos of the six sports from page 36, along with their French names, on the whiteboard. Ask students to deduce what the topic of this spread is and to guess how the sports may be pronounced in French. Give students two minutes with a partner to categorise the sports into two groups – any justifiable answers can be accepted, such as ping-pong and tennis are not team sports; basketball and rugby are the only sports where you can use your hands, etc.

> - Play Pictionary (either as a whole class or in pairs or small groups) using sports vocabulary. One student begins drawing a picture or symbol to represent a sport; the others try to guess as quickly as possible which sport it represents and name it in French, including gender. If correct, this student takes over and draws a picture to represent another sport. For an alternative version of this game, students could mime the sports instead of drawing them.

> ### Plenaries
> - Provide dictionaries and encourage students to find new sports in addition to those featured in Unit 5. Allow time for students to compare their responses with a partner and for whole class feedback.
> - Ask students to write down their three favourite sports. They should then go around the class trying to find someone who has written down the same choices.
> Student A: *Tu aimes le rugby?*
> Student B: *Non, je n'aime pas le rugby.*
> Student A: *Tu aimes le tennis?*
> Student C: *Oui! J'aime le tennis.*
> The winner is the first person to find an exact match for all three sports, or the person who finds most matches within a set time limit.

> ### Assessment opportunities
> - Reading: Students' Book page 37, exercise 6
> - Writing: Students' Book page 37, exercise 7

---

 **1 Relie les sports a–f aux photos 1–6.**
- Students match the name of each sport to its corresponding photo.

*Answers:* a 3; b 1; c 4; d 6; e 2; f 5

 **2 Écoute et répète.**
- Students listen to the pronunciation of the sports and repeat each one, taking care with pronunciation and intonation. The sentences use *J'aime* and *Je n'aime pas* with the sports. Before students listen, recap on these expressions to establish meaning.
- Ask students to point to the appropriate photo as they are speaking.
- Students could listen again and make the thumbs-up or thumbs-down sign, according to whether the speakers like the sports or not.

 **CD 3, track 11**  page 36, activité 2
- J'aime le tennis.
- J'aime le basket.
- J'aime le football.
- Je n'aime pas le ping-pong.
- Je n'aime pas le rugby.
- Je n'aime pas le hockey.
- Le sport, j'adore!

 **3 À deux.**
- Students work in pairs and take turns to throw a die. They say a sentence using *J'aime* and *Je n'aime pas* plus a sport, using the corresponding six numbered photos from exercise 1.

**AT 4.2** **4 Écris.**

- Students write six sentences to say which sports they like and don't like; they draw symbols for each.
- Ask students to check each other's work for accuracy of spelling.

### Preparation

- The next part of the spread focuses on *Je joue au* plus a sport. Look at the key language box and ask students to look at the patterns: *Je joue au* and *Je ne joue pas …* Ask students what *Je ne joue pas* means and establish that *ne … pas* is added to indicate the negative.
- If possible, hold up some sports pictures or show them on the whiteboard together with either a tick or a cross and ask students to say appropriate sentences.

**AT 1.2** **5 Regarde les photos. Écoute et note.**

- Students listen and note the number of the photos from exercise 1 in the order they are given in the teenagers' answers. They should only note the sports which the teenagers do play, not the ones which they don't.
- Ask students to listen again and note which sports are not played.

*Answers*: 6, 1, 5, 4, 2, 3

 **CD 3, track 12**                    page 37, activité 5

- Tu joues au football?
- Non, je joue au hockey.
- Dis, tu joues au football?
- Non, je joue au tennis.
- Tu joues au football?
- Non, je ne joue pas au football. Je joue au rugby.
- Tu joues au football?
- Non, je joue au ping-pong.
- Tu joues au football?
- Non, je ne joue pas au football. Je joue au basket.
- Tu joues au football?
- Oui! Je joue au football. J'aime bien le football. C'est mon sport préféré.
- Génial!

**AT 3.2–3** **6 Lis et décide.**

- Students read about which sports three people play and don't play. They note which person each symbol refers to.
- Read the texts out loud before students do the activity. Encourage students to read the texts out loud in pairs to practise pronunciation once they have completed the activity.

*Answers*: a Jojo; b Lou; c Jojo; d Lou; e Lou; f Pierre; g Jojo; h Pierre

**AT 4.2** **7 Et toi? Écris.**

- Students finish their work on this spread by writing sentences to say which of the six sports featured they play and don't play.

## 5.2    Fais du sport!                    pages 38–39

### *Planner*

> **Objectives**
> - Talk about more sports you do
> - Say how often you do sport

> **Resources**
> Students' Book, pages 38–39
> CD 3, tracks 13–15
> OxBox *Clic! 2 Star, Unité 5, Je fais du sport; J'aime faire du sport*
> Video clip 6, *Clic! 2 Star*
> Copymaster 58, *Clic! 2 Star*

> **Key language**
> *Je fais du ski, du jogging, du skateboard, du vélo, de la natation, de l'équitation.*
> *tous les jours, de temps en temps*
> *une, deux, trois fois par semaine*

> **Grammar**
> *du, de la, de l'* + sports

> **Framework reference**
> 1.2, 2.4, 4.4, 5.1

> **Starters**
> - Write on the board the six new sports from this spread: *le ski, le jogging, le skateboard, le vélo, la natation, l'équitation.* How many can students guess the meaning of? Give the English of any they cannot work out and ask them to try to find a match. For example, they may not have been able to guess *l'équitation*, but they may be able to work out once they see the English from equine/equestrian, etc.
> - Display four columns of words in a grid, as below:

| Je | joue | du | natation. |
|----|------|------|-----------|
|    | fais | de la | football. |
|    |      | de l' | équitation. |
|    |      |      | tennis. |
|    |      |      | basket. |
|    |      |      | vélo. |

Students choose an item from each column to write six sentences about doing different sports.

> **Plenaries**
> * Give students the names of the six sports. They have two minutes to work in pairs and put them in three categories: those which take *du*, *de la* and *de l'*. Can they do it in two minutes from memory?

Discuss the reasons as a class when pooling results.
* Ask students to name their favourite sports personalities. Try to ensure a range of sports is covered! Write the names on the board and invite students to choose their five favourites, pointing out that their list cannot have the same sport twice and must only have one footballer, one tennis player, one cyclist, etc. Challenge students to write a sentence for each personality, saying which sport they do and how often they train: *Salut! Je m'appelle Lance Armstrong. Je fais du vélo tous les jours.*

> **Assessment opportunities**
> * Writing: Students' Book page 39, exercise 7

---

 **1 Écoute, lis et répète.**

* Students listen to the expressions using *faire* and they repeat each one, taking care with pronunciation. Refer students to the point in the grammar box.
* If you have not already done so in the Starter, establish that students are clear about the meaning of all the sports.

**CD 3, track 13**          page 38, activité 1

– Tu fais quel sport?
1 Je fais du ski.
2 Je fais du jogging.
3 Je fais du skateboard.
4 Je fais du vélo.
5 Je fais de la natation.
6 Je fais de l'équitation.

## Grammaire

* The key language box points out that some sports use the verb *faire* and not *jouer* when it is more to do with 'doing' a sport rather than 'playing'. Often *jouer* is used for team games and *faire* for individual sports.
* Ask students why some sports take *du*, *de la* or *de l'* and establish that masculine sports take *du* feminine sports take *de la*, and sports beginning with a vowel take *de l'*.

**AT 1.3–4** **2 Regarde le clip. On parle de quels sports?**

* Students watch the first part of the video clip, where Joe and Nina are talking, and note the numbers of the corresponding sports from exercise 1 they mention.
* Students will have an opportunity to view the rest of the video at the end of the unit in Clic-vidéo.

*Answers*: 2, 6, 1, 5

 **Video clip 6**          page 38, activité 2

 **CD 3, track 14**

Nina: J'aime bien faire du sport. Je fais du jogging deux fois par semaine. Et toi?
Joe: Moi aussi, j'adore le sport. Devine quel sport je fais.
Nina: Euh … du judo?
Joe: Non.
Nina: De la musculation alors?
Joe: Non, c'est trop dur.
Nina: Du foot?
Joe: Oui, un peu. Je joue une fois par semaine avec mes copains. Mais je pratique un autre sport. Devine.
Nina: Ah … le basket!
Joe: Exactement. Je m'entraîne quatre heures par semaine.
Nina: Waouh! Tu es sportif.
Joe: Et toi? Tu fais un autre sport? De l'équitation?
Nina: Non.
Joe: Du ski?
Nina: Quelquefois.
Joe: De la natation?
Nina: Oui, exactement! Bon, on va chercher Max à son cours de tennis?
Joe: OK, on y va.

**AT 2.2** **3 À deux: interviews.**

* Students work in pairs. One student chooses a person (a–d) and answers their partner's questions about what sports they do. The student asking the questions must identify which letter, a–d, they chose.
* Demonstrate this activity first with a volunteer to show how it works.

**AT 4.2** **4 Écris.**

* Students write sentences for b, c and d in exercise 3 and then write another sentence saying which sports each person does.

*Answers*: a Je fais du ski, je fais du vélo et je fais du jogging. b Je fais de l'équitation, je fais de la natation et je fais du ski. c Je fais du skateboarding, je fais du vélo et je fais de l'équitation. d Je fais du jogging, je fais de la natation et je fais du skateboarding.

### Preparation

- The next part of the spread introduces frequency expressions, which students can use in relation to sports. You may want to introduce these separately in advance with students who may find the reading text a bit tricky. If necessary, write the French expressions on one side of the board and the English on the other. How many can students match from similarity with English expressions? Ask students to give their reasons when making suggestions of matches.

| AT 3.3 | **5 Lis et trouve l'équivalent.** |

- Students read the cartoon strip and find the French for the English expressions listed. Read the cartoon out loud before students do the activity, if they need more support.

*Answers*: a le dimanche matin; b deux fois par semaine; c le mercredi après-midi; d de temps en temps; e tous les jours

| AT 1.3 | **6 Écoute le rap.** |

- Students listen to the rap and put up their hand each time they hear one of the frequency expressions.
- Play the rap again and students do the same. Pause the audio each time and students repeat which expression they heard.
- Show the words of the rap, if appropriate, and ask students to note anything else they understand, such as sports mentioned, etc.

*Answers*: time expressions are underlined in the transcript

 **CD 3, track 15**   page 39, activité 6

<u>Tous les jours</u>, c'est gymnastique!
<u>Tous les jours</u>! C'est fantastique!

<u>De temps en temps</u>, je fais du yoga.
<u>De temps en temps</u>! C'est trop sympa!

<u>Le mercredi</u> <u>après-midi</u>,
j'aime bien faire du ski.

Et <u>le dimanche matin</u>,
Avec mon frère, je fais du patin … à roulettes.

Je <u>ne</u> fais <u>jamais</u> de vélo.
Le vélo, c'est pas rigolo.

<u>Deux fois par semaine</u>, j'ai judo.
<u>Deux fois par semaine</u>, ce n'est pas trop
Ce n'est pas trop, ce n'est pas trop.
<u>Deux fois par semaine</u>, ce n'est pas trop!
Yo!

| AT 4.2–3 | **7 Écris.** |

- Students adapt the speech bubble, changing the frequency expressions to suit Olenka, who is very sporty!

### Follow-up

 C58

- Further speaking practice of sports and frequency expressions can be found on Copymaster 58. Students carry out a survey in the class.

- Students could do the extension activities on sports and frequency expressions from OxBox, *Je fais du sport; J'aime faire du sport.*

## 5.3   Futur champion?   pages 40–41

### *Planner*

> **Objectives**
>   - Talk about daily routine
>   - Talk about healthy lifestyle

> **Resources**
> Students' Book, pages 40–41
> CD 3, tracks 16–18
> Copymaster 63, *Clic! 2 Star*

> **Key language**
> *Je me réveille à (huit heures).*
> *À midi, je mange un sandwich/des chips.*
> *Je joue (au basket).*
> *Je fais (de la natation).*
> *Je m'entraîne (une fois par semaine).*

> *Je fume. Je ne fume pas.*
> *Je me couche à (dix) heures.*

> **Grammar**
> Reflexive verbs: *je, tu*

> **Framework reference**
> 1.4, 4.5, 5.4

> **Starter**
>   - Before starting work on the spread, talk in English about what a healthy daily routine might consist of, such as getting up times and bed times, eating habits and sports activities. Ask students to predict any vocabulary for these areas from what they have already covered, including sports, frequency expressions, food and drink, etc. Make a note of their suggestions so you can compare them later

with what was actually covered on the spread.
- Students work in pairs with statements a–e from exercise 1. The aim is to adapt each statement by changing the sport, frequency expression and item of food/drink.
  *Je joue <u>au basket/football/rugby</u>.*

> **Plenaries**
- Display some sentences on the themes of the spread. Mix up the order of the words and phrases in each sentence, as below. Students rearrange the words of each sentence into the correct order.
  – *entraîne / Je / une fois / m' / par semaine*
  – *Je / couche / à / me / dix heures*

– *me / heures / six / Je / à / réveille / trente*
- Call out words or phrases from the spread. Working in pairs, students build two sentences around each word or phrase, one on behalf of a sports champion and the other on behalf of someone who is very unfit.
  *midi*
  – *À midi, je mange une salade.*
  – *À midi, je mange des chips et du chocolat.*
  Pool ideas and award points accordingly.

> **Assessment opportunities**
- Speaking: Students' Book page 41, exercise 6

 **1 Relie.**
- Students match the speech bubbles to the English sentences. Read the sentences out loud to students first and encourage them to use strategies met previously to aid understanding, such as using English, making sensible guesses, using the glossary, etc.
- Ask students to practise reading the sentences out loud in pairs to ensure good pronunciation.

*Answers*: a 5; b 2; c 4; d 3; e 1

 **2 Écoute Mathieu.**
- Students listen to the interview with Mathieu and note the order of the speech bubbles from exercise 1.

*Answers*: b, e, c, a, d

**CD 3, track 16**                    page 40, activité 2

– Alors, Mathieu … À quelle heure tu te réveilles?
– Je me réveille à six heures trente.
– Est-ce que tu fumes?
– Non, je ne fume pas.
– À midi, qu'est-ce que tu manges?
– Je mange des chips et je bois du soda.
– Tu fais du sport?
– Oui. Je joue au basket. Je m'entraîne une fois par semaine.
– Quand est-ce que tu te couches?
– Je me couche à dix heures tous les soirs.

## Grammaire
- Look at the pattern of reflexive verbs with students. Explain that some verbs have an extra pronoun before the verb; with *je* it is always *me* and with *tu* it is *te*. Remind students that they have met reflexive verbs before: *je m'appelle*.
- Ensure that students know the meaning of the three verbs listed and practise making different sentences with them, such as *Je me réveille* + different times.

 **3 Lis et relie.**
- Students match the questions listed to the speech bubbles from exercise 1. Recap on the meaning of questions *À quelle heure …?*, *Quand …?* and *Qu'est-ce que …?*

*Answers*: 1 b; 2 e; 3 c; 4 a; 5 d

**AT 1.3** **4 Écoute Mehdi. Choisis a ou b.**
- Students listen to Mehdi answering various questions and choose a or b for each sentence. Go over the meaning of both options first to provide more support and to ensure that students are adequately prepared for the listening.

*Answers*: 1 a; 2 b; 3 a; 4 b; 5 b; 6 b

**CD 3, track 17**                    page 41, activité 4

– Salut, Mehdi! Alors … À quelle heure tu te réveilles?
– Je me réveille à sept heures vingt.
– Est-ce que tu fumes?
– Je ne fume pas.
– À midi, qu'est-ce que tu manges?
– Je mange un sandwich.
– Tu t'intéresses aux activités sportives?
– Oui, je m'intéresse au football. Je m'entraîne une fois par semaine.
– Au collège, tu t'amuses en EPS?
– Bof, ça dépend. Je n'aime pas beaucoup le sport au collège.
– Quand est-ce que tu te couches?
– Je me couche à onze heures tous les soirs.
– D'accord, très bien. Merci, Mehdi.

 **5 Réponds pour Rachel.**
- Students use the notes in English to write answers for Rachel in response to the questions on the clipboard.
- For more support, show how students can use the key language box and change relevant parts of each sentence.

*Answers*: Je me réveille à sept heures trente. Je ne fume pas. À midi, je mange une pizza. Je joue au hockey. Je m'entraîne tous les jours. Je me couche à neuf heures trente.

### 6 À deux: interviews.

* Students work in pairs to ask and answer the questions from the questionnaire, again using the key language box as support.
* Model the interview first with a couple of volunteers.
* Choose a few interviews to perform for the rest of the class. The class can then vote on whose was the best interview.

AT 1.3 ### 7 Écoute la chanson.

* Students listen to the song and note the sports they hear. There are a couple of unfamiliar sports you might like to point out in advance: *canoë*, *plongée*.
* If students enjoy listening to the song, play it again, showing the words and see what else they can understand. Students can gradually start joining in with the song as they become more familiar with it, if they wish.

*Answers*: rugby, skiing, skateboard, canoeing, diving, swimming, badminton

 **CD 3, track 18**                    page 41, activité 7

**Je suis le champion!**

Je ne joue pas au rugby
Je n'ai jamais fait de ski
Mais en skateboard, ah oui,
En skateboard, je suis le champion!

*Refrain:*
Le sport, j'adore
Et je suis fort.
Tu sais ce que j'aime faire?
Il est le champion

Je n'fais pas de canoë
Je n'ai jamais fait de plongée
Mais en skateboard, ah oui,
En skateboard, je suis le champion!

*Refrain*

Je n'aime pas la natation
Je n'joue pas au badminton
Mais en skateboard, ah oui,
En skateboard, je suis le champion!

Je suis le champion!
Je suis le champion!
Je suis, je suis, je suis le champion!

### Follow-up

C63 * An extension reading activity containing language from the whole unit can be found on Copymaster 63.

*Answers*: **1** a célèbre; b l'équipe de France; c il a marqué beaucoup de buts; d il est passé professionnel; e date de naissance; f lieu de naissance; g Henri s'est marié; h le mannequin; i le couple a divorcé; j le sportif le plus riche

# 5.4   Vocabulaire
page 42

## *Planner*

> **Resources**
Students' Book, page 42

> **Objectives**
* *Vocabulaire*: to provide a theme-based summary of the key language of the unit, which students can use as a reference or as an aid to learning
* To practise pronunciation

> **Framework reference**
4.1, 5.5

### Using the vocabulary page

* Encourage students to use the *Vocabulaire* page as a reference point throughout the unit. It can also serve as a useful revision tool before students do the *Clic-test!*
* Vocabulary is listed spread-by-spread and you could either ask students to learn each section for homework after each spread is completed, or set the whole page as a homework task before starting work on the test. Most students learn shorter sections best, so often it is better to give them manageable chunks to learn at a time.

* Encourage students to use different techniques to help them learn the vocabulary:
  – Cover up the English and see what they can remember; write down any words they can't remember and test themselves again on those words.
  – Cover up the French and see if they can remember the words or phrases this way round.
  – Make word cards with English on one side and French on the other. Students can then test themselves to see what they can remember. Put any cards they can't remember on one side

and go over those again at the end.
  – Work in pairs to test each other, either using the vocabulary list or the word cards.
• Record themselves saying the words both in English and French. Saying words and phrases out loud can often help with memorising them.

## Sound French!

• *Aim:* To practise pronunciation
• The point practised here is the *tion* sound. Ask students to repeat the words listed after you and then ask them to find examples of *tion* words in the vocabulary list and practise saying them out loud.

## 5.4   Clic-test!                                      page 43

### *Planner*

The page is divided into four sections: listening, speaking, reading and writing.

➤ **Objectives**
  • To enable students to recap on the language and structures of the unit

• To provide an opportunity for quick testing of all four skills

➤ **Resources**
Students' Book, page 43
CD 3, track 19

➤ **Framework reference**
5.7, 5.8

---

| AT 1.1–2 | **1 Écoute! (1–6)** |

• Students listen and note the symbols in the order they hear the sports mentioned.

*Answers*: 1 d; 2 a; 3 f; 4 b; 5 c; 6 e

  **CD 3, track 19**               page 43, activité 1

1  – Tu fais du sport?
   – Oui, je fais du ski.
2  – Tu fais du sport?
   – Oui, je joue au football.
3  – Tu fais du sport?
   – Moi, je fais du jogging.
4  – Tu fais du sport?
   – Oui, je joue au ping-pong.
5  – Tu fais du sport?
   – Oui … de temps en temps … je joue au basket.

6  – Tu fais du sport?
   – Oui. Une fois par semaine, je fais de la natation.

| AT 3.2 | **2 Lis!** |

• Students read ten statements and choose six that could form part of a healthy lifestyle.

*Answers*: b, c, e, g, h

| AT 2.2 | **3 Parle!** |

• Students use the symbols to say sentences about sports they play and also how often they do them.

| AT 4.2–3 | **4 Écris!** |

• Students write sentences guided by English prompts. If possible, some students may be able to write a paragraph to include one or two connectives.

## À moi                                                 page 80

### *Planner*

➤ **Objectives**
  • To provide reinforcement activities for quiet work
  • To provide alternative class and homework material for students who finish other activities quickly

➤ **Resources**
Students' Book, page 80

➤ **Framework reference**
2.1, 2.2, 2.4

---

### Je suis en forme!

| AT 3.2–3 | **1 Read Moussa's answers (on the yellow strips). Finish the sentences below.** |

• Students complete the English phrases by looking at the information provided in Moussa's answers.

*Answers*: a 7.30; b 10; c cycling; d Wednesday; e plays football; f salad or a sandwich

| AT 3.2 | **2 Match the questions and the answers and write out an interview with Moussa.** |

• Students match the correct questions with the answers and write out the interview.

*Answers*: 1 b; 2 e; 3 a; 4 d; 5 c

 **En forme**

 AT 4.2

**3 Now write your own answers to questions 1–5.**

- Students write their own answers, using Moussa's interview as a model.

- For further practice, students can interview each other, using their prepared answers.

# Clic-vidéo

page 89

---

## Planner

> **Objectives**
- To provide extended listening practice recycling the language of the whole unit

> **Resources**

Students' Book, page 89
Video clip 6, *Clic! 2 Star*
CD 3, track 20

> **Framework reference**
1.2, 1.3

---

 AT 1.3–4

**1 Watch the whole video clip. Who has the tennis lesson: Joe, Max or Nina?**

- Students can now watch the whole of the video clip, which they started on spread 5.2. Firstly, students familiarise themselves with the general theme and simply look for one fact.

*Answer:* Max

**CD 3, track 20**      page 89, activités 1, 2, 3 et 4

Nina: J'aime bien faire du sport. Je fais du jogging deux fois par semaine. Et toi?
Joe: Moi aussi, j'adore le sport. Devine quel sport je fais.
Nina: Euh … du judo?
Joe: Non.
Nina: De la musculation alors?
Joe: Non, c'est trop dur.
Nina: Du foot?
Joe: Oui, un peu. Je joue une fois par semaine avec mes copains. Mais je pratique un autre sport. Devine.
Nina: Ah … le basket!
Joe: Exactement. Je m'entraîne quatre heures par semaine.
Nina: Waouh! Tu es sportif.
Joe: Et toi? Tu fais un autre sport? De l'équitation?
Nina: Non.
Joe: Du ski?
Nina: Quelquefois.
Joe: De la natation?
Nina: Oui, exactement! Bon, on va chercher Max à son cours de tennis?
Joe: OK, on y va.
Coach: Très bien … Attention ta main gauche … allez … OK, très bien … vise la balle avec ta main gauche, voilà … OK, Max … eh, pas mal … Hop allez, on attaque bientôt Roland-Garros, là!
Nina: Tu as déjà joué au tennis? Moi, j'ai jamais essayé.
Joe: Oui, j'ai déjà essayé avec mes cousins, mais j'ai jamais pris de leçons.
Coach: Reste bien les pieds au sol, Max.
Nina: Max, il joue bien. Il a des grandes jambes. Lui, il fait de la danse. Il est souple, c'est un sportif.
Joe: Oui, et pour le tennis, il faut des bras musclés.

Nina: Ouais. Ça y est. Il a fini.
Max: À mardi.
Coach: Super.
Max: Merci beaucoup.
Coach: Bien joué. Très, très bien. À mardi.
Nina: Alors, Max, le tennis, c'est dur?
Max: Mais, écoute. Le coup droit, c'est facile, mais le revers, c'est plus difficile déjà.
Nina: Et tu n'as pas trop mal aux jambes?
Max: J'ai mal au bras. J'ai mal aux jambes. J'ai mal aux genoux et j'ai mal aux pieds.
Nina: Alors, on fait quoi maintenant? On va faire du footing?
Max: Sûrement pas. Je préfère aller au cinéma. Au moins, je pourrai m'asseoir.
Joe: Bonne idée. Le cinéma, c'est mon sport préféré!

**Point langue**
J'aime bien faire du sport.
Je fais du jogging deux fois par semaine.
J'ai mal au bras.
J'ai mal aux jambes.

 AT 1.3–4

**2 Watch the first part again. Choose a or b.**

- Students watch the first part of the video clip again and look at more of the detail.

*Answers:* 1 b; 2 a; 3 b; 4 a

AT 1.3–4

**3 Watch the second part of the video. Which of the following do you hear the tennis coach say?**

- Students watch the second part of the video and concentrate on the phrases the tennis coach uses. Go over the phrases first to ensure students are clear about meaning.

*Answers:* a, b, c, e

AT 1.3

**4 Watch again. Can you match these parts of the body (a–d) with their French equivalents (1–4)?**

- Students have not met parts of the body but, from watching the tennis game carefully, they should be able to deduce the answers.

*Answers:* a 4; b 2; c 3; d 1

# 6

# Mon temps libre

| Page reference | Contexts and objectives | Grammar | Language strategies and pronunciation | Key language | Framework | AT level |
|---|---|---|---|---|---|---|
| **Unité 6: Mon temps libre** | Overview grid | | | | | |
| 44–45<br>**6.1 Je fais du shopping!** | • Say what you do in your free time<br>• Say how often you do something | • Frequency expressions | Using the same verbs with different endings | *Je vois des copains/ma famille.*<br>*Je vais au cinéma/sur Internet.*<br>*Je fais du sport/du shopping.*<br>*Je regarde la télé/des films.*<br>*Je joue à des jeux vidéo/dans un groupe.*<br>*J'écoute la radio/de la musique.*<br>*tous les jours, le weekend, de temps en temps* | 1.2, 4.5, 5.2, 5.6 | 1.1–3<br>2.2<br>3.1–3<br>4.2 |
| 46–47<br>**6.2 C'est combien?** | • Use numbers 70–1 000<br>• Say what you'd like to buy | • *je voudrais* | Patterns of high numbers | Numbers 70–1 000 (just tens)<br>*C'est combien? C'est environ 100 euros.*<br>*C'est entre 60 et 70 euros.*<br>*Si j'étais riche, je voudrais…un ordinateur portable, une Wii, une PSP, des chaussures Ugg, des baskets Converse, un jean Diesel* | 4.2, 5.1, 5.5 | 1.1–2<br>2.1–2<br>3.1<br>4.2 |
| 48–49<br>**6.3 L'argent de poche** | • Say how much pocket money you get<br>• Say what you bought with your pocket money | • Negative: *je n'ai pas acheté de* | Using little words to make longer sentences: *et, mais, alors* | *J'ai environ dix euros par mois.*<br>*J'ai 20 euros par mois.*<br>*J'ai entre 20–30 euros par semaine.*<br>*et, alors, mais*<br>*C'est/Ce n'est pas assez/bien super.*<br>*J'ai acheté… des vêtements, des affaires d'école, des accessoires, des magazines, des livres, des chansons, des jeux vidéo, des sucreries, des places de cinéma*<br>*Je n'ai pas acheté de…* | 1.4, 4.4, 4.6 | 1.2<br>2.2–3<br>3.2<br>4.2 |
| 50<br>**6.4 Vocabulaire** | • Practise pronunciation | | Nasal sound *in* | | 4.1, 5.5 | |
| 51<br>**6.4 Clic-test!** | • Recap on the language and structures of the unit<br>• Provide an opportunity for quick testing of all four skills | | | | 1.5, 5.8 | 1.2–3<br>2.2–3<br>3.2–3<br>4.2–3 |
| 81<br>**À moi** | • Provide reinforcement activities for self-access work | | | | 2.1, 2.2 | 3.2<br>4.2 |
| 90<br>**Clic-vidéo** | • To provide extended listening practice recycling the language of the whole unit through a video | | | | 1.2, 1.3, 3.1, 3.2 | 1.3-4 |

| MEDIUM TERM GRID Week-by-week overview (assuming six weeks' work or approximately 10–12.5 hours) |
| --- |

**About Unit 6, *Mon temps libre***

In this unit, students learn to talk about free time activities and pocket money with a variety of present tense verbs. They use *je voudrais* and learn about patterns of higher numbers. They also continue to use the perfect tense, including the negative, and they make longer sentences with connectives.

New vocabulary includes verbs to express free time activities (*voir, aller, faire, regarder, jouer, écouter*), numbers 70–1000, items they would buy if they were rich, items bought with pocket money. Revised language includes frequency expressions, numbers 1–70 and opinion phrases with *c'est*.

Reading, listening and comprehension skills are developed through a variety of text, audio and video materials.

| Week | Resources | Objectives |
| --- | --- | --- |
| 1 | 6.1 Je fais du shopping! | Using verbs to say what you do in your free time (*voir, faire, aller, regarder, jouer, écouter*) <br> Saying how often you do something with frequency expressions <br> Using the above verbs with other endings to say different things |
| 2 | 6.2 C'est combien? | Using numbers 70–1000 to say how much something costs <br> Saying what you would like to buy if you were rich (*si j'étais riche, je voudrais*) <br> Looking at patterns of high numbers |
| 3 | 6.3 L'argent de poche | Saying how much pocket money you get and how often <br> Saying what you bought with your pocket money and what you didn't buy (*j'ai acheté/je n'ai pas acheté*) <br> Using little words, *et, mais, alors*, to make longer sentences |
| 4 | Sound French! (p50) <br> À moi (p81) <br> Clic-vidéo (p90) | Practising pronunciation (nasal sound *in*) <br> Additional reading and writing practice <br> Using the video for reinforcement, extension and follow-up work |
| 5 | 6.4 Vocabulaire <br> Clic-test! | Learning vocabulary <br> Recapping on vocabulary of unit <br> Preparing and carrying out of assessment in all four skills <br> Reviewing progress |
| 6 | Copymasters (*Feuilles*) <br> OxBox | Reinforcement and extension of the language of the unit using extra resources <br> Reviewing progress via the Checklist on page 50, *Vocabulaire* <br> Going back over aspects of the unit which need reviewing after *Clic-test!* |

# 6.1 Je fais du shopping!

## *Planner*

> ### Objectives
> - Say what you do in your free time
> - Say how often you do something

> ### Resources
> Students' Book, pages 44–45
> CD 3, tracks 21–22
> OxBox *Clic! 2 Star, Unité 6, Qu'est-ce que tu fais pendant ton temps libre? Que fais-tu pendant ton temps libre? Nina et Max*
> Copymaster 71, 72, *Clic! 2 Star*

> ### Key language
> *Je vois des copains/ma famille.*
> *Je vais au cinéma/sur Internet.*
> *Je fais du sport/du shopping.*
> *Je regarde la télé/des films.*
> *Je joue à des jeux vidéo/dans un groupe.*
> *J'écoute la radio/de la musique.*
> *tous les jours, le weekend, de temps en temps*

> ### Framework reference
> 1.2, 4.5, 5.2, 5.6

> ### Starters
> - Before looking at the spread in the Students' Book, ask students to work in pairs to come up with a list of what they consider to be the eight most popular leisure activities for young people. If possible, they could list words and short phrases in French, recycling previously learned language and using dictionaries, where necessary. Then look together at the photos on page 44 and compare their lists with the pictures. Students score a point for each activity they predicted correctly.
> - Students play a memory game in pairs or small groups using the six leisure activities A–F.
> Student A: *J'écoute de la musique.*
> Student B: *J'écoute de la musique et je vais au cinéma.*
> Student C: *J'écoute de la musique, je vais au cinéma et je fais du sport.*
> Student D: *J'écoute de la musique, je vais au cinéma, je fais du sport et …*

> ### Plenaries
> - Working in pairs, students estimate how many of the six leisure activities A–F they think they can list, from memory. Ask them to make a note of their estimate – this avoids disagreements later on! Explain that they will score a point for each item they recall, but will lose points if they fail to meet their estimated figure and that they cannot attempt more than the number of items they estimate. For example, a student estimates six items but can only manage five, so he/she wins five points but loses a point because of failing to meet the original estimate.
> - Ask students to write down three activities they like doing. They should then move around the class trying to find someone else who shares their tastes. The winner is the first person to find an exact match within a set time.

> ### Assessment opportunities
> - Writing: Students' Book page 45, exercise 6

---

**AT 3.1** **1a Lis. Relie 1–6 aux photos A–F.**
- Students match six photos to the correct entries on the list of top hobbies. They should be able to do this using vocabulary they already know, even if they have not met the exact expressions.

*Answers*: A 4; B 3; C 2; D 1; E 6; F 5

**AT 1.1** **1b Écoute et vérifie.**
- Students listen to check they matched the photos and text correctly.
- Play the audio again for students to repeat and go over the meaning of the verbs. If necessary, do a matching activity on the board where students match the French verbs to their English equivalents.

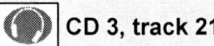 **CD 3, track 21**      page 44, activité 1b

**A**
J'écoute de la musique.
**B**
Je regarde la télé.
**C**
Je fais du sport.
**D**
Je vois mes copains.
**E**
Je vais au cinéma.
**F**
Je joue à des jeux vidéo.

**AT 2.2** **2 À deux.**

- Students work in pairs. They choose three activities in secret and note them down. Their partner asks questions to find out which activities they have chosen. Who can guess their partner's activities with the fewest number of questions?

**AT 4.2** **3 Écris ton hit-parade.**
- Students write out the six activities from the hit-parade in their order of preference. Ask them to take care with accuracy.

### Top Tips!

- This box points out that you can say many different things using the same verb. Take each verb in turn and brainstorm different endings which could be added to say different things in a number of contexts.

 **4 Décris les activités.**

- Students use the verbs from exercise 1 and put different endings on each one to describe the pictures.

*Answers*: 1 J'écoute la radio. 2 Je fais du shopping. 3 Je regarde des films. 4 Je vais sur Internet. 5 Je vois ma famille. 6 Je joue dans un groupe.

### Follow-up

- For further practice in using these verbs in a variety of expressions, students could do the OxBox activity, *Qu'est-ce que tu fais pendant ton temps libre?*

**AT 3.3** **5 Lis et écoute. Que fait Alex?**

**AT 1.3**
- Students listen while following the text in their books. They then answer the questions in English.
- Encourage students to read the text out loud in pairs once they have completed the activity.

*Answers*: a listens to radio/goes on the internet; b plays in a band/sees family; c watches a film/goes shopping

 **CD 3, track 22**      page 45, activité 5

Alors, euh ... j'écoute la radio et je vais sur Internet tous les jours.
Je joue dans un groupe et je vois ma famille le weekend.
Je regarde des films et je fais du shopping de temps en temps.

**AT 4.2** **6 Écris des phrases.**

- Students write twelve different sentences about their free time activities, using the phrases in the grid.

### Follow-up

**C71**
- A card game practising leisure activities and frequency expressions is provided on Copymaster 71 for additional speaking practice.

**C72**
- Copymaster 72 provides extension reading activities.

*Answers*: **1** <u>Both</u>: rugby, computer games, TV; <u>Jacob</u>:listening to music; <u>moi</u>: tennis, piano
Answers: **2** ensemble – *together*; sans lui – *without him*; ami – *friend (m.)*; mêmes goûts – *same interests*; beaucoup de – *lots of*; chez lui – *at his house*; chez moi – *at my house*
Answers: **3** a mon meilleur ami; b beaucoup de choses; c nous jouons au rugby ensemble; d le samedi; e chez lui; f sans lui

- For further practice on this topic, there are two suitable activities on OxBox, *Que fais-tu pendant ton temps libre?* and *Nina et Max*.

## 6.2    C'est combien?            pages 46–47

### *Planner*

➤ **Objectives**
- Use numbers 70–1 000
- Say what you'd like to buy and how much it costs

➤ **Resources**
Students' Book, pages 46–47
CD 3, tracks 23–26

➤ **Key language**
Numbers 70–1 000 (just tens)
*C'est combien? C'est environ 100 euros.*
*C'est entre 60 et 70 euros.*
*Si j'étais riche, je voudrais ...un ordinateur portable, une Wii, une PSP, des chaussures Ugg, des baskets Converse, un jean Diesel*

➤ **Framework reference**
4.2, 5.1, 5.5

➤ **Starters**
- Play some number games to revise numbers 1–30. In pairs or groups, students could play a version of Fizz Buzz, counting from one to 31 and replacing every multiple of a certain number (e.g. two, five) with an agreed word or phrase in French (e.g. *Bof! Sport!*). For a quieter activity, set some simple sums for students to do against the clock. Gradually include the tens up to 60 too.
- Once multiples of ten from 70–1 000 have been introduced, play a team game whereby you call out a number very slowly. The first person to shout out the correct number in English wins a point for his/her team. If he/she says a wrong answer, that team loses its chance to have a go and the other team can have more time to work it out.

➤ **Plenaries**
- Divide the class into two teams and practise

numbers by starting a number sequence; students provide the next number in the sequence. The first team to call out the correct number wins a point.

*vingt, trente, quarante …(cinquante)*
*onze, douze, treize …(quatorze)*

- Have different prices (in euros) displayed on the board. Point to one of the prices and ask, *C'est combien?* Set up two teams and the first person to call out the correct price in French wins a point for that team.

> **Assessment opportunities**
- Speaking: Students' Book page 47, exercise 7
- Writing: Students' Book page 47, exercise 8

**AT 3.1** **1a Lis et écris dans l'ordre.**

- This activity revises numbers up to 50, which students have already met. Ask students to write each group of numbers in numerical order, starting with the smallest.
- If you have not already done so in the Starter, play games to recap on numbers, such as counting round the class and for each multiple of five, students say a specific word (Fizz Buzz). You could also practise counting backwards, playing *Loto*, asking students to count in pairs giving alternate numbers, etc.

*Answers*: dix, onze, douze, treize, quatorze, quinze, seize, dix-sept, dix-huit, dix-neuf; vingt, trente, quarante, cinquante, soixante

**AT 1.1** **1b Écoute et vérifie.**

- Students listen and check they got the numerical order correct.

 **CD 3, track 23** page 46, activité 1b

- dix, onze, douze, treize, quatorze, quinze, seize, dix-sept, dix-huit, dix-neuf
- vingt, trente, quarante, cinquante, soixante

**AT 1.1** **2 Écoute, lis et répète.**
**AT 2.1**

- Students now listen to the new numbers, tens between 70–1 000, and repeat each one.
- Look at the patterns of the numbers with students. *soixante-dix* = 60 + 10 and *quatre-vingts* = 4 x 20. Brainstorm ways to help students remember these numbers.
- Only tens are introduced here, but if students can cope, you may wish to introduce the numbers in between.

 **CD 3, track 24** page 46, activité 2

soixante-dix
quatre-vingts
quatre-vingt-dix
cent
deux-cents
mille

**AT 1.1** **3 Écoute et continue. (a–f)**
**AT 2.1**

- Students listen to the number sequences and note the numbers down, along with the next one in the sequence after the beep.

*Answers*: a (50, 60, 70) 80; b (20, 30, 40) 50; c (70, 80, 90) 100; d (100, 90, 80) 70; e (60, 70, 80) 90; f (10, 100) 1 000

 **CD 3, track 25** page 46, activité 3

**A**
cinquante, soixante, soixante-dix …
**B**
vingt, trente, quarante …
**C**
soixante-dix, quatre-vingts, quatre-vingt-dix …
**D**
cent, quatre-vingt-dix, quatre-vingts …
**E**
soixante, soixante-dix, quatre-vingts …
**F**
dix, cent …

**AT 2.1** **4 À deux.**

- Students work in pairs to see how quickly they can say each line of numbers correctly. They can make several attempts for each line and try to say it in the shortest time.

**AT 3.1** **5 Lis et écris les résultats.**

- Students read the sums and select the correct answer. Encourage them to write the sums in figures to assist the working out.

*Answers*: a quatre-vingt-dix; b soixante; c quatre-vingt-dix; d soixante-dix; e quatre-vingts; f cent

### Preparation

- The next part of this spread concentrates on objects students might buy if they were rich. Look at the six photos together and name each object in turn for students to repeat.

**AT 1.2** **6a Écoute et note. (1–5)**

- Students listen and note the letter of the object mentioned by each person.

*Answers*: 1 C; 2 D; 3 A; 4 F; 5 E

 **CD 3, track 26** page 47, activités 6a et 6b

1. – Si j'étais riche, je voudrais un ordinateur portable.
   – C'est combien?
   – C'est environ 300 euros.

2 – Si j'étais riche, je voudrais des chaussures
Ugg.
– C'est combien?
– C'est entre 80 et 90 euros.
3 – Si j'étais riche, je voudrais une Wii.
– C'est combien?
– C'est entre 100 et 200 euros.
4 – Si j'étais riche, je voudrais un jean Diesel.
– C'est combien?
– C'est environ 70 euros.
5 – Si j'étais riche, je voudrais des baskets
Converse.
– C'est combien?
– C'est environ 80 euros.

mentioned. They can select from the options
provided in the box.

*Answers:* 1 300€; 2 80–90€; 3 100–200€; 4 70€;
5 80€

**AT 2.2** **7 À deux.**

- Students work in pairs to ask each other about
the prices of the items pictured in exercise 6.
The student who gives the price, should try to
do so from memory.

**AT 4.2** **8 Et toi? "Si j'étais riche, je voudrais…"**

- Students complete the sentence for themselves and
they imagine how three friends might answer it.
Encourage them to use a dictionary to look up any
items they don't know.
- Pool ideas and create a graph with the results.
What is the most popular item and what is the most
unusual?

**AT 1.2** **6b Réécoute. C'est combien? (1–5)**

- Students listen again and note the amount of money

# 6.3 L'argent de poche

pages 48–49

## *Planner*

> **Objectives**
- Say how much pocket money you get
- Say what you bought with your pocket money

> **Resources**
Students' Book, pages 48–49
CD 3, track 27–29
OxBox *Clic! 2 Star, Unité 6, Avec mon argent
j'achète …; L'argent de poche*
Copymaster 69, 70 *Clic! 2 Star*
CD 3, tracks 64–65

> **Key language**
*J'ai environ dix euros par mois.*
*J'ai 20 euros par mois.*
*J'ai entre 20–30 euros par semaine.*
*et, alors, mais*
*C'est/Ce n'est pas assez/bien super.*
*J'ai acheté … des vêtements, des affaires d'école,
des accessoires, des magazines, des livres, des
chansons, des jeux vidéo, des sucreries, des places
de cinéma*
*Je n'ai pas acheté de …*

> **Framework reference**
1.4., 4.4, 4.6

> **Starters**
- For quick number practice (to prepare for talking
about sums of money), play Speed Duel. Two

students stand up. Call out two numbers, such
as *quatre-vingts, soixante-dix!* The two students
compete to name the highest number. The fastest
student remains standing while the other student
sits down and is replaced by another challenger.
Continue in the same way until students are
confident with the higher numbers.
- Before working on the second part of the spread,
ask students to close their books and list nine
items they recently bought with their pocket
money. Encourage them to do this in French,
recycling previously learned language and using
dictionaries where necessary. Students can then
compare their list with the survey results on page
49 to see how many items are the same.

> **Plenaries**
- Display a few sentences from the spread on
the theme of pocket money with the words in a
jumbled order. Students work in pairs to rewrite
the sentences with the words in the correct order.
For an extra challenge, ask students to write
similar sentences to swap with a partner.
- Challenge students to write from memory as
many items as possible that they could buy with
pocket money. They can work in pairs. How many
items can they remember and how many can they
write with the correct spelling?

> **Assessment opportunities**
- Writing: Students' Book, page 49 exercise 5
- Speaking: Students' Book, page 49 exercise 6

## Top Tips!

- Before looking at the texts, remind students of the importance of using little words, such as *et* 'and', *mais* 'but' and *alors* 'so', to make longer and more natural sentences. Encourage students to use these expressions in any writing or speaking tasks they do.

 **AT 1.2**
**AT 3.2**

**1 Lis, écoute et réponds.**

- Students listen while reading the texts in their books. Before giving students time to answer the questions, ask them to tell you anything they can understand after a first hearing. Can they understand the numbers? Go over the opinion phrases in each and explain any they cannot work out.

*Answers*: a Raphaël and Simon; b Raphaël; c Morgane; d Chloé

**CD 3, track 27**         page 48, activité 1

- Morgane, tu as combien d'argent de poche?
- J'ai environ soixante-dix euros par mois et c'est assez.

- Raphaël, tu as combien d'argent de poche?
- J'ai dix euros par semaine mais ce n'est pas assez!

- Chloé, tu as combien d'argent de poche?
- J'ai vingt-cinq euros par semaine alors c'est super!

- Simon, tu as combien d'argent de poche?
- Je n'ai pas d'argent de poche alors c'est nul!

**AT 1.2**

**2 Écoute et note en anglais. (1–5)**

- Students listen and note how much pocket money each person receives and what they think of it. Ask students to concentrate on the amount on the first listening, including whether it is weekly or monthly, and on the opinion on a further listening.

*Answers*: 1 60€ per month, not enough; 2 70–80€ per month, enough; 3 20€ per week, super; 4 30€ per week, not great; 5 0€, rubbish

**CD 3, track 28**         page 48, activité 2

1 J'ai environ 60 euros par mois mais ce n'est pas assez!
2 J'ai entre 70 et 80 euros par mois et c'est assez.
3 J'ai 20 euros par semaine alors c'est super!
4 J'ai environ 30 euros par mois mais ce n'est pas super!
5 Je n'ai pas d'argent de poche alors c'est nul!

**AT 4.2**

**3 Écris.**

- Students use the key language box to write ten sentences about pocket money.

 **AT 1.2**

**4 Écoute et note l'ordre. (1–9)**

- This activity introduces a range of items which teenagers have recently bought with their pocket money. It introduces the past tense *j'ai acheté*. If you have not already done so in the Starter, look at the pictures and captions and see how many students already know and how many are new. Read them out loud and ask students to repeat them, with correct pronunciation.
- You could ask students to notice any patterns in the words, such as they all use *des* and they are all in the plural.
- Students listen to nine French teenagers and note down the item from the list they each bought with their pocket money.

*Answers*: 1 F; 2 D; 3 G; 4 I; 5 H; 6 C; 7 E; 8 A; 9 B

**CD 3, track 29**         page 49, activité 4

1 – Tu as acheté quoi avec ton argent de poche?
  – J'ai acheté des chansons.
2 – Tu as acheté quoi avec ton argent de poche?
  – J'ai acheté des magazines.
3 – Et toi?
  – J'ai acheté des jeux vidéo.
4 – Et toi? Tu as acheté quoi avec ton argent de poche?
  – J'ai acheté des places de cinéma.
5 – Et toi?
  – J'ai acheté des sucreries.
6 – Tu as acheté quoi avec ton argent de poche?
  – J'ai acheté des accessoires.
7 – Et toi?
  – J'ai acheté des livres.
8 – Tu as acheté quoi avec ton argent de poche?
  – J'ai acheté des vêtements.
9 – Et toi?
  – J'ai acheté des affaires d'école.

### Follow-up

- Students could do further work on pocket money items from OxBox, *Avec mon argent j'achète …*

**AT 4.2**

**5 Écris A–I en deux colonnes.**

- Students write sentences about the items covered in the hit-parade, using *J'ai acheté* and *Je n'ai pas acheté*. Firstly, write *Je n'ai pas acheté* on the board and ask students what it means. If necessary, remind them that the addition of *ne … pas* always indicates a negative.

**AT 2.2–3**

**6 À deux.**

- Students work in pairs to ask each other questions about what they bought with their pocket money, i.e. their sentences from exercise 5. They should answer in full sentences, using either *J'ai acheté* or *Je n'ai pas acheté …*

### Follow-up

 • Copymaster 69 provides extension activities on the subject of pocket money.

*Answers*: **2** aller: au cinéma, sur Internet; écouter: de la musique; jouer: de la guitare, du piano, dans une équipe, à des jeux vidéo; faire: du sport, du shopping

C70 • Copymaster 70 provides listening activities on the subject of pocket money.

*Answers*: **1**

|   | Qui? | Combien? | Quand? |
|---|------|----------|--------|
| 1 | parents | 5 euros | par semaine |
| 2 | mère | 30 euros | par mois |
| 3 | grands-parents | 10 euros | si je travaille bien au collège |
| 4 | père | 8 euros | par semaine |
| 5 | parents | 100 euros<br>6 euros | pour son anniversaire (100 euros), si elle aide à la maison le weekend (6 euros) |

*Answers*: **2** 1 cinema, shopping, friends; 2 listening to music, computer games, TV; 3 sport, internet; 4 guitar, friends, internet

 **CD 3, track 64** Feuille 70, *Clic! 2 Star*, activité 1

1 – Tu reçois de l'argent de poche, Max?
   – Oui, mes parents me donnent cinq euros par semaine.
2 – Et toi, Vanessa, on te donne de l'argent de poche?
   – Oui, ma mère me donne 30 euros par mois.
3 – Sam, tu reçois de l'argent de poche?
   – Ça dépend. Si je travaille bien au collège, mes grands-parents me donnent dix euros.

4 – Et Saïd, on te donne de l'argent de poche?
   – Oui, si j'aide à la maison, mon père me donne huit euros par semaine.
5 – Naïma, tu reçois de l'argent de poche chaque semaine?
   – Non, je reçois de l'argent pour mon anniversaire et si j'aide à la maison.
   – Ah bon. Et combien reçois-tu?
   – D'habitude, mes parents me donnent 100 euros pour mon anniversaire et six euros si j'aide à la maison le weekend.

 **CD 3, track 65** Feuille 70, *Clic! 2 Star*, activité 2

1 – Chloé, que fais-tu le weekend?
   – Le samedi, j'aime faire des courses et aller au cinéma. J'aime aussi passer du temps avec mes copines.
2 – Et toi, Enzo, qu'est-ce que tu fais quand tu as du temps libre?
   – J'écoute de la musique sur mon iPod, je regarde la télé et j'aime aussi jouer aux jeux vidéo.
3 – Rachida, qu'est-ce que tu aimes faire?
   – Je suis très sportive, moi. Je fais beaucoup de sport. J'aime aussi surfer sur Internet quand je suis chez moi.
4 – Et toi, Rémi, que fais-tu le weekend?
   – Euh, je joue de la guitare dans un groupe: ça me prend beaucoup de temps.
   – Et à part cela?
   – Je surfe sur Internet et je sors aussi avec des amis.

 • A further listening activity on pocket money is provided on OxBox, *L'argent de poche*.

# 6.4    Vocabulaire

page 50

---

## *Planner*

> **Resources**
Students' Book, page 50

> **Objectives**
• *Vocabulaire*: to provide a theme-based summary of the key language of the unit, which students can use as a reference or as an aid to learning
• To practise pronunciation

> **Framework reference**
4.1, 5.5

---

### Using the vocabulary page

• Encourage students to use the *Vocabulaire* page as a reference point throughout the unit. It can also serve as a useful revision tool before students do the *Clic-test!*
• Vocabulary is listed spread-by-spread and you could either ask students to learn each section for homework after each spread is completed, or set the whole page as a homework task before starting work on the test. Most students learn shorter sections best, so often it is better to give them manageable chunks to learn at a time.
• Encourage students to use different techniques to help them learn the vocabulary:
  – Cover up the English and see what they can remember; write down any words they can't remember and test themselves again on those words.
  – Cover up the French and see if they can remember the words or phrases this way round.

- Make word cards with English on one side
  and French on the other. Students can then test
  themselves to see what they can remember.
  Put any cards they can't remember on one side
  and go over those again at the end.
- Work in pairs to test each other, either using
  the vocabulary list or the word cards.
- Record themselves saying the words both in
  English and French. Saying words and phrases out
  loud can often help with memorising them.

### Sound French!

- *Aim:* To practise pronunciation
- The point practised here is the nasal sound *in.*
- Demonstrate and practise the sound with the
  words listed.
- Ask students to find examples of the *in* sound in
  any of the vocabulary lists and practise saying
  them out loud.

# 6.4    Clic-test!                                            page 51

---

## *Planner*

The page is divided into four sections: listening,
speaking, reading and writing.

➤ **Objectives**
- To enable students to recap on the language and
  structures of the unit

- To provide an opportunity for quick testing of all
  four skills

➤ **Resources**
Students' Book, page 51
CD 3, track 30

➤ **Framework reference**
1.5, 5.8

---

| AT 1.2–3 | **1 Écoute!** |

- Students listen and note the activities in the order
  they hear them mentioned.

*Answers:* c, a, d, b, e, f

 **CD 3, track 30**          page 51, activité 1

- Katie, qu'est-ce que tu fais pendant ton temps
  libre?
- Alors, euh … je fais du sport … je joue au
  football, c'est super! Euh … Et je fais du
  shopping le weekend. Tous les jours, je regarde
  la télé, et euh … j'écoute de la musique aussi.
- Tu joues à des jeux vidéo?
- Euh … de temps en temps, je joue sur la
  PlayStation avec mes copains.
- Et tu vas sur Internet?

- Oui, je vais sur Internet tous les jours.
- Merci!

 **2 Lis!**

- Students read the passage and choose the correct
  option.

*Answers:* 1 a; 2 b; 3 b; 4 b; 5 a; 6 b

 **3 Écris!**

- Students write five things they do in their spare
  time, including frequency expressions. Encourage
  some students to write a short paragraph, if they
  can, using connectives met in the unit.

| AT 2.2–3 | **4 Parle!** |

- Students say a few sentences about their pocket
  money. For those who can, ask them to prepare and
  memorise a mini-presentation about pocket money.

# À moi                                                        page 81

---

## *Planner*

➤ **Objectives**
- To provide reinforcement activities for quiet work
- To provide alternative class and homework material
  for students who finish other activities quickly

➤ **Resources**
Students' Book, page 81

➤ **Framework reference**
2.1, 2.2

---

### Le temps libre

AT 3.2
**1 Read the survey. Can you spot the French for the following?**

- Students write the French for the phrases listed in English.

*Answers*: a Je lis (des livres, des magazines); b je fais des activités musicales ou artistiques; c je joue à des jeux vidéo; d je vais au concert/spectacle; e je visite un musée/un monument/une exposition; f je joue à des jeux de société

AT 3.2
**2 What percentage of French teenagers…**

- Students note the correct percentage for each activity listed in English.

*Answers*: a 97%; b 65%; c 78%; d 92%; e 97%; f 92%

AT 4.2
**3 Copy the survey list under two headings:**

- Students write two lists: the activities they often do and those they don't often do. Encourage them to be careful with accurate copying.

# Clic-vidéo

page 90

## *Planner*

> **Objectives**
- To provide extended listening practice recycling the language of the whole unit

> **Resources**
Students' Book, page 90
Video clip 7, *Clic! 2 Star*
CD 3, track 31

> **Framework reference**
1.2, 1.3, 3.1, 3.2

**1 Watch the clip. In which order do you see these activities?**

- Students watch the video clip and note the order they see the sports listed.

*Answers*: c, b, e, a, d

 **Video clip 7**  page 90, activités 1 et 2

 **CD 3, track 31**

Joe: Wouah! C'est super comme endroit. Qu'est-ce qu'il y a à faire ici?
Max: Il y a plein de choses à faire. Il y a la pelouse, il y a les jeux pour enfants. Il y a la fontaine. On peut aussi faire du vélo, du skateboard, du roller. Moi, je retrouve Nina tous les samedis après-midi, ici.

Nina: Salut les gars!
Joe: Salut!
Max: Salut, Nina.
Nina: Ça va?
Max: Très bien, et toi?
Nina: Oui, ça va.
Joe: Alors, Max, Nina c'est ta meilleure copine?
Max: Oui. Nina, c'est ma meilleure amie. Elle est super sympa.
Nina: Oui, Max, il est super cool. On a les mêmes goûts et en plus, on fait tout ensemble.
Max: Nous allons au cinéma ensemble. Nous nous téléphonons plusieurs fois par jour et nous écoutons de la musique.

Nina: Je lui raconte tout. Je lui fais confiance.
Nina: Tu as déjà essayé de faire du skate, toi?
Joe: Quand j'étais petit, j'aimais faire du skate.
Max: Moi aussi. Quand j'étais petit, je faisais du skate. Tu as déjà essayé le monocycle?
Joe: Non.
Nina: Non, moi … bof.
Joe: Mais on peut tous essayer ensemble! Nina: Tu es sûr?
Max: Allez. On essaie.
Nina: Bon, d'accord.
Joe: Max et Nina sont super sympa! J'adore le français. Paris, c'est super!

**Point langue**
On a les mêmes goûts et en plus, on fait tout ensemble.
Nous allons au cinéma ensemble.
Nous nous téléphonons plusieurs fois par jour.
Je lui raconte tout. Je lui fais confiance.

AT 1.3–4
**2 Listen carefully and select the correct option: a or b.**

- Students watch the clip again and choose a or b to answer the questions correctly.

*Answers*: 1 a; 2 b; 3 a; 4 a

# 7 Premiers contacts

| Unité 7: Premiers contacts  Overview grid | | | | | | |
|---|---|---|---|---|---|---|
| Page reference | Contexts and objectives | Grammar | Language strategies and pronunciation | Key language | Framework | AT level |
| 53–53 **7.1 Salut!** | • Find out about someone you have just met • Tell someone a bit about yourself | • Useful question words | | Ça va? Ça va bien! Ça ne va pas! Comment tu t'appelles? Je m'appelle (Alex). Tu as quel âge? J'ai (treize) ans. Tu es français? Non, je suis (anglais). Tu habites ou? J'habite à (Manchester). | 1.1, 1.4, 4.2, 4.6 | 1.2–3 2.2–3 3.2–3 4.2–3 |
| 54–55 **7.2 Tu veux venir?** | • Ask someone out • Accept or refuse an invitation | • tu veux …? | | Tu veux venir …? au cinéma, au café, au match de foot, au centre commercial, à la piscine, à la plage lundi, mardi … Désolé(e), je ne peux pas. Oui, je veux bien! On se retrouve à quelle heure? On se retrouve à 6h. | 1.5, 2.5, 4.6, 5.2 | 1.2 2.2 3.1–2 4.2–3 |
| 56–57 **7.3 Garder contact** | • Say how you will keep in touch with friends | • Say what you are going to do in the future • Using on | | Je vais téléphoner. Je vais envoyer des emails. Je vais envoyer des SMS. Je vais communiquer sur mon profil web. Je vais organiser une fête Je ne vais pas garder contact. Tu vas …? On va … | 2.4, 4.5, 5.4 | 1.2 2.2 3.2–3 4.2–3 |
| 58 **7.4 Vocabulaire** | • Practise pronunciation | | qu = k | | 4.1, 4.2 | |
| 59 **7.4 Clic-test!** | • Recap on the language and structures of the unit • Provide an opportunity for quick testing of all four skills | | | | 5.8 | 1.2–3 2.2–3 3.2 4.2–3 |
| 82 **À moi** | • Provide reinforcement activities for self-access work | | | | 2.2, 2.3, 2.5 | 3.2–3 4.2–3 |

| MEDIUM TERM GRID Week-by-week overview (assuming six weeks' work or approximately 10–12.5 hours) | |
|---|---|

**About Unit 7, *Premiers contacts***

In this unit, students learn to have a conversation with someone they have just met and find out about them by asking and answering questions, and understanding question words. They use *tu veux* + infinitive to ask someone out and they say what they are going to do in the future using *aller* + infinitive. They use on to mean 'we' and that using word for word translation is not always a good idea.

New vocabulary includes places in town, invitations, accepting or refusing an invitation and future expressions with *je vais* + infinitive. Revised language includes greetings, saying name, age, nationality and where they live, *au/à la* + venue, days of the week and times.

Reading, listening and comprehension skills are developed through a variety of text, audio and video materials.

| Week | Resources | Objectives |
|---|---|---|
| 1 | **7.1 Salut!** | Finding out about someone you have just met by asking their name, age, nationality and where they live<br>Telling someone about yourself<br>Using and understanding question words<br>Realising that word for word translation does not always work |
| 2 | **7.2 Tu veux venir?** | Using *tu veux venir* + place to ask someone out<br>Using *au* and *à la* with places<br>Accepting or refusing an invitation<br>Using *on* to suggest when to meet |
| 3 | **7.3 Garder contact** | Saying how you will keep in touch with friends<br>Using *je vais* + infinitive phrase to say what you are going to do in the future<br>Using *tu vas* and *on va* with future expressions |
| 4 | **Sound French!** (p58)<br>**À moi** (p82)<br>**Copymasters, OxBox** | Practising pronunciation (*qu* = k)<br>Additional reading and writing practice<br>Using the video for reinforcement, extension and follow-up work<br>Using additional resources, such as Copymasters and OxBox activities, to reinforce and extend language met |
| 5 | **7.4 Vocabulaire**<br>**Clic-test!** | Learning vocabulary<br>Recapping on vocabulary of unit<br>Preparing and carrying out of assessment in all four skills<br>Reviewing progress |
| 6 | **Copymasters (*Feuilles*)**<br>**OxBox** | Reinforcement and extension of the language of the unit using extra resources<br>Reviewing progress via the Checklist on page 58, *Vocabulaire*<br>Going back over aspects of the unit which need reviewing after *Clic-test!* |

# 7.1 Salut!

## *Planner*

> **Objectives**
> - Find out about someone you have just met
> - Tell someone a bit about yourself

> **Resources**
> Students' Book, pages 52–53
> CD 3, tracks 32–33
> OxBox *Clic! 3 Star, Unité 1, Questions et réponses; Salut!*

> **Key language**
> *Ça va? Ça va bien! Ça ne va pas!*
> *Comment tu t'appelles? Je m'appelle (Alex).*
> *Tu as quel âge? J'ai (treize) ans.*
> *Tu es français? Non, je suis (anglais).*
> *Tu habites où? J'habite à (Manchester).*

> **Framework reference**
> 1.1, 1.4, 4.2, 4.6

> **Starters**
> - To revise greetings, introductions and exchanging personal information, ask students to imagine they are about to meet other young people on summer camp in France. What questions might they be asked? What questions would they want to ask?

In pairs or groups, students gather useful language. Share ideas as a whole class.
- Display a jumble of key questions and answers. Students race against the clock to match the questions to their corresponding answers.

> **Plenaries**
> - Call out an answer from the spread, such as *J'habite à Manchester*. Students compete to provide the corresponding question: *Tu habites où?* Once students are confident with this activity, do it in reverse, by calling out a question and students compete to provide an answer.
> - Show the class two photos of anonymous people (not famous people) taken from magazines. Divide the class into two teams. Team A takes on the identity of the person in photo A while team B acts as the person in photo B. Teams build a conversation between the two people, imagining they are meeting each other for the first time. They take turns to ask and answer questions. Depending on the ability of the class, you may need to provide support on the board or OHP for this activity, such as lists of key questions and model answers for students to choose from.

> **Assessment opportunities**
> - Writing: Students' Book page 53, exercise 7

---

**AT 3.2** **1 Fais le jeu-test.**
- Students read the quiz about getting to know people, and choose answer a or b for each question. If students need more support, go over the questions first to help them with meanings.

*Answers*: 1 a; 2 b; 3 b; 4 b; 5 a

**AT 1.2** **2 Vérifie. Écoute, lis et répète les questions et**
**AT 2.2** **les bonnes réponses.**
- Students can now listen to check their answers. They also repeat the questions and answers to ensure good pronunciation.

 **CD 3, track 32**          page 52, activité 2

1 – Salut! Ça va?
  – Ça va bien! Et toi?
2 – Tu t'appelles comment?
  – Je m'appelle Alex.
3 – Tu as quel âge?
  – J'ai treize ans.
4 – Tu es français?
  – Non, je suis anglais.
5 – Tu habites où?
  – J'habite à Manchester.

**AT 2.2–3** **3 À deux.**

- Students read the questions and answers from the quiz in pairs. One student reads the question, while the other reads the correct answer.

**Follow-up**
- If appropriate for your students, point out that word for word translation from French to English does not always work: *J'ai 13 ans* = 'I have 13 years'. Encourage students not to look at individual words in such phrases, but to try to get the gist of the meaning from the whole sentence.
- Compare also other phrases students have met that cannot be translated literally, including *Ça va* and *Comment tu t'appelles*?

**AT 4.2–3** **4 Écris.**
- Students write a conversation based on the quiz questions and answers. They write out the questions first and then adapt the answers so they refer to themselves
- You could do some oral practice of the answers around the class in advance to remind students of relevant vocabulary, such as nationalities and ages.

**AT 1.3** **5 Écoute. Choisis a or b.**
- Students listen to several teenagers talking and choose the correct option for each sentence. Look

at the sentences before playing the recording and prepare students for the language they will hear.

*Answers*: 1 a; 2 a; 3 b; 4 a; 5 b; 6 b

 **CD 3, track 33**　　　　　　　　　　page 53, activité 5

- Salut! Je m'appelle Ben. Et vous?
- Salut, Ben! Moi, c'est Éric. Et voici ma copine, Lisa.
- Salut, Ben! Tu es français?
- Non, je suis anglais. Je viens de Londres. Et toi, Lisa?
- Moi, je suis italienne. J'habite à Rome. Je parle un peu le français.
- Tu parles super bien le français, Lisa!
- Tu as quel âge, Ben?
- J'ai 14 ans. Et toi?
- Moi aussi. Mon anniversaire, c'est le 23 février.
- C'est quand, ton anniversaire, Lisa?
- Le 4 août.
- Moi aussi! C'est incroyable! On fait la fête, d'accord?
- OK, OK, viens, Lisa. Salut, Ben!

### Top Tips!

- Before students work on exercise 6, go over the question words with them in the *Top Tips!* box.

Ask them to find examples of each question word in the quiz.

 **6 Lis et complète la conversation.**

- Students read the gapped text and complete it with the words from the box.
- If more support is needed, work with the class first, reading out the text and ensuring that students understand what each sentence means. What sort of words would they expect in each gap?
- For more writing practice, students could write out the whole conversation.

*Answers*: 1 salut; 2 comment; 3 quel; 4 où

 **7 Écris.**

- Students write a conversation where they invent Dracula's answers to the quiz questions.
- Ask pairs of students to read out their conversations, taking on the character of Dracula.

### Follow-up

- An extension activity which practises questions and answers met on this page, plus additional questions and answers, can be found on OxBox, *Questions et réponses*.
- An extension listening activity on this topic can also be found on OxBox, *Salut!*

# 7.2　Tu veux venir?　　　　　　　　　　pages 54–55

## *Planner*

> **Objectives**
- Ask someone out
- Accept or refuse an invitation

> **Resources**
Students' Book, pages 54–55
CD 3, tracks 34–35
OxBox *Clic! 3 Star, Unité 1, Je veux bien*
Copymaster 7, *Clic! 3 Star*

> **Key language**
*Tu veux venir ...?*
*au cinéma, au café, au match de foot, au centre commercial, à la piscine, à la plage*
*lundi, mardi ...*
*Désolé(e), je ne peux pas.*
*Oui, je veux bien!*
*On se retrouve à quelle heure?*
*On se retrouve à 6h.*

> **Framework reference**
- 1.5, 2.5, 4.6, 5.2

> **Starters**
- Set a time limit for students to work in pairs or groups thinking of activities that they might want to invite someone to do: *aller au cinéma, jouer*

*au foot, regarder une vidéo, faire du shopping.* If they cannot provide complete phrases, single words will do, such as *cinéma*. Collect ideas on the board.
- Call out places in a town. Students respond by including it in an invitation, which other students should reply to. Ask them to include a day of the week in their invitations once they are more fluent. Recap on days of the week: list them on the board in a jumbled order for students to write them out in the correct order as quickly as possible.

> **Plenaries**
- Display a dialogue on the OHP or board, including two or three suggestions, a couple of refusals and an acceptance. Blank out some key words and phrases and ask students to read the dialogue out loud in pairs, filling in the missing words. Blank out more words and phrases and encourage students to read the dialogue again. Continue doing this, blanking out more words each time. Challenge students to recall the whole dialogue from memory.
- In pairs, students invent their own dialogue between two famous figures or cartoon characters. They perform their dialogue for the class.

> **Assessment opportunities**
- Speaking: Students' Book page 55, exercise 4b
- Writing: Students' Book page 55, exercise 6

**AT 1.2**
**AT 2.2**

## 1 Écoute, lis et répète.

- Look at the key language box with students first. Can they recognise the places mentioned? Compare with the list they came up with in the Starter activity. Point out the meaning of *Tu veux venir ...?*
- Students listen to the invitations, while looking at the key language box, and repeat each one as closely as they can, copying intonation as well as pronunciation. Recap on using rising intonation at the end of sentences to ask questions.

  **CD 3, track 34**  page 54, activité 1

1 Tu veux venir au cinéma?
2 Tu veux venir au café?
3 Tu veux venir au match de foot?
4 Tu veux venir au centre commercial?
5 Tu veux venir à la piscine?
6 Tu veux venir à la plage?

**AT 3.1**

## 2 Relie les images (a–f) aux questions (1–6).

- Students match the pictures with each question in the key language box to ensure understanding of the places.

*Answers*: a 5; b 2; c 3; d 1; e 4; f 6

**AT 1.2**

## 3a Écoute (1–6). On va où?

- Students listen to each invitation and note the letter of the correct place from exercise 2.

*Answers*: 1 c; 2 d; 3 b; 4 a; 5 e; 6 f

  **CD 3, track 35**  page 54, activités 3a et 3b

1 – Salut! Tu veux venir au match de foot?
  – Oui, je veux bien!
2 – Salut! Tu veux venir au cinéma?
  – Oui, je veux bien!
3 – Mariam, tu veux venir au café?
  – Ah non, désolée! Je ne peux pas!
4 – David, tu veux venir à la piscine?
  – Ah non, désolé! Je ne peux pas!
5 – Sarah, tu veux venir au centre commercial avec moi?
  – Oui, je veux bien!
6 – Salut, Mylène! Ça va?
  – Oui, ça va bien!
  – Tu veux venir à la plage?
  – Ah non, désolée! Je ne peux pas!

**AT 1.2**

## 3b Réécoute. On accepte (✓) ou on refuse (✗)?

- Look together at the key language box before playing the audio. Ask students to repeat both the positive and the negative replies, exaggerating intonation.
- Students then listen again and note whether

each person accepts or refuses the invitation. An alternative would be that students put up their hand only when someone accepts.

*Answers*: 1 ✓ 2 ✓ 3 ✗ 4 ✗ 5 ✓ 6 ✗

**AT 4.2**

## 4a Écris.

- Students write a list of the places in the order they would like to go to them. Before they write out the phrases, display them on the board and ask students to explain what *au* and *à la* mean and why each is used (masculine and feminine places). They have met this before in earlier units.

**AT 2.2**

## 4b À deux: invitations.

- Students work in pairs, with one partner inviting the other to each of the six places. Their partner replies, accepting the first three on their list from exercise 4a and refusing the other three. Model first with a volunteer, if more support is needed.
- Students could note their partner's answers and write them up as six mini-conversations.

**AT 3.2**

## 5 Lis et note en anglais pour chaque message:

- Students read the two text messages and answer the questions in English.
- Read out the messages for more support and ask students to read them out loud with a partner to practise pronunciation.
- Look at the key language which gives the structures about arranging to meet at a certain time: *On se retrouve à quelle heure? On se retrouve à six heures.* Ask students to adapt the second sentence, changing the time to one you show on a large clock.

*Answers*: A a swimming pool; b Wednesday; c 3 o'clock; B a beach; b Saturday; c 2.30

**AT 4.2–3**

## 6 Écris une conversation.

- Students write a little play, using as much language as they can from the spread. They can use the key language as support.
- Ask confident pairs to perform their play for the rest of the class. The class must evaluate which one was best, giving reasons.

### Follow-up

- For further oral practice of invitations and responses, an interactive activity using the places met on this spread, as well as some additional places, is provided on OxBox, *Je veux bien*.

- Further speaking practice on this topic is provided on Copymaster 7.

**175**

# 7.3　Garder contact

## *Planner*

> ### Objectives
> • Say how you will keep in touch with friends

> ### Resources
> Students' Book, pages 56–57
> CD 3, track 36

> ### Key language
> *Je vais téléphoner.*
> *Je vais envoyer des emails.*
> *Je vais envoyer des SMS.*
> *Je vais communiquer sur mon profil web.*
> *Je vais organiser une fête*
> *Je ne vais pas garder contact.*
> *Tu vas …?*
> *On va …*

> ### Grammar
> Say what you are going to do in the future
> Using *on*

> ### Framework reference
> 2.4, 4.5, 5.4

> ### Starters
> • Before looking at the Students' Book, students work in groups to come up with ideas of ways of keeping in touch with someone they have met on holiday. Do this in English first and then see if they can come up with any related French words. Note all their suggestions on the board, then display the following phrases from page 56 and see if students mentioned any of them: *téléphoner; envoyer des emails; envoyer des SMS; communiquer sur mon profil web; organiser une fête*. Ask students to try to work out what these phrases mean.
> • Display the six phrases from page 56 on the board with just the first letter of each word showing: J. v… t……… (*Je vais téléphoner.*). Give students a few minutes to try to write them all out from memory in pairs. How many could they remember? Did they spell them correctly?

> ### Plenaries
> • Write the six phrases from page 56, but jumble the words in each sentence: *vais SMS des Je envoyer*. Students work in pairs to see how fast they can unjumble them all. They should work with their books closed, if possible.
> • Write the following verbs on the board: *écouter, regarder, manger, boire, envoyer, organiser*. Challenge students to write as many sentences as they can in three minutes, using these verbs: *Je vais manger une pizza*, etc. Pool ideas to see who came up with the most novel sentence.

> ### Assessment opportunities
> • Reading: Students' Book page 57, exercise 5
> • Writing: Students' Book page 57, exercise 6

---

 **AT 3.2** 　**1 Relie.**

• Before giving students time to do this activity, look at the six phrases together, if you have not already done so in the Starter. Which phrases can they work out? Encourage them to use the photos and to try to work out those they did not know.
• Students then match each sentence to a picture.

*Answers*: 1 b; 2 e; 3 f; 4 a; 5 c; 6 d

**AT 1.2** 　**2 Écoute.**

• Students listen and note the letters of the pictures in the order they are mentioned.

*Answers*: f, e, b, a, c, d

 **CD 3, track 36**　　　　　　page 56, activité 2

– Comment garder contact avec les copains de vacances? Qu'est-ce que tu vas faire?
– Je vais envoyer des SMS.
– Je vais envoyer des emails.
– Je vais téléphoner.
– Je vais communiquer sur mon profil web.
– Je vais organiser une fête.
– Je ne vais pas garder contact.

**AT 4.2** 　**3 Écris.**

• Students list the sentences in order of preference, starting with the action which is their favourite.

### Grammaire

• Write *Je vais …* on the board. Ask students if they remember what it means. Once you have established it means 'I'm going …' ask if they can accurately translate each of the speech bubbles in exercise 1. Explain that *je vais* in this instance is used to talk about something they are going to do in the future.

- Look at the grammar box together and establish the meaning of: *Je ne vais pas ...*, *Tu vas...?* To practise the negative, ask students to make each of the speech bubbles in exercise 1 negative.

 **4 À deux.**

- Students work in pairs. One reads out sentences 1–6 in random order and their partner points to the relevant photo on page 56.

AT 3.3 **5 Lis et trouve le français.**

- Students read the text and find the French for the English phrases listed.

*Answers*: a Nous, on va garder contact. b On ne va pas téléphoner. c On va organiser une grande fête. d On va envoyer des emails. e Les copines, c'est important!

## Grammaire

- Point out the use of *on* to mean 'we'. *On va* can replace *Je vais* in the expressions already met. Do some oral practice by calling out a number of a picture from exercise 1 and students say a corresponding phrase, starting with *On va* ...

 **6 Écris.**

- Students use the verbs given to write about what they and their friends are going to do at a party.
- Point out that *On va ...* can be used with any verb to say what you are going to do. Demonstrate a few expressions on the board first, if more support is needed.

# 7.4 Vocabulaire

page 58

---

## *Planner*

➤ **Resources**
Students' Book, page 58

➤ **Objectives**
- *Vocabulaire*: to provide a theme-based summary of the key language of the unit, which students can use as a reference or as an aid to learning
- To practise pronunciation

➤ **Framework reference**
4.1, 4.2

---

### Using the vocabulary page

- Encourage students to use the *Vocabulaire* page as a reference point throughout the unit. It can also serve as a useful revision tool before students do the *Clic-test!*
- Vocabulary is listed spread-by-spread and you could either ask students to learn each section for homework after each spread is completed, or set the whole page as a homework task before starting work on the test. Most students learn shorter sections best, so often it is better to give them manageable chunks to learn at a time.
- Encourage students to use different techniques to help them learn the vocabulary:
  - Cover up the English and see what they can remember; write down any words they can't remember and test themselves again on those words.
  - Cover up the French and see if they can remember the words or phrases this way round.

  - Make word cards with English on one side and French on the other. Students can then test themselves to see what they can remember. Put any cards they can't remember on one side and go over those again at the end.
  - Work in pairs to test each other, either using the vocabulary list or the word cards.
- Record themselves saying the words both in English and French. Saying words and phrases out loud can often help with memorising them.

### Sound French!

- *Aim:* To practise pronunciation
- The point practised here is the *qu* spelling which sounds like *k* in French.
- Practise saying the words and phrases listed, before asking students to find more examples in any of the vocabulary lists.

# 7.4 Clic-test!

## *Planner*

The page is divided into four sections: listening, speaking, reading and writing.

➤ **Objectives**
* To enable students to recap on the language and structures of the unit
* To provide an opportunity for quick testing of all four skills

➤ **Resources**
Students' Book, page 59
CD 3, track 37

➤ **Framework reference**
5.8

**AT 1.2–3** **1 Écoute!**
* Students listen to the conversation and choose option a or b in each English sentence.

*Answers*: 1 a; 2 b; 3 b; 4 a; 5 b

 **CD 3, track 37** page 59, activité 1

– Salut! Moi, c'est Sophie. Tu t'appelles comment?
– Je m'appelle Yann.
– Tu es français, Yann?
– Oui, je suis français. Et toi?
– Moi aussi, je suis française. J'habite à Dijon. Tu habites où?
– J'habite à Paris.
– Cool! Tu as quel âge, Yann?
– J'ai quinze ans.
– Écoute … tu veux venir au café?
– Désolé, je ne peux pas.
– Dommage!

**AT 3.2** **2 Lis!**
* Students read the statements and say how each person is going to stay in touch.

*Answers*: a phone; b email; c web profile page; d won't keep in touch; e organise a party; f text/phone

**AT 4.2–3** **3 Écris!**
* Students write sentences to complete each of the English prompts given. If students are able to, they could write a paragraph including some connectives.

**AT 2.2–3** **4 Parle!**

* Students work with a partner and invite each other to the places pictured. The other partner must either accept or refuse, according to the symbol.
* For extension, you could ask students to include a time to meet.

# À moi

## *Planner*

➤ **Objectives**
* To provide reinforcement activities for quiet work
* To provide alternative class and homework material for students who finish other activities quickly

➤ **Resources**
Students' Book, page 82

➤ **Framework reference**
2.2, 2.3, 2.5

### Au camp de vacances

**AT 3.2** **1 Read the cartoon strip. Where does Sam ask Flo, Lola and Marie to go?**
* The cartoon strip concentrates on invitations and responses. Students identify the places.

*Answers*: Flo cinema; Lola swimming pool; Marie café

**AT 3.2–3** **2 Answer in English.**
* Students now look at more of the detail of the invitations and answer questions in English.

*Answers*: a refuse; b beach; c refuse; d beach; e accept; f because he has an invitation he can accept

**AT 4.2–3** **3 Continue the story.**
* Students write four more frames where Sam finds out something about the girl (name, age, nationality and where she lives).
* Encourage students to continue the conversation, using the language they have met in this unit, such as name, age, where people live, nationality, etc.

# 8 Les médias

| Unité 8: Les médias  Overview grid | | | | | | |
|---|---|---|---|---|---|---|
| Page reference | Contexts and objectives | Grammar | Language strategies and pronunciation | Key language | Framework | AT level |
| 60–61<br>**8.1 À la télé** | • Name types of TV programmes<br>• Say which programmes you like and don't like | | Remember new words by making connections | J'aime (bien), J'adore, Je n'aime pas, Je déteste … les films, les documentaires, les dessins animés, les jeux, les feuilletons, les émissions sportives, les émissions musicales, les émissions de télé réalité, les informations<br>Bof! C'est … génial, marrant, intéressant, pas mal, nul, ennuyeux. | 5.1, 5.2, 5.3 | 1.1–2<br>2.1–2<br>3.2<br>4.1–2 |
| 62–63<br>**8.2 Au cinéma** | • Name different types of film<br>• Give your opinion of films | • Revision of some perfect tense<br>• c'était + adjective | | J'ai vu, adoré, aimé, détesté …<br>une comédie, un dessin animé, un film d'action, un film romantique, un film d'horreur, un film de science-fiction<br>C'était … amusant, drôle, génial, long, ennuyeux, nul. | 1.4, 1.5, 2.4, 4.5 | 1.1–3<br>2.1–3<br>3.3<br>4.2–3 |
| 64–65<br>**8.3 Je peux?** | • Say what you can and can't do | • je peux, je ne peux pas | | Je peux … Je ne peux pas …<br>avoir une télé dans ma chambre, télécharger de la musique, avoir mon profil sur Internet, aller au cinéma avec mes copains, échanger mes jeux électroniques, avoir mon portable au collège<br>C'est bien/nul. Ce n'est pas juste. | 1.1, 3.1, 4.6, 5.4 | 1.2<br>2.2<br>3.2–3<br>4.2–3 |
| 66<br>**8.4 Vocabulaire** | • Practise pronunciation | | j sound | | 4.1, 5.5 | |
| 67<br>**8.4 Clic-test!** | • Recap on the language structures of the unit<br>• Provide an opportunity for quick testing of all four skills | | | | 5.8 | 1.2–3<br>2.2<br>3.2<br>4.2 |
| 83<br>**À moi** | • Provide reinforcement activities for self-access work | | | | 2.1, 2.2, 2.4 | 3.2–3<br>4.2–3 |

## MEDIUM TERM GRID Week-by-week overview (assuming six weeks' work or approximately 10–12.5 hours)

**About Unit 8, *Les médias***

In this unit, students learn to talk about television programmes and films and to say what they are and are not allowed to do. They use plurals of nouns and say what they saw and liked in the perfect tense. They give opinions using *c'était* + adjective. They also use *je peux* and *je ne peux pas* to say what they are and are not allowed to do. They learn the technique of remembering new words by making connections.

New vocabulary includes types of television programmes and films, opinion phrases in the perfect tense, adjectives to describe films and infinitive expressions with *peux*. Revised language includes expressing opinions with *c'est* and *c'était*, *j'aime*, *je n'aime pas*, *j'adore*, *je déteste* and perfect tense verbs.

Reading, listening and comprehension skills are developed through a variety of text, audio and video materials.

| Week | Resources | Objectives |
|------|-----------|------------|
| 1 | 8.1 À la télé | Naming types of television programmes<br>Using *j'aime*, *je n'aime pas*, *j'adore* and *je déteste* to say which programmes you like and don't like<br>Using *c'est* + adjective to express your opinion |
| 2 | 8.2 Au cinéma | Naming different types of film<br>Saying which films you have seen<br>Using the perfect tense to say which films you liked or disliked<br>Using *c'était* + adjective to express your opinion in the past |
| 3 | 8.3 Je peux? | Using *je peux* and *je ne peux pas* to say what you are and are not allowed to do<br>Saying whether you think something is fair or not |
| 4 | Sound French! (p66)<br>À moi (p83)<br>Copymasters, OxBox | Practising pronunciation (*j* sound)<br>Additional reading and writing practice<br>Using additional resources, such as Copymasters and OxBox activities, to reinforce and extend language met |
| 5 | 8.4 Vocabulaire<br>Clic-test! | Learning vocabulary<br>Recapping on vocabulary of unit<br>Preparing and carrying out of assessment in all four skills<br>Reviewing progress |
| 6 | Copymasters (*Feuilles*)<br>OxBox | Reinforcement and extension of the language of the unit using extra resources<br>Reviewing progress via the Checklist on page 66, *Vocabulaire*<br>Going back over aspects of the unit which need reviewing after *Clic-test!* |

# 8.1 À la télé

## *Planner*

➢ **Objectives**
- Name types of TV programme
- Say which programmes you like and don't like

➢ **Resources**
Students' Book, pages 60–61
CD 3, tracks 38–39
OxBox, *Clic! 3 Star, Unité 2, À la télé; J'aime ça*
Copymaster 18, 23, *Clic! 3 Star*

➢ **Key language**
*J'aime (bien), J'adore, Je n'aime pas, Je déteste …
les films, les documentaires, les dessins animés,
les jeux, les feuilletons, les émissions sportives, les
émissions musicales, les émissions de télé réalité, les
informations
Bof! C'est … génial, marrant, intéressant, pas mal,
nul, ennuyeux.*

➢ **Framework reference**
5.1, 5.2, 5.3

➢ **Starters**
- Display the types of television programmes from page 60, together with a list of English equivalents. Students work in pairs and race against the clock to match the French programme types to the English words. They should be able to work some out because of the similarity with English words – the others they could guess. How many can they get correct?

- Ask all students in the class to stand up. Begin by calling out the name of a television programme and nominating someone in the class. Without hesitating, this student says something about the programme, such as what type of programme it is and/or an opinion, then names another programme for another student to do likewise. The student then sits down again. The nominated student says something about the programme, names another programme for another student, then sits down. Continue until all students are sitting down. You could do this with pairs of students to make it quicker.

➢ **Plenaries**
- Give students a couple of minutes, working in pairs, to list as many different types of television programmes as they can, giving an example of each. When the time is up, they compare their list with another pair, scoring a point for each type of programme not mentioned by the other pair.
- Play a version of Word Tennis with the class divided into two teams. The aim is to build sentences expressing opinions of television programmes.
  Team A: *J'aime …*
  Team B: *… les dessins animés*
  Team A: *C'est …*
  Team B: *marrant et …*
  Provide key words and phrases on the board as support, if necessary, for students to choose from.

➢ **Assessment opportunities**
- Speaking: Students' Book page 61, exercise 6
- Writing: Students' Book page 61, exercise 7

---

 **AT 1.2**
 **AT 2.2**

**1 Écoute, lis et répète.**
- Students listen, read the captions and repeat the types of television programmes.
- Ask students to look at the words and see if they can detect a pattern: all the programmes use *les* so must be plural; all the nouns have *s* at the end apart from *jeux* which has *x*. Establish the fact that most nouns add *s* for plural, but there are exceptions, such as *jeux*.

**CD 3, track 38**      page 60, activité 1

1 les films
2 les documentaires
3 les dessins animés
4 les jeux
5 les feuilletons
6 les émissions sportives
7 les émissions musicales
8 les émissions de télé réalité
9 les informations

 **AT 2.1**

**2 À deux.**
- Students work in pairs. One partner says a television programme type and the other gives an example of that sort of programme.

## Top Tips!
- Point out to students that, to remember new words, it is often useful to make connections with words they already know. Look at each type of television programme and see if students can give ideas of connections and how they might remember them best.

### Follow-up

- A matching activity on the types of television programmes from this unit, as well as a couple of additional ones, is provided on OxBox, *À la télé*.

AT 4.1 **3 Écris ton hit-parade (1–9). Donne des exemples.**

- Students write the nine types of television programmes in order of personal preference, giving examples of each type.
- To provide more support, you may like to display a prepared *hit-parade* on the board and ask a few questions to ensure comprehension.
  *Le hit-parade de Julie*
  *1 = les films, 2 = les dessins animés,*
  *3 = les jeux, 4 = les documentaires,*
  *5 = les émissions musicales, 6 = les feuilletons*

| Lis le hit-parade de Julie. Vrai (✓) ou faux (✗)? | Vrai ✓ | Faux ✗ |
|---|---|---|
| a | Her favourite programmes are films. | | |
| b | She likes cartoons. | | |
| c | She is not so keen on soaps. | | |
| d | She prefers documentaries to game shows. | | |
| e | She doesn't mention music shows. | | |

- For extra speaking practice, students could compare their list with that of a partner. Do they have any the same?
  Student A: *Le numéro un, c'est les films.*
  Student B: *Moi, le numéro un, c'est les feuillletons.*

## Preparation

- The rest of the spread revises opinions, using *j'aime / j'adore* and *je n'aime pas / je déteste*. It also covers *c'est* + adjectives.
- Practise *j'adore, j'aime, je n'aime pas* and *je déteste* first by asking questions about television programmes: *Tu aimes EastEnders? Tu aimes les informations?*
- Gradually encourage students to justify their opinions: *C'est … génial, marrant, intéressant, pas mal, nul, ennuyeux.* If necessary, recap on the meaning of these adjectives. If more support is needed, write the adjectives on the board and ask students to match them with their English equivalents.

AT 3.2 **4 Lis les phrases. C'est positif ☺, négatif ☹ ou entre les deux 😐?**

- Students read the various opinions about television programmes and indicate whether the opinion is positive, negative or a bit of both.

*Answers:* a ☺ b ☹ c 😐 d ☺ e ☹ f ☺

AT 1.2 **5 Écoute. C'est positif ☺, négatif ☹ ou entre les deux 😐? (1–7)**

- Students listen to seven opinions and say again whether each one is negative, positive or in

between.

- Ask students to listen again and note one detail from each opinion offered, such as the type of programme, a specific opinion, an opinion word, etc.

*Answers:* 1 ☹ 2 ☺ 3 ☹ 4 ☺ 5 ☹ 6 😐 7 ☺

 **CD 3, track 39**  page 61, activité 5

1 Je déteste les feuilletons! C'est nul, ça!
2 J'aime bien. C'est marrant, les émissions de télé réalité.
3 Oh non, encore un documentaire – c'est ennuyeux.
4 Je préfère la musique. J'adore les émissions musicales.
5 Je n'aime pas du tout les informations!
6 Les dessins animés? Bof, pas mal.
7 Super! Je préfère les émissions sportives.

AT 2.2 **6 À deux: interviews.**

- Students work in pairs to ask and answer questions about what they think about different types of television programmes.
- Modal an interview with a volunteer first and encourage students to try to keep their conversation going for as long as possible.
- Students could record their interviews, if possible.

AT 4.2 **7 Écris.**

- Students write four to six sentences saying what they think of different types of television programmes.

**Follow-up**

- Students choose a celebrity and imagine what he/she likes and dislikes watching on television. They write a few sentences on behalf of the celebrity, expressing opinions of different programmes.
-  Extension listening practice on this topic can be found on OxBox, *J'aime ça.*
-  C18 Further speaking practice on types of television programmes is provided on Copymaster 18.
-  C23 Students could carry out the extension reading activities on Copymaster 23.

*Answers:* 1 a it's a game show; b *Wheel of Fortune*; c a detective/police series; d at 17.30 on Arte; e (1) La Roue de la fortune, Questions pour un champion, Êtes-vous plus fort qu'un élève de 10 ans?; (2) *How I met your mother, Little Britain*; (3) *Star Academy, Topmodel*; (4) CD-aujourd'hui, On n'a pas tout dit, Le meilleur de Florence Foresti, Le grand journal de Canal +, Histoires incroyables; (5) Un livre, un jour, Le journal de culture

# 8.2 Au cinéma

## *Planner*

> ### Objectives
> * Name different types of film
> * Give your opinion of films

> ### Resources
> Students' Book, pages 62–63
> CD 3, tracks 40–41
> OxBox, *Clic! 3 Star, Unité 2, On parle des films;*
> *Au ciné-club*
> Copymaster 15, *Clic! 3 Star*

> ### Key language
> *J'ai vu, adoré, aimé, détesté …*
> *une comédie, un dessin animé, un film d'action,*
> *un film romantique, un film d'horreur, un film de*
> *science-fiction*
> *C'était … amusant, drôle, génial, long, ennuyeux, nul.*

> ### Grammar
> Revision of some perfect tense
> *c'était* + adjective

> ### Framework reference
> 1.4, 1.5, 2.4, 4.5

> ### Starters
> * Display the types of film from page 62 in French and English on the board. Students match them. Afterwards, ask students to tell you what strategies they used, such as working out from similarity to English words, process of elimination, etc.
> * Display a list of current film titles that students are likely to be interested in, in English and in French, and set a time limit for students to match them. The latest film titles can be looked up online.

> ### Plenaries
> * Challenge students to think of two or three film titles (in English) to represent each of the film genres listed on page 62. Set a strict time limit, then ask them to compare lists with a partner. Students score one point for each film they have listed that their partner does not have.
> * Students decide on a film they would take with them to a desert island. Provide some key phrases and ask students to prepare two or three sentences about the film, mentioning type of film, title, their opinion of it, etc. Students then try to speak enthusiastically about their chosen film, aiming to 'sell' it to the class. On the strength of the presentations, the class vote for the film they would choose as their desert island movie.

> ### Assessment opportunities
> * Writing: Students' Book page 63, exercise 6

---

**AT 1.1**
**AT 2.1**

**1 Écoute, lis et répète.**

* Students listen to the types of films and repeat each one, following the captions in their books.
* Do some quick oral practice on film genres by calling out a type of film. Students say the number of the corresponding picture on page 62 as quickly as possible. Alternatively, you say a number and students call out the type of film.

 **CD 3, track 40**      page 62, activité 1

1 une comédie
2 un dessin animé
3 un film d'action
4 un film romantique
5 un film d'horreur
6 un film de science-fiction

**AT 2.2** **2 À deux.**

* Before students work in pairs, look at the film titles together and discuss what types of films they think they are.
* Students work in pairs and one student says he/she has seen a certain type of film. Students use the structure *j'ai vu* plus one of the film genres met in exercise 1; recap with students that they are talking about a film they have seen in the past. The other student then says a matching title from the *Ciné-club* list.
* For more speaking practice, students can play a memory game in pairs or small groups.
  Student A: *J'ai vu une comédie.*
  Student B: *J'ai vu une comédie et un film d'horreur.*
  Student A: *J'ai vu une comédie, un film d'horreur et un film d'action.*

**AT 4.2** **3 Tu as vu quels films? Écris six phrases.**

* Students write six sentences stating which films they have seen recently. They should name the film and say what type of film it is. Students can use the film titles provided or add their own.

**4a Lis les emails. Qui a préféré le film: Annie ou Mario?**

- Read the two emails out loud with students as preparation for this task.
- Students can then read the emails again and say whether Mario or Annie liked the film they saw most. Point out to students they are reading for gist at this stage and they do not have to understand every word to answer the question.
- Students could read the emails out loud with their partner, being as expressive as they can.

*Answer:* Mario

 **4b Relis. Note en anglais pour chaque personne:**

- Students now look at more of the detail in the emails and answer the questions in English.
- If students need more support with opinions, you could do a matching activity. Write the French adjectives, *amusant, long, ennuyeux, drôle, génial, nul* on the board, along with their English equivalents. Students should match them.

*Answers:* Mario: a Pirates of the Caribbean; b action film; c liked it – great, funny; Annie: a Mr Hulot's Holiday; b comedy; c hated it – long, boring, rubbish

 **5 Écoute. Ils ont aimé le film? Pourquoi? Prends des notes. (1–6)**

- Students listen to six people stating their opinion of films they have recently seen. Students make notes in English with as much detail as they can. Pause the audio at appropriate places, if necessary.

*Answers:* 1 no, boring; 2 no, long; 3 yes, very funny; 4 yes, great; 5 no, rubbish; 6 yes, loved it, great, excellent

 **CD 3, track 41**          page 63, activité 5

– Tu as aimé le film?
**1** Non, je n'ai pas aimé le film. C'était ennuyeux.
**2** Non, je n'ai pas aimé le film. C'était long!
**3** J'ai adoré le film parce que c'était très drôle.
**4** Oui, j'ai aimé le film. C'était génial!
**5** Euh … moi, non … je n'ai pas aimé le film. C'était nul!
**6** J'ai vu un excellent film. J'ai adoré! C'était génial!

 **6 Écris ton email.**

- Students write an email about a film they have seen.

- Go through the key language box with students and recap on the phrases *j'ai adoré, j'ai aimé* and *j'ai détesté* to refer to opinions in the past tense. Remind students also to use *c'était* plus an adjective to talk about opinions in the past tense.
- Demonstrate on the board how students can adapt the example to talk about their chosen film.

**Follow-up**

- Two further extension activities on the subject of films can be found on OxBox. There is a matching activity, *On parle des films* and an extension listening activity which includes types of films from this spread, plus a few more, *Au ciné-club*.
- Copymaster 15 provides further reading practice.

*Answers:* **1** un documentaire, les informations, une pub, un jeu télévisé, une émission musicale, la météo; *the highlighted squares spell out:* un dessin animé

| u | n | d | o | c | u | m | e | n | t | a | i | r | e |   |   |   |   | l |
|---|---|---|---|---|---|---|---|---|---|---|---|---|---|---|---|---|---|---|
|   |   |   |   |   |   |   |   |   |   |   |   |   |   |   |   |   |   | a |
| l | e | s | i | n | f | o | r | m | a | t | i | o | n | s |   |   |   | m |
|   |   |   |   |   |   |   |   |   |   |   |   |   |   |   |   |   |   | é |
| u | n | e | p | u | b |   |   |   |   |   |   |   |   |   |   |   |   | t |
|   |   |   |   |   |   |   |   | u | n | j | e | u | t | é | l | é | v | i | s | é |
|   |   |   |   |   |   |   |   |   |   |   |   |   |   |   |   |   |   | o |
| u | n | e | é | m | i | s | s | i | o | n | m | u | s | i | c | a | l | e |

*Answers:* **2** a émissions; b feuilletons; c trouves; d vu, était; e trouvé, trop
*Answers:* **3** a I love reality TV shows. They're great! b Do you prefer documentaries or soap operas? c What do you think of action films? d I saw/watched a romantic film that was very good. e I found the film too long.

## 8.3 Je peux?

pages 64–65

### *Planner*

➤ **Objectives**
- Say what you can and can't do

➤ **Resources**
Students' Book, pages 64–65
CD 3, tracks 42–43

➤ **Key language**
*Je peux … Je ne peux pas …*
*avoir une télé dans ma chambre, télécharger de la musique, avoir mon profil sur Internet, aller au cinéma avec mes copains, échanger mes jeux électroniques, avoir mon portable au collège*
*C'est bien/nul. Ce n'est pas juste.*

➤ **Grammar**
*je peux, je ne peux pas …*

➤ **Framework reference**
1.1, 3.1, 4.6, 5.4

➤ **Starters**
- Before beginning work on this spread, students keep their books closed and discuss in pairs, in English, any issues that tend to come up for discussion between themselves and their parents, such as what they are and are not allowed to do. Students can then open their books and look at the expressions on page 64 together. Can they work out what they mean? How does this list compare to what they discussed in English?
- Play Hangman with the expressions from exercise 1.

➤ **Plenaries**
- Give students a minute to try to memorise the six key expressions from page 64. Display them on the board with key words blanked out. Students try to complete the sentences from memory. To add an element of competition, you could play this as a team game.
- Invite a volunteer to the front of the class. He/She stands facing the class. Give the volunteer one of the phrases from exercise 1 with a tick or a cross to show whether it is allowed or not. The other students cannot see what you have written and they must make statements to find out what the phrase is. The student at the front can only answer *oui/non*.
  Class: *Je peux télécharger de la musique.*
  Student A: *Non!*
  Class: *Je ne peux pas avoir un portable au collège.*
  Student A: *Non!*
  See how many attempts it takes to get the correct answer.

➤ **Assessment opportunities**
- Writing: Students' Book page 65, exercise 5
- Speaking: Students' Book page 65, exercise 6

---

AT 3.2 **1 Relie.**
- Students match each picture to its corresponding sentence. They should be able to do this by understanding key words.
- Look with students at the detail of each sentence and lead them to work out what each one means. For example, they have not met *télécharger* but they will understand *musique*. Encourage students to look at the picture and deduce what *télécharger* might mean. Do something similar with each sentence in turn.

*Answers:* 1 e; 2 b; 3 a; 4 d; 5 f; 6 c

AT 1.2
AT 2.2 **2 Écoute, lis et répète.**
- Students listen and repeat the sentences while following the phrases in the key language box. Can students guess what *je peux* means?

 **CD 3, track 42**      page 64, activité 2

Je peux avoir une télé dans ma chambre.
Je peux télécharger de la musique.
Je peux avoir mon profil sur Internet.
Je peux aller au cinéma avec mes copains.
Je peux échanger mes jeux électroniques.
Je peux avoir mon portable au collège

AT 1.2 **3a Écoute Marie. Tu entends combien de fois …?**
- Before students listen, point out *je ne peux pas*. If students know what *je peux* means, what do they think *je ne peux pas* means? Compare to *j'aime / je n'aime pas* and *je joue / je ne joue pas*. Establish that *ne … pas* indicates a negative.
- Students listen to Marie talking about what she is and isn't allowed to do. Students listen and note how many times she says *Je peux …* and *Je ne peux pas …*

*Answers:* a 3; b 3

**CD 3, track 43**        page 64, activités 3a et 3b

Ma mère est sympa. Je peux télécharger de la musique. C'est bien.
Pourtant, je ne peux pas avoir mon profil sur Internet. C'est nul.
Je ne peux pas avoir mon portable au collège. Ce n'est pas juste.
Je peux aller au cinéma avec mes copains. Ça, c'est bien.
Et je peux échanger mes jeux électroniques. C'est bien aussi.
Mais je ne peux pas avoir une télé dans ma chambre. Ce n'est pas juste!

**AT 1.2**   **3b Réécoute.**

• Students listen again and note the numbers of the key phrases 1–6 in activity 1 in the order they hear them.

*Answers*: 2, 3, 6, 4, 5, 1

**AT 3.3**   **4 Lis et complète.**

• Before students work independently, look at the gapped text together. Read it out loud, stopping at each gap. Establish what each sentence means. Can students suggest the type of word they think might fill the gap?
• Give students a few minutes to select the word for each gap from the box. You could ask them to write out the whole passage for more writing practice, if liked.

*Answers*: 1 peux; 2 je ne peux pas; 3 portable; 4 aller; 5 jeux; 6 avoir

**AT 4.2**   **5 Écris ce que tu peux faire (six phrases). C'est juste?**

• Before students do this activity, display the three expressions on the board and elicit what they mean: *C'est bien. C'est nul. Ce n'est pas juste.* Call out a volunteer, who should come up with a phrase from exercise 1 to match the opinion you have given (in his/her view).
Teacher: *Ce n'est pas juste.*
Student: *Je ne peux pas avoir mon portable au collège.*
• Students then write six sentences to say what they can and cannot do and say whether it is fair or good, using one of the expressions from above.

**AT 2.2**   **6 À deux. Combien de points en commun?**

• Students work in pairs and compare their lists from exercise 5. How many points did they have the same?

**AT 4.2–3**   **7 Tu peux ou tu ne peux pas? Fais des phrases.**

• Students are now encouraged to use *je peux* or *je ne peux pas* with the new phrases listed. Go over the phrases together first, before asking students to write whether they are allowed or not allowed to do each one.
• The aim here is to broaden out the structures and encourage students to say different things. You may like to gather together other possible phrases on the board first, such as manger *des frites, me réveiller à midi*.
• Students could create a survey using some of the new phrases. What are other students allowed and not allowed to do?

# 8.4   Vocabulaire

page 66

## *Planner*

➤ **Resources**
Students' Book, page 66

➤ **Objectives**
• *Vocabulaire*: to provide a theme-based summary of the key language of the unit, which students can use as a reference or as an aid to learning
• To practise pronunciation

➤ **Framework reference**
4.1, 5.5

## Using the vocabulary page

• Encourage students to use the *Vocabulaire* page as a reference point throughout the unit. It can also serve as a useful revision tool before students do the *Clic-test!*
• Vocabulary is listed spread-by-spread and you could either ask students to learn each section for homework after each spread is completed, or set the whole page as a homework task before

starting work on the test. Most students learn shorter sections best, so often it is better to give them manageable chunks to learn at a time.
• Encourage students to use different techniques to help them learn the vocabulary:
  – Cover up the English and see what they can remember; write down any words they can't remember and test themselves again on those words.

- Cover up the French and see if they can remember the words or phrases this way round.
- Make word cards with English on one side and French on the other. Students can then test themselves to see what they can remember. Put any cards they can't remember on one side and go over those again at the end.
- Work in pairs to test each other, either using the vocabulary list or the word cards.
- Record themselves saying the words both in English and French. Saying words and phrases out loud can often help with memorising them.

### Sound French!

- *Aim:* To practise pronunciation
- The point practised here is the pronunciation of the *j* sound in French.
- Look at the words on the page and ask students to repeat them after you.
- Ask students to find examples of more words with the *j* sound in the vocabulary list from this and previous units and to practise saying them out loud.

## 8.4   Clic-test!                                                     page 67

---

### *Planner*

The page is divided into four sections: listening, speaking, reading and writing.

➢ **Objectives**
- To enable students to recap on the language and structures of the unit

- To provide an opportunity for quick testing of all four skills

➢ **Resources**
Students' Book, page 67
CD 3, track 44

➢ **Framework reference**
5.8

---

**AT 1.2–3**   **1 Écoute!**

- Students listen and note the types of film in the order mentioned.
- You could ask students to listen again and note opinions, if they are able to.

*Answers*: d, f, a, e, c, b

 **CD 3, track 44**                page 67, activité 1

- Dis, Lucas … Tu aimes les films romantiques?
- Les films romantiques! Ah non, je déteste les films romantiques!
- Tu aimes les films de science-fiction?
- Les films de science-fiction? Non, c'est ennuyeux!
- Tu aimes les comédies?
- Oui, les comédies, c'est pas mal.
- Et les films d'horreur?
- Oui, j'adore les films d'horreur. Et toi?
- Moi, j'aime bien les films d'action.
- Oui, c'est génial.
- Et j'adore les dessins animés.
- Les dessins animés? Tu adores les dessins animés? Oh là là. Les dessins animés, c'est complètement nul!

**AT 3.2**   **2 Lis!**

- Students give the meanings of the French sentences.

*Answers*: a have my page on the Internet; b go to the cinema with my friends; c have a TV in my bebroom; d swap video games; e download music; f take my mobile phone to school

**AT 2.2**   **3 Parle!**

- Students choose three types of television programmes they like and three they don't like and give reasons for each.

**AT 4.2**   **4 Écris!**

- Students write sentences on the subject of films they have seen and add an opinion for each one.

*Answers*: J'ai vu … C'était … a un dessin animé; b un film d'action; c un film d'horreur; d un film romantique; e un film de science-fiction; f une comédie

# À moi

## *Planner*

> **Objectives**
> - To provide reinforcement activities for quiet work
> - To provide alternative class and homework material for students who finish other activities quickly

> **Resources**
> Students' Book, page 83

> **Framework reference**
> 2.1, 2.2, 2.4

### Opinions télé

 **1 Read the bubbles. Who is it?**

- Students read the three speech bubbles of people talking about their television likes and dislikes and say who each English sentence refers to.

*Answers:* a Noémie; b Bastien; c Janila; d Janila; e Noémie; f Bastien; g Janila; h Bastien

AT 3.3 **2 Who would you rather spend an evening watching TV with? Bastien, Noémie or Janila? Translate that person's speech bubble into English.**

- Students say who they agree with most regarding television likes and dislikes and then concentrate on the detail by translating their chosen one into English.

*Answers:* Bastien: I've got a TV in my room. I love sports programmes. They are great! I don't like reality shows. Janila: I hate sports programmes and I don't like cartoons. They are stupid. I like game shows and reality shows. Noémie: I like the news and documentaries. I also like music shows. I hate soaps. They are boring.

 **3 Write a similar speech bubble with your own opinions. Then write one for a friend or family member.**

- Students use the speech bubbles as models to write their own. Model an example on the board first, highlighting the words students can change to personalise them.

# 9 L'avenir

| Unité 9: L'avenir  Overview grid | | | | | | |
|---|---|---|---|---|---|---|
| Page reference | Contexts and objectives | Grammar | Language strategies and pronunciation | Key language | Framework | AT level |
| 68–69 **9.1 Je vais faire français** | • Say what subjects you do at school<br>• Say what subjects you will do next year, and why | • *je vais* + infinitive (immediate future)<br>• Masculine and feminine adjectives (revised) | Giving reasons | *Cette année, je fais … anglais, dessin, sport, français, histoire-géographie, maths, musique, sciences, technologie et informatique*<br>*L'année prochaine, je vais faire/je ne vais pas faire …*<br>*parce que je suis nul/ nulle, fort/forte, je n'aime pas ça/j'aime ça* | 4.4, 4.5, 4.6 | 1.1–3<br>2.1–2<br>3.1–3<br>4.1–2 |
| 70–71 **9.2 Mon petit boulot** | • Say what part-time job you are going to do<br>• Give opinions of jobs | • *je vais, je ne vais pas* + infinitive (immediate future) | | *Je vais … Je ne vais pas …*<br>*travailler dans un magasin, faire du baby-sitting, sortir les chiens, aider à la maison, faire les courses, distribuer les journaux*<br>*parce que je n'aime pas ça/j'aime ça, c'est bien/ mal payé* | 5.2, 5.4, 5.6 | 1.2<br>2.2<br>3.2<br>4.2 |
| 72–73 **9.3 Je voudrais être styliste!** | • Say which job you would like to do<br>• Say why you would or wouldn't like a job | • Masculine and feminine forms of jobs titles | Finding new words in a dictionary | *Je suis …*<br>*styliste, acteur/ actrice, infirmier/ infirmière, chanteur/ chanteuse, fooballeur/ footballeuse, mécanicien/ mécanicienne*<br>*Je voudrais être … Je ne veux pas être …*<br>*parce que c'est bien/mal payé, c'est/ce n'est pas intéressant* | 1.1, 1.4, 4.3, 5.5 | 1.1–3<br>2.1–3<br>3.2–3<br>4.1–3 |
| 74 **9.4 Vocabulaire** | • Practise pronunciation | | c, ç and vowels | | 4.1, 5.5 | |
| 75 **9.4 Clic-test!** | • Recap on the language structures of the unit<br>• Provide an opportunity for quick testing of all four skills | | | | 5.7, 5.8 | 1.2<br>2.2–3<br>3.3<br>4.2 |
| 84 **À moi** | • Provide reinforcement activities for self-access work | | | | 2.2, 2.3, 2.5 | 3.2–3<br>4.2–3 |

| | MEDIUM TERM GRID Week-by-week overview (assuming six weeks' work or approximately 10–12.5 hours) | |
|---|---|---|

**About Unit 9, *L'avenir***

In this unit, students learn to talk about the future. They talk about which subjects they will be doing at school next year, which part-time job they are going to do and which job they would like to do later in life. Students use *je vais* and *je ne vais pas* + infinitive to talk about their future plans and they use adjectives in both the masculine and feminine form.

They also learn to give reasons, use masculine and feminine forms of jobs and find new words in a dictionary.

New vocabulary includes reasons for doing or not doing subjects next year, part-time jobs, future jobs and reasons for doing or not doing jobs. Revised language includes school subjects and opinions.

Reading, listening and comprehension skills are developed through a variety of text, audio and video materials.

| Week | Resources | Objectives |
|---|---|---|
| 1 | 9.1 Je vais faire français | Saying which subjects you do at school this year<br>Saying which subjects you are going to do next year<br>Using *je vais* and *je ne vais pas* + infinitive to talk about future plans<br>Giving reasons with *parce que*<br>Using masculine and feminine forms of adjectives |
| 2 | 9.2 Mon petit boulot | Using *je vais* and *je ne vais pas* + infinitive to say which part-time jobs you are going and not going to do<br>Giving reasons with parce que<br>Using *c'est* + reason |
| 3 | 9.3 Je voudrais être styliste! | Saying which job you would like to do later in life<br>Using *je voudrais être* and *je ne veux pas être* + job to say why you would or would not like a particular job<br>Using masculine and feminine forms of jobs<br>Finding new jobs in a dictionary |
| 4 | Sound French! (p74)<br>À moi (p84)<br>Copymasters, OxBox | Practising pronunciation (*c*, *ç* with different vowels)<br>Additional reading and writing practice<br>Using additional resources, such as Copymasters and OxBox activities, to reinforce and extend language met |
| 5 | 9.4 Vocabulaire<br>Clic-test! | Learning vocabulary<br>Recapping on vocabulary of unit<br>Preparing and carrying out assessment in all four skills<br>Reviewing progress |
| 6 | Copymasters (*Feuilles*)<br>OxBox | Reinforcement and extension of the language of the unit using extra resources<br>Reviewing progress via the Checklist on page 74, *Vocabulaire*<br>Going back over aspects of the unit which need reviewing after *Clic-test!* |

# 9.1 Je vais faire français

## Planner

> **Objectives**
> - Say what subjects you do at school
> - Say what subjects you will do next year, and why

> **Resources**
> Students' Book, pages 68–69
> CD 3, tracks 45–47
> OxBox, *Clic! 3 Star, Unité 6, Mon emploi du temps*
> Copymaster 65, 71, *Clic! 3 Star*
> CD 3, track 66

> **Key language**
> *Cette année, je fais …*
> *anglais, dessin, sport, français, histoire-géographie, maths, musique, sciences, technologie et informatique*
> *L'année prochaine, je vais faire/je ne vais pas faire …*
> *parce que je suis nul/nulle, fort/forte, je n'aime pas ça/j'aime ça*

> **Framework reference**
> 4.4, 4.5, 4.6

> **Starters**
> - To revise school subjects, display the names of the subjects on the board with all the vowels missing. Challenge students to write them out in full within a set time limit.
> - Students answer the register by saying a sentence about a subject they are doing this year or next year:

*Cette année, je fais français; L'année prochaine, je vais faire / je ne vais pas faire informatique.*

> **Plenaries**
> - Challenge students to see how many school subjects they can write accurately from memory. They must state how many they think they can remember in advance and they get a point for each subject they write correctly. Give the class two minutes, before asking them to check their partner's work. Students can only get a maximum score of how many subjects they stated they could remember, and a point must be deducted for each one they get wrong!
> - Play a game with a soft ball to practise the immediate future. Start by throwing the ball to a student who starts a sentence: *Je vais faire / Je ne vais pas faire …* The student then throws the ball to someone else who adds a comment or opinion about the subject mentioned, before throwing the ball to a third person, who begins a new sentence.
> Student A: *Je vais faire musique …*
> Student B: *parce que j'aime ça!*
> Student C: *Je ne vais pas faire sport …*
> Student D: *parce que je suis nul!*
> To make sure that everyone has a turn, ask the class to stand up before the game starts and when someone gives a correct response, he/she sits down.

> **Assessment opportunities**
> - Speaking: Students' Book page 69, exercise 7
> - Writing: Students' Book page 69, exercise 8

---

**AT 3.1** **1 Lis et relie.**
- Students match the nine pictures to their corresponding French word, to revise school subjects.

*Answers*: 1 d; 2 a; 3 f; 4 e; 5 h; 6 c; 7 i; 8 b; 9 g

**AT 1.1** **2 Écoute et répète tes matières.**
**AT 2.1**
- Students listen to the school subjects being listed and repeat the ones they are doing this year, taking care to pronounce them correctly.

 **CD 3, track 45**       page 68, activité 2

Cette année, …
1 je fais français
2 je fais anglais
3 je fais maths
4 je fais histoire-géographie
5 je fais sciences
6 je fais sport
7 je fais technologie et informatique
8 je fais dessin
9 je fais musique

**AT 4.1** **3 Écris tes matières dans l'ordre de préférence.**
- Students write a list of their school subjects in order of personal preference. Ask them to be careful about accurate spelling and explain that *Cette année je fais …* means 'This year I'm doing …'

**AT 3.2** **4 Écoute et lis. Trouve les quatre matières mentionnées.**
- Students listen to Caroline and François talking about what they are going to do next year, while following the text in their books. They note in English the four subjects mentioned.
- Point out the box which explains that *je vais faire / je ne vais pas faire* refers to what you are <u>going to do</u> whereas *je fais* refers to the present, what you are <u>doing</u>. Compare to the English immediate future which is very similar.

*Answers*: Caroline: French, music; François: science, sport

**CD 3, track 46**  page 69, activité 4

– Caroline, tu vas faire quelles matières l'année prochaine?
– L'année prochaine, je vais faire français parce que j'aime ça. Je ne vais pas faire musique parce que je suis nulle.

– François, tu vas faire quelles matières l'année prochaine?
– L'année prochaine, je vais faire sciences parce que je suis fort. Je ne vais pas faire sport parce que je déteste ça!

**AT 3.3** **5 Relis. Choisis a ou b.**

• Before students work on their own, explain that *parce que* means 'because'. Ask them to read the texts again and choose option a or b for each sentence.

*Answers:* 1 a; 2 a; 3 b; 4 b; 5 a; 6 b

## Grammaire

• Go over the expressions, *je suis fort(e)* and *je suis nul(le)*. Establish the meaning of both and ask students why there are two different versions of each adjective (masculine and feminine). Remind students that adjectives always agree with the person or thing they refer to.

**AT 1.2–3** **6 Écoute. Quelles matières?**

• Students listen to Curtis and Cerise and note which subjects they are going to do and not going to do next year. Remind students that *ne ...pas* indicates a negative.
• Ask students to listen again and note the reasons given.

*Answers:* Cerise: history ✓ (likes it), art ✗ (no good at it); Curtis: maths ✓ (good at it), English ✗ (hates it)

 **CD 3, track 47**  page 69, activité 6

– Cerise, tu vas faire quelles matières l'année prochaine?
– L'année prochaine, je vais faire histoire parce que j'aime ça. Je ne vais pas faire dessin parce que je suis nulle.

– Curtis, tu vas faire quelles matières l'année prochaine?
– L'année prochaine, je vais faire maths parce que je suis fort. Je ne vais pas faire anglais parce que je déteste ça!

**AT 2.2**  **7 À deux.**

• Prepare this pairwork by asking students which subjects they are going to do next year: *Tu vas faire français?* Students answer using *parce que* plus one of the reasons from the key language box. Encourage students to give a variety of answers and they could also use other adjectives they have learned previously with *c'est*, such as *intéressant, bien, nul* and *ennuyeux*.
• Students then work in pairs to ask each other which subjects they are going to do next year, giving reasons.

**AT 4.2** **8 Écris tes matières pour l'année prochaine. Explique.**

• Students list the subjects they will be doing next year and explain why they have chosen them.

### Follow-up

• Further work on school subjects can be found on OxBox, *Mon emploi du temps*.
**C65** • Students could carry out the listening activities on Copymaster 65.

*Answers:* **1a** English, Spanish, sport, ICT, design and technology, maths
*Answers:* **1b** traducteur, reporter
*Answers:* **2** a i; b ii; c ii; d ii; e i; f i; g ii

 **CD 3, track 66**  Feuille 65, *Clic! 3 Star*, activités 1 et 2

Je m'appelle Marc. J'ai 15 ans et je suis en troisième au Collège Jules Ferry. Cette année je passe le brevet. Ma matière préférée, c'est l'anglais, je suis fort en anglais. J'aime bien l'espagnol et l'EPS. Je fais aussi informatique, je trouve ça facile. La technologie ne m'intéresse pas. Je déteste les maths, je suis nul. Malheureusement, c'est obligatoire alors j'en ferai encore l'année prochaine. Plus tard, je voudrais continuer mes études. J'aimerais étudier l'anglais à l'université et travailler à l'étranger. Mon rêve, c'est d'être traducteur ou même reporter aux États-Unis. Il faut être très fort en langues et c'est pour ça que j'espère travailler comme au pair en Grande-Bretagne cet été. J'ai envie d'apprendre plus de choses sur la culture britannique et en même temps améliorer mon anglais en vivant avec une famille.

**C71** • Copymaster 71 has a text about *classes découvertes* (discovery classes) in French schools which could be used here, if appropriate for your students.

*Answers:* 1 1 g; 2 c; 3 b; 4 f; 5 a; 6 d; 7 e

# 9.2 Mon petit boulot

## *Planner*

> ### Objectives
> - Say what part-time job you are going to do
> - Give opinions of jobs

> ### Resources
> Students' Book, pages 70–71
> CD 3, tracks 48–49
> OxBox, *Clic! 3 Star, Unité 6, Les petits boulots.*
> Copymaster 63, *Clic! 3 Star*

> ### Key language
> *Je vais … Je ne vais pas …*
> *travailler dans un magasin, faire du baby-sitting,*
> *sortir les chiens, aider à la maison, faire les courses,*
> *distribuer les journaux*
> *parce que je n'aime pas ça/j'aime ça, c'est bien/mal*
> *payé*

> ### Grammar
> *je vais, je ne vais pas* + infinitive (immediate future)

> ### Framework reference
> 5.2, 5.4, 5.6

> ### Starters
> - Before students open their books, tell them that the theme is part-time jobs and that six jobs are going to be introduced – all of them are types of jobs that teenagers might do. Challenge students to work in pairs predicting what the jobs might be in English. Then look at the photos on page 70

together. How many jobs did they predict correctly? Look at the French phrases together. Are there any jobs they did not predict?
- To begin a lesson after the six part-time jobs have been introduced, give students 30 seconds to try and memorise the order (1–6) of the pictures. In pairs, they then test each other on the phrases. Student A looks at page 70 and says the number of a picture; student B says the corresponding sentence from memory.
Student A: *Numéro 6!*
Student B: *Je vais distribuer des journaux.*
Student A continues until Student B has attempted all six pictures, then the roles are reversed. Students win a point for each correct sentence.

> ### Plenaries
> - Students play a memory game in small groups to practise the six part-time jobs.
> Student A: *Je vais faire les courses.*
> Student B: *Je vais faire les courses et je vais travailler dans un magasin.*
> Student C: *Je vais faire les courses, je vais travailler dans un magasin et je vais …*
> - Call out a word or phrase from the spread and ask students to put it into a sentence.
> Teacher: *chiens*
> Student: *Je vais sortir les chiens.*
> Teacher: *parce que*
> Student: *parce c'est mal payé!*

> ### Assessment opportunities
> - Speaking: Students' Book page 71, exercise 5
> - Writing: Students' Book page 71, exercise 6

---

AT 1.2

AT 2.2

**1 Écoute, lis et répète.**
- Students listen, while following the captions in their books, and repeat each one, taking care with pronunciation.
- Ensure, if you have not already done so in the Starter, that students are clear about what each phrase means. Ask students to work out what the whole sentence means, deducing from words they already know. Recap on the meaning of *je vais* plus verb ('I'm going to') and establish the theme of this spread is to talk about which part-time jobs they are going to do, not ones they already do.

 **CD 3, track 48**          page 70, activité 1

Tu vas faire un petit boulot?
**1** Je vais travailler dans un magasin.
Tu vas faire un petit boulot?
**2** Je vais faire du baby-sitting.
Tu vas faire un petit boulot?
**3** Je vais sortir des chiens.
Tu vas faire un petit boulot?
**4** Je vais aider à la maison.
Tu vas faire un petit boulot?
**5** Je vais faire les courses.
Tu vas faire un petit boulot?
**6** Je vais distribuer des journaux.

**2 À deux: jeu de mime.**

- Students work in pairs. One partner mimes a job and the other student guesses in French what it is.

 **3 Écris les petits boulots dans l'ordre pour toi.**

- Students list the six jobs in order of personal preference.

**4 Lis, écoute et réponds.**

- Students listen, while following the text in their books, and then answer the questions in English.
- Before students work individually, point out the box which shows the expressions *mal/bien payé* and establish meaning. Also remind students of the negative *je ne vais pas*.
- Once students have completed the task, they can read the texts out loud in pairs, using as much expression as they can to convey the opinions.

*Answers:* a Chloé; b badly paid; c Laeticia; d doesn't like it; e likes it and well paid

**CD 3, track 49**        page 71, activité 4

- Laeticia, tu vas faire un petit boulot l'année prochaine?
- Je vais travailler dans un magasin de sport parce que j'aime ça.

- Lucas, tu vas faire un petit boulot l'année prochaine?
- Je ne vais pas distribuer des journaux parce que c'est mal payé!

- Chloé, tu vas faire un petit boulot l'année prochaine?
- Je vais faire du baby-sitting parce que j'aime ça!

- Lucie, tu vas faire un petit boulot l'année prochaine?
- Moi, je ne vais pas faire du baby-sitting parce que je n'aime pas ça!

- Matthieu, tu vas faire un petit boulot l'année prochaine?
- Je ne vais pas faire les courses parce que je n'aime pas ça!

- Jules, tu vas faire un petit boulot l'année prochaine?
- Moi, je vais aider à la maison parce que j'aime ça et c'est bien payé!

**5 À deux.**

- Do some class oral work in preparation for the pairwork activity. Ask questions, such as: *Tu vas sortir les chiens?* Students reply giving a reason, using the key language box as support; *Non, parce que je n'aime pas ça. / Oui, parce que c'est bien payé.*
- Students then work in pairs, asking and answering questions about part-time jobs and giving reasons.

**6 Écris six phrases.**

- Students write six sentences about the jobs, saying why they will or won't do them.

### Follow-up

 • A matching activity on jobs covered in this spread, along with a few others, is provided on OxBox, *Les petits boulots.*

 • Copymaster 63 provides extension reading activities on part-time jobs and school subjects.

*Answers:* **1** a 6; b 2; c 3; d 1; e 4; f 5
*Example answers:* **2** a brevet (*it isn't an adjective/ it's the only qualification*); b obligatoire (*it's the only adjective/ the others are all school subjects*); c arts plastiques (*it's the only school subject/the others are all jobs*); d nul (*the others are all personal qualities*); e l'étranger (*the others are all places to study*); f arrêter les études (*the others are all part-time jobs*)
Answers: **3** les matières: anglais, français, sciences physiques, technologie; les qualités: organisé/ organisée, travailleur/travailleuse, actif/active, dynamique; les métiers: pilote de ligne, reporter, infirmier/infirmière, acteur/actrice

# 9.3 Je voudrais être styliste!

## *Planner*

> ### Objectives
> - Say which job you would like to do
> - Say why you would or wouldn't like a job

> ### Resources
> Students' Book, pages 72–73
> CD 3, tracks 50–51
> Copymaster 67, 68, *Clic! 3 Star*

> ### Key language
> *Je suis …*
> *styliste, acteur/actrice, infirmier/infirmière, chanteur/*
> *chanteuse, fooballeur/footballeuse, mécanicien/*
> *mécanicienne*
> *Je voudrais être … Je ne veux pas être …*
> *parce que c'est bien/mal payé, c'est/ce n'est pas*
> *intéressant.*

> ### Grammar
> Masculine and feminine forms of job titles

> ### Framework reference
> 1.1, 1.4, 4.3, 5.5

> ### Starters
> - Write up the six jobs from page 72, including both masculine and feminine forms. Write the English equivalents and ask students to match the French and English words. Ask students to explain how they could do it, for example, by seeing which jobs look like the English words, see if they have met it before or through a process of elimination. Ask students why there are two forms of most of the jobs in French. Elicit that the words for jobs often change for masculine and feminine forms. Compare to English where they sometimes change, such as actor/actress.
> - To begin a lesson once students are familiar with the masculine and feminine endings for job titles, display a jumble of masculine and feminine jobs, including new jobs that don't appear on the spread, together with jumbled English

translations. Words might include:
*caissier/caissière*/cashier;
*journaliste/journaliste*/journalist;
*coiffeur/coiffeuse*/hairdresser;
*agent de police/agente de police*/police officer;
*agriculteur/agricultrice*/farmer;
*électricien/ électricienne*/electrician;
*cuisinier/cuisinière*/cook;
*vendeur/vendeuse*/sales assistant.
Students race against each other to match up the masculine/feminine forms and their English translations within a time limit.

> ### Plenaries
> - Invite a volunteer to the front of the class and give him/her the name of a job (either the masculine or feminine form) written on a piece of paper. The other students try to identify the job. The volunteer may answer only *oui* or *non*. How many guesses do students need before they get it correct?
>   Class: *C'est un homme?*
>   Volunteer: *Non!*
>   Class: *Elle est actrice?*
>   Volunteer: *Non!*
>   Class: *Elle est chanteuse?*
>   Volunteer: *Oui, c'est ça!*
>   Continue with other volunteers. To keep the game moving quickly, limit the number of guesses to a maximum of five – if the class doesn't come up with the answer in five guesses, the volunteer wins and beats the class!
> - Give students three to four minutes to work in pairs with a dictionary and find the masculine and feminine words for six jobs that you write on the board, such as teacher, model, bus driver, baker, farmer, postman. How quickly can they find the six jobs and write them down correctly?

> ### Asessment opportunities
> - Speaking: Students' Book page 73, exercise 6
> - Writing: Students' Book page 73, exercise 7

## Preparation
- Point out, if you have not already done so in the Starter, that names of jobs are often different for men and women. Can students spot any patterns in the six jobs listed in activity 1?

| AT 1.1 |
| AT 2.1 |

## 1a Écoute, lis et répète.
- Students listen to the jobs, while looking at their books, and repeat each one carefully. They should listen for the difference in pronunciation between the male and female versions.
- For more practice, do some oral discrimination activities whereby you read out jobs in the masculine and feminine forms and students note 'm' or 'f' according to the gender.

**CD 3, track 50**      page 72, activités 1a et 1b

**1** – Je suis styliste.
   – Je suis styliste.
**2** – Je suis acteur.
   – Je suis actrice.
**3** – Je suis infirmier.
   – Je suis infirmière.
**4** – Je suis chanteur.
   – Je suis chanteuse.
**5** – Je suis footballeur.
   – Je suis footballeuse.
**6** – Je suis mécanicien.
   – Je suis mécanicienne.

**AT 1.1** **1b Réécoute. Répète les bons mots pour toi.**

- Students listen again and only repeat the version (male or female) that applies to them.

**AT 2.1** **2 À deux: jeu de mémoire.**

- Students play a memory game. One partner says a job (using the correct version to suit them) and the other says the corresponding number of the picture it exercise 1. Give students a minute or two to look at the pictures before they start to try to memorise which is which.

**AT 4.1** **3 Écris six autres jobs. Cherche dans le dictionnaire.**

- After looking at the *Top Tips!* box with students, ask them to use a dictionary to find six other jobs they are interested in. They must note both the masculine and feminine forms.

## Top Tips!

- Work with students to help them look up new French words. Give out one dictionary per person or per pair. Name a job for students to look up in the English-French section, for example 'butcher'. They find it and note both the masculine and feminine forms. They double check they have the correct word by looking it up in the French-English section.

**AT 1.3** **4 Écoute et lis. Relie les textes aux photos.**

**AT 3.2–3**

- Students listen to the four people speaking, while following the texts in their books. They then match each photo to a speech bubble.
- This activity introduces the expression *Plus tard, je voudrais être …* Explain what this means and also point out the negative *je ne veux pas être …*
- Do some oral work, asking the class: *Qu'est-ce que tu voudrais être? Pourquoi?* Students can use the key language box as support for their answers.

*Answers*: 1 C; 2 D; 3 B; 4 A

 **CD 3, track 51**      page 73, activité 4

**1** – Yacin, tu voudrais être footballeur plus tard?
   – Oui, plus tard, je voudrais être footballeur parce que c'est bien payé!
**2** – Marie, tu voudrais être chanteuse plus tard?
   – Moi, non, plus tard, je ne veux pas être chanteuse parce que ce n'est pas intéressant!
**3** – Marcus, tu voudrais être infirmier plus tard?
   – Non, plus tard, je ne veux pas être infirmier parce que c'est mal payé!
**4** – Camille, tu voudrais être actrice plus tard?
   – Oui, plus tard, je voudrais être actrice parce que c'est intéressant.

**AT 3.2–3** **5 Relis. Corrige ces résumés.**

- Students read the speech bubbles in activity 4 again, this time in more detail and correct mistakes in the English summaries.
- Encourage students to read the texts out loud in pairs. They could then practise changing one detail in each sentence, such as the job itself or the reason.

*Answers*: a Yacin wants to be a footballer because it's <u>well paid</u>. b Marie doesn't want to be <u>a singer</u> because it's not interesting. c Marcus doesn't want to be a <u>nurse</u> because it's badly paid. d Camille wants to be an actress because it is <u>interesting</u>.

**AT 2.2–3** **6 À deux.**

- Students work in pairs to ask and answer questions about the six jobs on page 72. They say whether they would or wouldn't like to do each job and give a reason to justify their choices.

**AT 4.2–3** **7 Écris six phrases sur des jobs.**

- Students write six sentences about what they would or would not like to do as a job, using the key language box and the jobs they looked up in exercise 3. Students should give reasons for each job they mention.
- Students can then compare their sentences with a partner. Did they have any the same?

**Follow-up**

**C67**

- Copymaster 67 provides extension reading and writing activities on future jobs and personal qualities.

*Answers*: **1** a Elle est chanteuse. Elle est passionnée, extravertie et active. b Il est styliste. Il est dynamique, extraverti et travailleur. c Il est infirmier. Il est passionné, organisé et travailleur.
*Answers*: **3** Elle est professeur. Il est rugbyman/joueur de rugby. (*Accept any appropriate qualities*)

C68 • Copymaster 68 provides extension reading and writing activities on future jobs and plans.

*Answers:* **1** b, c, d, g
*Answers:* **2a** Moi, je vais faire des <u>langues</u> parce que ça <u>m'intéresse</u> beaucoup. Je suis très fort en français. Je voudrais beaucoup <u>voyager</u>. Plus <u>tard</u>, je voudrais être <u>professeur</u>. Mon <u>rêve</u>, c'est d'aller en Chine.

# 9.4   Vocabulaire
page 74

## *Planner*

> **Resources**
Students' Book, page 74

> **Objectives**
• *Vocabulaire*: to provide a theme-based summary of the key language of the unit, which students can use as a reference or as an aid to learning
• To practise pronunciation

> **Framework reference**
4.1, 5.5

## Using the vocabulary page

• Encourage students to use the *Vocabulaire* page as a reference point throughout the unit. It can also serve as a useful revision tool before students do the *Clic-test!*
• Vocabulary is listed spread-by-spread and you could either ask students to learn each section for homework after each spread is completed, or set the whole page as a homework task before starting work on the test. Most students learn shorter sections best, so often it is better to give them manageable chunks to learn at a time.
• Encourage students to use different techniques to help them learn the vocabulary:
    – Cover up the English and see what they can remember; write down any words they can't remember and test themselves again on those words.
    – Cover up the French and see if they can remember the words or phrases this way round.
    – Make word cards with English on one side and French on the other. Students can then test themselves to see what they can remember. Put any cards they can't remember on one side and go over those again at the end.
    – Work in pairs to test each other, either using the vocabulary list or the word cards.
• Record themselves saying the words both in English and French. Saying words and phrases out loud can often help with memorising them.

## Sound French!

• *Aim:* To practise pronunciation
• The point practised here is the *c* and *ç* sounds with different vowels. Explain the combinations listed and practise saying the words together.
• Ask students to find more examples of each type in other vocabulary lists. How many can they find in four minutes?

# 9.4    Clic-test!

## *Planner*

The page is divided into four sections: listening, speaking, reading and writing.

> ## Objectives
> * To enable students to recap on the language and structures of the unit

* To provide an opportunity for quick testing of all four skills

> ## Resources
> Students' Book, page 75
> CD 3, track 52

> ## Framework reference
> 5.7, 5.8

---

 **1 Écoute! (1–5)**
* Students listen and select the correct picture for each speaker.

*Answers*: 1 e; 2 c; 3 a; 4 b; 5 d

---

**CD 3, track 52**          page 75, activité 1

1 L'année prochaine, je vais faire musique parce que je suis forte.
2 Je ne vais pas faire histoire parce que je n'aime pas ça.
3 L'année prochaine, je vais faire du baby-sitting.
4 Je voudrais être mécanicien parce que c'est intéressant.
5 Je ne veux pas être mécanicien parce que ce n'est pas intéressant.

---

AT 3.3 **2 Lis!**
* Students read Lisa's message and select the correct option in each sentence.

*Answers*: 1 a; 2 a; 3 b; 4 b; 5 a

---

AT 4.2 **3 Écris!**
* Students write sentences for each picture clue, using the key language box provided as support.

*Answers*: 1 Plus tard, je ne veux pas être mécanicien parce que ce n'est pas intéressant. 2 Plus tard, je veux être chanteuse parce que c'est bien payé. 3 Plus tard, je veux être styliste parce que c'est intéressant. 4 Plus tard, je veux être mécanicienne parce que c'est bien payé. 5 Plus tard, je ne veux pas être infirmier parce que c'est mal payé. 6 Plus tard, je ne veux pas être actrice parce que ce n'est pas intéressant.

---

AT 2.2–3 **4 Parle!**
* Students complete the sentences for themselves, using the support provided.

---

# À moi

## *Planner*

> ## Objectives
> * To provide reinforcement activities for quiet work
> * To provide alternative class and homework material for students who finish other activities quickly

> ## Resources
> Students' Book, page 84

> ## Framework reference
> 2.2, 2.3, 2.5

---

### Mon CV

 **1 Read Caroline's CV. Match each heading (a–f) to the information below.**
* Students match each English sentence to the correct section in the French CV.

*Answers*: 1 b; 2 a; 3 f; 4 e; 5 d; 6 c

---

 **2 Have a go at writing your own CV. Replace Caroline's details with yours.**
* Demonstrate on the board, if necessary, how students could adapt Caroline's details to write their own CV.